For Better, For Worse

For Better, For Worse

The Marriage Crisis That Made Modern Egypt

Hanan Kholoussy

Stanford University Press

Stanford, California

Stanford University Press
Stanford, California

Printed in the United States of America on acid-free, archival-quality paper

Library of Congress Cataloging-in-Publication Data
Kholoussy, Hanan.
  For better, for worse : the marriage crisis that made modern Egypt / Hanan
Kholoussy.
     p. cm.
  Includes bibliographical references and index.
  ISBN 978-0-8047-6959-4 (cloth : alk. paper) — ISBN 978-0-8047-6960-0 (pbk. :
alk. paper)
     1. Marriage—Egypt—History—20th century. 2. Nationalism—Egypt—
History—20th century. I. Title.
  HQ691.7.K46 2010
  306.810962'0904—dc22
                                    2009035618

Typeset by Bruce Lundquist in 11/13.5 Adobe Garamond Pro

Contents

Acknowledgments

I AM INDEBTED to so many individuals and institutions for their support while I researched and wrote this book. For nearly a decade, my dissertation committee of exceptional scholars, Khaled Fahmy, Zachary Lockman, Mary Nolan, Linda Gordon, and Manu Goswami, shared their invaluable time, knowledge, and guidance without which this book would not have been possible. Funding from New York University (NYU), the American Research Center in Egypt, the Foreign Language Area Studies Research Abroad Program, and the Social Science Research Council's International Dissertation Research Fellowship Program sponsored my research in Egypt, and a grant from the American University in Cairo (AUC) helped cover the indexing costs of this book.

The staff and scholars working in the Egyptian National Archives and Library were incredibly accommodating, and I could not have completed my research without their assistance. Madame Nadia Mustafa, Madame Nagwa Mahmud, Mr. Muhammad, and Ms. Esther were especially gracious. More fellow researchers than I can list shared their experience, helped decipher illegible words, and located documents. Hibba Abugideiri, Laura Bier, Magdi Guirgis, Dana Hearn, Emad Hilal, Wilson Jacob, Jennifer Peterson, Mario M. Ruiz, Mona Russell, and Ahmed Zaki were particularly generous. I owe a special thanks to Farida Makar for helping me find and choose the caricatures that appear in this book.

NYU and AUC provided funding that enabled me to present parts of this book at various conferences. I am very grateful for the feedback from the many people who attended my talks at AUC, NYU, Sarah Lawrence College, the Oriental Library in Tokyo, Sabancı University, Tokyo University, the Social Science Research Council, the American Research

Center in Egypt, the University of Chicago, the University of Illinois, Columbia University, and City University of New York.

The professionalism, attention, and timeliness of my editors, Kate Wahl, Carolyn Brown, and Mimi Braverman have made the experience of writing my first book easier than I had ever anticipated. They and the anonymous reviewers of the manuscript provided meticulous readings and important suggestions that only made the manuscript stronger. Of course, I alone am responsible for any oversights or errors. I would also like to thank AUC Press for permission to use the main argument and a short segment for Chapter 4 from my article, "The Nationalization of Marriage in Monarchical Egypt," in *Re-Envisioning Egypt, 1919–1952*, edited by Arthur Goldschmidt Jr., Amy J. Johnson, and Barak Salmoni (Cairo: American University in Cairo Press, 2005), 317–350.

I am especially indebted to Joel Beinin, Khaled Fahmy, Zachary Lockman, Lisa Pollard, and Omnia El Shakry, who helped me in more ways than they can know in the process of transforming my dissertation into this book. Beth Baron, David Blanks, Kenneth Cuno, Michael Gilsenan, Ann Lesch, Saba Mahmood, Chris Payne, Mike Reimer, Amira Sonbol, Chris Toensing, and Judith E. Tucker also offered great advice along the way. My colleagues, students, and the staff at AUC offered a warm environment while I finished the writing and editing of this book. My dear friends Jehan Agha, Ozlem Altan, Reham Barakat, Liat Kozma, Mia Lee, Shane Minkin, Amy Motlagh, Sherene Seikaly, and Shareah Taleghani supported me through personal and academic trials, provided important insights into various chapters, and sparked my ideas in numerous brainstorming sessions.

My cousin Walid Fathi and his wife, Mona Mohy, who sparkled my stays in Egypt with their love and laughter, kindly allowed me to use their July 1991 wedding photo as inspiration for the book cover. That they chose to represent early twentieth-century Egyptian wedding attire and deportment on the most meaningful day of their lives captures the essence of my book. Their embodiment of this era exemplifies its historic significance to modern times, the critical role that marriage continues to play in the formation of modern Egyptian national identity, and the relevance of early twentieth-century marital issues to contemporary Egyptians. The image of my stoic cousin donning a fez and sporting a mustache and cane in true effendi fashion while his wife cheekily peers at the camera in a modest but modern wedding dress worn by the new Egyptian woman left an indelible impression on me as a teenager. It eventually stirred me to study this period so that I could tell the story of how it came to be that marriage helped to make modern Egypt.

Most of all, I thank my family, who nurtured me throughout this arduous process with their love, faith, and encouragement. Mom, Dad, and Tarek: This book was inspired and sustained by you. You have left your mark on every page. It is your story as much as it is mine. Marwan: Even when you forced me to type one-handed, you made every sleepless night working worth every daytime moment together. Nayer: Your appearance just as this book went to press motivated me to meet its final deadlines so that I could be all yours when you arrived. Walid: This book is for you. Your support, patience, and understanding made it possible.

Note on Transliteration, Translation, and Currency

I HAVE FOLLOWED the system of transliteration adopted by the *International Journal of Middle East Studies* (*IJMES*), which reduces diacritics to a minimum so that only the Arabic letters *'ayn* (') and *hamza* (') are demarcated. The Arabic letter *jim* has been translated as *j*, except in those cases where the Egyptian pronunciation (*gim*) is used (for example, the male name Gamal). Other exceptions include the transliteration of Arabic names whose owners have their own English renderings. I use commonly accepted transliterations of Arabic words like *effendi* and *galabiya*, and I have occasionally anglicized plural renditions of Arabic words by adding an "s" (for example, beys and pashas).

The titles of all Arabic primary and secondary sources have been translated in the bibliography. Although the Arabic language does not use capitalization, I have followed the *IJMES* system, which applies English capitalization rules to transliterated titles. The definite article *al-* (the) that often precedes nouns and names is not capitalized, unless it begins a sentence or endnote. Unless otherwise indicated, translations of all foreign sources, words, and excerpted passages are my own. In cases where my renditions needed further clarification, I have indicated such additions in brackets.

After the first mention of the full name of a female primary writer or female court litigant in the text, I either use her forename or reiterate her full name. Because most Egyptians used their father's first name or masculine family name for their last name, reference to a female author by her masculine moniker can be confusing. I do not follow this system with men's names or female or male scholars' names, whether in English or Arabic.

All financial amounts in the book appear in their original Egyptian currency, the Egyptian pound (LE), which is divisible into 100 piasters. Between 1885 and 1914, LE 1 = 7.4375 grams of pure gold. From 1914 to 1962, the Egyptian pound was pegged to the British pound at a rate of LE 0.975 = £1 sterling ($4.86).

1

The Making and Marrying
of Modern Egyptians

Social crises are just as important and dangerous as their
political or economic counterparts, if not more so, because their
repercussions can destroy the entire nation and foreshadow its
annihilation. Is there anything more indicative of this than the
marriage crisis that threatens the Egyptian nation at its core, erodes
its backbone, and forewarns of its ruin? The government and people
must urgently unite to solve this crisis.

William Gayyid

IN THIS 1929 LETTER TO THE EDITOR, the lawyer William Gayyid
underscored the alarming anxieties that the Egyptian middle class shared
about the marriage crisis and the fate of their fledgling nation.[1] Writers
and readers deployed the term *marriage crisis* in the press to refer to a
supposed rise in the number of middle-class men who were choosing
bachelorhood over marriage in early twentieth-century urban Egypt.
For many like Gayyid, the biggest problem facing Egypt was not British domination or the Great Depression but the marriage crisis, which
demanded nothing short of government intervention because it signified
the potential demise of the nation. When Egyptians were discussing this
crisis in the press, they were not simply voicing their concerns about

the purported greater prevalence of bachelorhood. They were also using marriage as a metaphor to critique larger socioeconomic and political turmoil and to envision a postcolonial nation free of social ills. Marriage was not just a political act and a patriotic duty for these Egyptians; it was also a microcosm of their nation.

The marriage crisis was a middle-class urban phenomenon limited to the large cities of Egypt, most notably its capital, Cairo.[2] It was most clearly articulated by middle-class exponents for middle-class consumption and was said to affect middle-class bachelors. Egypt's Arabic-language press (as opposed to its upper-class French-language press) was a middle-class forum in which the founders, editors, and writers of the various newspapers and periodicals wrote in the language of the urban middle class.[3] Although this group was a minority in Egypt, its domination of the press and its control of the struggle for national independence led it to claim middle-class perceptions as the norm in its attempts to define new hegemonic notions of marriage, law, gender, and nationalism in the early twentieth century.

Even though the middle-class writers and readers of the press represented a small portion of the population, they differed immensely in the plethora of reasons they offered to explain middle-class men's evasion of marriage. Some writers argued that these men could not afford the costs of marriage given the various economic crises sweeping early twentieth-century Egypt. Others faulted materialistic women and their parents for demanding extravagant dowers from their suitors. Still others blamed the bachelors themselves, accusing them of squandering their money and time in idle places, such as the coffeehouse, or on illicit diversions, such as prostitution and alcohol. Certain observers argued that the customs of arranged marriage and female seclusion deterred educated men from marrying women with whom they could not become acquainted before marriage. Some readers and writers claimed that middle-class men were repelled by uneducated women who could not provide stimulating companionship, run homes efficiently, and raise future citizens for the nation. Yet others contended that men were turned off by educated women, who were too immodest and liberal to make honorable obedient wives and mothers. Still others faulted the high divorce rate, evidenced in protracted disputes in the Islamic courts, for discouraging single middle-class men from entering into unstable unions that would likely fall apart.

Cases from the Islamic courts, however, paint a different picture of marriage in early twentieth-century Cairo. They reveal the improvisations of couples from all social classes and their creative responses to the changing circumstances of early twentieth-century Egyptian life. Contrary to the portrayals by middle-class writers, couples of all classes used a variety of strategies to manipulate the courts to their advantage. Whereas the middle class conceptualized certain notions of marital rights and duties in the press, lower-class, middle-class, and elite couples in the courtrooms exercised and understood these rights and duties in different ways. Many litigants and judges did not necessarily subscribe to the new notions of marriage, masculinity, and femininity that were being disseminated in the press. Others, however, were influenced by ideas about the roles men and women should play in marriage and the nation. Although the middle-class press argued that marriage was supposed to be a permanent hierarchical relationship, various legal possibilities were available to both sexes to escape the institution. When husbands or wives divorced, when wives tried to force absent husbands to provide alimony, or when couples wrestled for custody over children, many turned to the legal system for redress. Egyptians petitioned judges to challenge apparently fixed doctrinal understandings because they viewed law as a crucial and flexible sociopolitical resource. Their extensive use of the Islamic courts suggests that they did not consider law a last resort. It also indicates that Egyptians of all classes were aware of their legal and socially acceptable options, even if they were not all aware of or influenced by the middle-class debates over marriage.

Marriage was a site of contested national identity formation that attracted the growing social attention of the middle-class press and the legal attention of the Egyptian administration under British rule. Egyptian men and women conceptualized the nation and understood their rights and duties through marriage in the early twentieth century. During this period, new ideas of marriage, law, nationalism, and gender were being shaped and redefined in an unprecedented manner. In this book, I examine a sample of marriage and divorce cases filed in Cairo's Islamic courts in order to situate them within the widespread press debates over the alleged marriage crisis. By undertaking a discursive analysis of middle-class understandings of marriage in the press with those of the urban lower, middle, and upper classes in the courts, I demonstrate how marriage, law, nationalism, and gender were portrayed and practiced in a semicolonial context between 1898 and 1936.

The year 1898 marked the first year of the existence of the newly reorganized Islamic court system, and it roughly coincided with the controversial publication of Qasim Amin's *The Liberation of Women.*[4] Amin, commonly if inaptly considered "the father of Arab feminism," was the first Egyptian to perceive a phenomenon of bachelorhood long before an ostensible marriage crisis riveted the nation in the 1920s and 1930s.[5] The proposals set forth in Amin's book also served as the basis for marriage and divorce legislation in Egypt.

Although many writers and readers advanced similar arguments and explanations for bachelorhood during the first two decades of the twentieth century, the term *marriage crisis* was not coined until after the 1919 Egyptian revolution for independence began. 'Abdu al-Barquqi, a frequent contributor to the secular women's monthly *al-Mar'a al-Misriyya*, was the first writer to call the supposed rise in middle-class bachelorhood a marriage crisis in an article he penned in the magazine's February 1920 issue.[6] Al-Barquqi argued that the problem of middle-class bachelorhood had come to constitute a full-fledged crisis that threatened the fledgling Egyptian nation amid its struggle for independence from the British. The failure to secure political and economic independence led many Egyptians to view their nation as being in turmoil and to imagine marriage—their microcosm of the nation and the locus of the ways and means for producing and reproducing—as being in crisis.

Debates over the marriage crisis started to fade by 1936, when national identity began to acquire new and different meanings in a more sovereign Egypt and when discussions of bachelorhood ceased to dominate the pages of the press. The assumption of power in 1936 by King Faruq, a new and different kind of royal ruler, upon the death of his father, King Fu'ad (r. 1917–1936); the Anglo-Egyptian Treaty of 1936, which granted Egypt more sovereignty; the end of the Great Depression; and the impending World War II all helped to distract the literate Egyptian public from a crisis in marriage at least for the next several decades.

Historical Background

Although Britain occupied Egypt militarily in 1882 and established a new colonial regime, Egypt nominally remained a province of the Ottoman Empire. At the onset of World War I in 1914, however, the British placed Egypt under a protectorate, ending its legal ties with the Ottoman Empire. When the British neglected to remove this protectorate status and grant Egypt political independence after World War I, Egyptian nationalists initiated an intense struggle for independence, beginning with the 1919 revolution. After three years of Anglo-Egyptian negotiations, the British unilaterally imposed a limited form of independence in 1922 by establishing a parliamentary monarchy. Egyptians assumed responsibility for their internal affairs, and the British retained a political and military presence to safeguard their interests and maintain influence over Egyptian and foreign affairs. As historian Afaf Lutfi al-Sayyid Marsot puts it, "That independence was hedged by a number of restrictions that rendered it well nigh void."[7] This status quo lasted until the Anglo-Egyptian Treaty of 1936. This treaty established Egypt as a sovereign nation but permitted Britain to maintain a military presence along the Suez Canal and impose martial law and censorship. The British finally evacuated Egypt after Gamal Abdel Nasser led a revolution that overthrew the pro-British monarchy in 1952 and declared Egypt independent in 1954.

Because of this unique but awkward relationship of quasi-independence and semicolonial rule, Egyptian experiences in marriage, law, nationalism, and gender in the early twentieth century differed from those of other European colonies in a number of ways. First, unlike in colonial India, British officials did not reform the Islamic legal system in Egypt, despite their frequent criticisms of its courts.[8] The Egyptian administration reformed this system on its own accord and drafted, debated, and passed Islamic laws on marriage and divorce without any direct interference from the British.[9] Second, the discourses on marriage and gender in the press were constructed by and for indigenous Egyptian subjects. Studies of colonialism tend to concentrate on colonizers' assumptions and perceptions of marriage and gender more than on those of the colonized.[10] In contrast, the marriage crisis discussions were internal dialogues among Egyptians not steeped in debates on racial difference. Third, the Egyptian case does not compare with the Bengali one because Bengali nationalists began to overlook women's issues in favor of political issues, seeking to situate women in an inner domain of spirituality, localized within the home and embodied by the feminine.[11] Egyptian discussions on marriage were very much about women's issues *and* political issues, and women's issues were characterized by attempts to advance and develop women as *both* an inner domain of culture and an outer domain of progress for the nation.

What the Egyptian case did share with its colonial counterparts was an obsession with modernity. New marital legislation that regulated the marriage of female minors in colonial India, for example, was more concerned with promoting modernity than with improving the status of women for their own sake, and this legislation marked a crucial turning point between the delegitimization of colonialism as the agent of modernity and the advent of a new nationalist Indian modernity.[12] Concerns over bachelorhood likewise provide evidence of the political and cultural anxieties that often underwrote experiments in colonial modernity. Paul Rabinow has argued that instead of attempting to define modernity, one must track the diverse ways in which claims to being modern are made.[13] Egyptian claims to being modern can be examined through marriage, an arena in which notions of colonial modernity were produced and reproduced as a condition for the political independence of the emerging Egyptian nation and its national subjects. Male and female writers used marriage to critique Egyptian society and to construct visions of modern marriage and nation and of modern husbands, wives, and national subjects. At the same time, their constructions of modern marriage, nation, and subjects were also uniquely and authentically Egyptian and Islamic. Although Egyptians occasionally deployed Western models of marriage and nation as positive examples of modernity, they welcomed neither wholesale adoption nor complete rejection of them. Like early twentieth-century advocates of modernity elsewhere, they tailored their own visions of modernity to their individual political, class, religious, cultural, and economic situations.[14]

Parameters and Perceptions

Marriage crisis observers focused on a small and select subcategory of middle-class bachelors and constructed them as a distinct social group that aroused anxiety in contrast to other early twentieth-century Western societies that reconstituted single women as such.[15] The emerging middle class was an evolving and amorphous group in early twentieth-century Egypt. It was loosely composed of a lower middle class of government employees, merchants, and urban and agricultural workers; a rural petty bourgeoisie of small landowners; and an urban middle class of students, teachers, professionals, government bureaucrats, technocrats, and intellectuals who were educated in Egyptian state schools and universities.[16] The bachelor of the marriage crisis was a member of this last subgroup: The educated urban professional male middle class that usually resided in the capital of Cairo, spoke a Western language, dressed in European attire, worked in a white-collar occupation, and regularly consumed and sometimes produced periodicals and books.[17] A man who belonged to this small but powerful segment within the middle class and between the landless peasantry and the landowning elite minority assumed the title *effendi*, which connoted a somewhat bourgeois identity that most closely resembles a gentleman in English.[18] These men were crucial to the development of Egyptian anticolonial nationalism, as their intellectual contributions and political activities proved central in urban culture and politics.[19]

Ahmad al-Sawi Muhammad, who often dedicated his column in the daily *al-Ahram* to marital issues, outlined the unique predicament of the middle-class bachelor.

> You are the victims of this society that . . . gives you a paltry salary . . . and forces you at the same time to become an effendi, wear a fez and suit, . . . ride the tram, read the paper, and sit in a coffeehouse. But if you were, my brother, to wear a galabiya . . . you would find thousands . . . happy to marry you.[20]

By highlighting the explicit urban-rural divide that marked early twentieth-century Egypt, al-Sawi distinguished between two types of Egyptian men: the urban educated effendi, visibly demarcated by his Western-style suit and fez, versus the rural illiterate peasant farmer, marked by his galabiya (a simple loose long dress).[21] Both figures were commonly and perhaps contradictorily deployed as symbols of Egyptian nationalism during the struggle for complete independence: The effendi represented the modern Westernized Egyptian man, whereas the peasant symbolized his authentic traditional counterpart. According to al-Sawi, only the middle class fell victim to the trappings of Egyptian modernity and materialism and, as a result, could not afford to marry. Although approximately 70 percent of the population was composed of peasants, who were the hardest hit by the various economic depressions, they were not facing a crisis in marriage because they continued to marry to reproduce children, who would help them work the fields, and because their class did not place outrageous financial demands on them in marriage.[22]

Egypt's elite beys (an honorific title for distinguished professional men) and pashas (the highest honorific title reserved for prominent landowners and political officials) also were not facing a bachelorhood epidemic because they could afford to marry. Their urban members, however, frequented the Cairo Islamic courts just as often as their lower-class and middle-class counterparts did. They also occasionally took part in marriage crisis debates in the press as observers, and they formed the core of the Egyptian administration that passed marriage and divorce legislation in the 1920s.

Despite the repeated claims in the press that large numbers of middle-class men were shunning marriage, writers and readers rarely offered data to substantiate their arguments. Even those who mentioned that the Islamic courts were recording fewer marriages annually did not cite statistics. Because the registration of marriage was not required before a 1931 law mandated it, it is impossible to ascertain whether or not middle-class men were avoiding marriage.[23] Ironically, a comparison of the percentage of never-married Cairene men during the height of the crisis reveals a sharp drop: 57 percent had never married in 1927 versus 34 percent in 1937.[24] These figures, however, are unreliable because they come from problematic census registers that included males of all ages, did not distinguish between classes, and were accurate only at the moment the census was conducted.[25]

More significant is the widespread *perception* that middle-class bachelorhood was on the rise: the reasons offered to explain this purported phenomenon, why it caused such alarm, and what those apprehensions said about Egyptian men, women, their economy, their society, and their political situation. The marriage crisis reflected escalating anxieties about the political, social, and economic state of the fragile nation more than realities of widespread bachelorhood. Specifically, middle-class Egyptians worried about whether and when they would achieve full independence from the British. They were concerned about what role Islamic and secular law, education, and culture would play and what kind of government would rule in a postcolonial Egypt. They fretted over foreign economic domination, middle-class materialism, low salaries, unemployment rates, periods of inflation, and cycles of depression at various points during the early decades of the twentieth century. Perhaps most of all, the writers and readers in the press were anxious about how all these factors would affect their own gendered, marital, and national identities as well as those of middle-class men and women like themselves.

A few scholars have mentioned the growing concerns over Egyptian bachelorhood in the 1930s. According to Margot Badran, journalists and social reformers blamed spousal incompatibility in age and education as well as economic problems that made it difficult for middle-class men to marry.[26] Bruce Dunne and Laura Bier, on the other hand, attribute the marriage crisis to social reformers who blamed widespread bachelorhood on the easily accessible outlet of prostitution, which made sex available without the responsibilities of marriage.[27] Their focus on sexuality and prostitution oversimplifies the multiple manifestations of the marriage crisis. Although the 1930s were characterized by campaigns to end official prostitution, there was nothing new about prostitution or calls for its eradication. Prostitution had been regulated by the British until the postcolonial government outlawed state-regulated prostitution in 1953.[28] Nor were the early 1930s concerns that middle-class men preferred bachelorhood to marriage new. As early as 1899, social reformers such as Qasim Amin lamented the supposed rise in bachelorhood and the decline in marriage rates. Although the 1930s debates were connected to the 1929–1933 economic depression and high levels of unemployment, this economic crisis was not the first that early twentieth-century Egypt had experienced. The country had also faced one in 1907, which led many in the press to bemoan the financial preoccupations behind marriage because they deterred men from marriage.

Marriage, Nationalism, and Gender

Theorists of nationalism have underscored the utility of examining the family because it is often viewed as the basic building block of a nation.[29] Recent works have been instrumental in establishing a solid foundation for this sort of research on Egyptian nationalism. Beth Baron has demonstrated how the nation has invariably been imagined by means of metaphors of the family, and Marilyn Booth has shown how women found it difficult to escape the nationalist ideal of the nuclear family.[30] Lisa Pollard further illustrated the extent to which the home served as an arena where Egyptian men and women learned to be modern nationalists in the late nineteenth and early twentieth centuries.[31] These scholars have interrogated the rigid divide traditionally posited by scholars of nationalism between the public nationalist domain of men and the private cultural sphere of women and the family, revealing that women and the family were fundamental to the constitution of Egyptian national identity.[32]

I largely draw on and seek to contribute to this pioneering body of scholarship. Rather than women or the family, however, I use marriage as the central lens for studying anticolonial nationalism. We must first examine marriage in order to better understand the production of the family, the nation, and gender.[33] My focus on marriage, however, does not mean that I do not consider the family. On the contrary, the two are inextricably linked: Marriage is the fundamental foundation of the Egyptian family and, by extension, the nation because it is the institution that makes and breaks families. Because the ultimate goal of Egyptian marriage was to produce offspring, a study of marriage is also a study of the family. Marriage, however, is more significant for a variety of reasons.

The Egyptian middle class often constructed marriage as a fundamental national duty. As a result, conjugal ties and identities provide a useful way to examine how men and women were turned into husbands and wives and how both were made into modern national subjects. Egyptian legislators also viewed marriage as paramount to the nation because the bulk of state intervention into the so-called private sphere focused on marriage and divorce laws in order to secure their public objectives of political independence and national modernity. By focusing on marriage, we can better grasp the competing articulations of the nation that reveal the nuanced and polycentric variants of nationalism.

Marriage is also important because it serves as one of the most effective, yet largely ignored, ways of studying gender in normative heterosexual contexts because "the whole system of attribution and meaning that we call gender relies on and to a great extent derives from the structuring provided by marriage. Turning men and women into husbands and wives, marriage has designated the way both sexes act in the world."[34] Rather than a parallel women's history that marginalizes men, in this book I offer a national history that uses gender instead of women as both a primary tool and an object of analysis.[35] Because notions of masculinity and femininity are constantly being redeployed and renegotiated in relation to one another, we cannot begin to understand how one is being reworked without considering the other.

I do not mean to suggest that marriage played the only role in the construction of gender in early twentieth-century Egypt. Gender is constructed by a variety of institutions, discourses, and processes, as the aforementioned scholars have shown. Marriage remains pivotal, however, because gender identities and marital identities are mutually constitutive. Likewise, gender is a useful tool for studying marriage and nationalism.[36] Although consideration of the gendered connotations of nationalist discourse can take a variety of scholarly routes, I am most interested in how national identity was constructed differently for men and for women and how notions of femininity and masculinity were deployed in the formation of national identity.

In using gender as a category of analysis, I employ an understanding of gender similar to that of historian Mary H. Blewett, who characterizes it as the "appropriate masculine and feminine behaviors that are worked out in political controversy and become socially established as expressions of the fundamental 'natures' of men and women."[37] Building on Blewett's definition, I investigate the ways in which men and women manipulated constantly changing notions of manhood and womanhood to better suit their interests as husbands, wives, and Egyptian national subjects. Although constructions of manhood and womanhood were indeed shaped and reshaped by a variety of socioeconomic and political forces, I focus on the contradictory ways in which Egyptians in the press and in the courtrooms understood and used their gender identity to affect their marital and national identities and vice versa. This does not mean, however, that these Egyptians were completely free to create, assert, and manipulate their individual gender, marital, and national identities. They were constrained by larger religious, political, and socioeconomic processes, such as Islamic law, British rule, and foreign economic domination, as well as by powerful figures in positions of authority, such as the Islamic judges who presided over their cases and the British and Egyptian politicians who determined their political and legal systems.

I loosely refer to the middle-class (and occasionally upper-class) writers and readers in this book as nationalists, even though they come from a variety of political leanings and religious convictions. I use the term *nationalist* broadly to include any writer who used marriage as a lens to critique a social, political, or economic ill that he or she perceived was linked to the Egyptian political or economic dependency on the British. As a result, the term includes liberal and conservative reformers, secular and religious activists, and patriarchs and feminists. The Islamic judges and lower-class, middle-class, and upper-class litigants in the courts, however, are not referred to as nationalists because their views on the political status of the nation are impossible to detect from case transcripts. At the same time, however, I do not assume that these Islamic judges and litigants were not nationalists. They were often influenced by the nationalist discourses circulating in the newspapers and magazines that the literate among them read. Although Islamic law, which was designed by medieval jurists and later reformed by modern legal scholars and politicians, often departed from Egyptian nationalist discourses, law and nationalism often influenced and informed one another in early twentieth-century Egypt.

Most nationalists showed a deep respect for Islamic law. For example, members of the Egyptian Feminist Union (EFU), which Huda Sha'rawi founded in 1923 when Egyptian nationalist leaders failed to enfranchise women who had participated in the 1919 revolution, were careful not to criticize Islam. They did not challenge Islamic conceptions of unequal complementary gender roles in their 1920s campaign to reform the laws of personal status (marriage, divorce, child custody, and inheritance) because they did not want to be seen as advocating the abandonment of Egypt's Islamic heritage. Nevertheless, this nationalist secular movement of Muslim and Christian middle-class and upper-class urban women had little success in influencing legislators to restrict polygamy and limit men's access to divorce. Similarly, EFU members played only a minor role in marriage crisis debates and instead focused most of their efforts on campaigning for women's rights in education, work, and suffrage, establishing social services for poor women, and outlawing state-regulated prostitution.[38]

Sources and Methods

I analyze court records and press sources in tandem to produce a nuanced conceptualization of marriage, gender, and nationalism in early twentieth-century Egypt. In combining the two sources, I strive to bridge the theoretical and methodological divide in Middle East studies between academic works that rely primarily on periodicals and those that make use of court records. Scholars of twentieth-century Egypt who have relied largely on the press to examine elite articulations of nationalism, feminism, and the family understandably cannot address how financially destitute and politically disfranchised nonelites, who constituted the vast majority of the Egyptian population, participated in the nationalist and feminist struggles against colonialism. Likewise, scholars of the Ottoman-era courts, who obviously did not have a flourishing press to consult before its emergence in the 1870s, rarely situate their litigants and personnel beyond the walls of the courtroom. Merging the two sources provides a more telling story of marriage and the nation in early twentieth-century Egypt.

In 1897, only 5.8 percent of Egypt's population was literate (0.2 percent of women versus 8 percent of men).[39] Nevertheless, 169 periodicals were reported to be in circulation in 1898, although many admittedly were short-lived enterprises.[40] Literacy rates were much lower for women than for men, but Egypt also had a vibrant women's press, with more than thirty Arabic-language weeklies and monthlies produced by, for, and about women between 1892 and 1919 (and several others that emerged from the 1920s onward).[41] During the first two decades of the twentieth century, various women's journals estimated their circulation in the high hundreds or at most a few thousand, whereas most male-run newspapers published several thousands of copies a day. None, however, compared to the top-selling *al-Ahram*, which was selling 20,000 daily copies in 1919, 30,000 by 1929, and up to 50,000 by 1937.[42] The higher sales reflected an increasingly educated society. By 1937, 17.1 percent of Egypt's population was literate (9.5 percent of women versus

24.7 percent of men), and more than 250 Arabic-language periodicals were in circulation.[43]

At the same time, literacy rates and circulation figures cannot provide an accurate glimpse of the number of Egyptians who were exposed to debates in the newspapers. Actual readership in the early twentieth-century Middle East was much higher than the literacy rates or number of subscribers reveal when the likely large number of listeners, the shared subscriptions, and the practice of passing periodicals around are taken into consideration.[44] As an Egyptian observed in 1897, "We often see servants, donkey-rearers and others who cannot read, gather around one who reads while they listen. The streets of Cairo and of other towns in the region are full of this."[45] Popular sites of collective (male) reading included the streets, the marketplace, and, most notably, the coffeehouse, the traditional gathering place for entertainment and the exchange and discussion of information where men read newspapers and talked politics. Although female listeners did not frequent these public places, periodicals were read aloud to middle-class and upper-class women in the classroom and at home.[46]

We may never know how many Egyptians were aware of the marriage crisis, but we know that discussions of the crisis picked up such steam by the early 1930s that several popular newspapers, such as *al-Ahram* and *al-Usbu'*, and women's journals, such as *al-Mar'a al-Misriyya* and *al-Nahda al-Nisa'iyya*, introduced regular columns titled "The Marriage Crisis" to publish the influx of letters from concerned readers. These letters help to capture a broader view because they provide a crucial way to hear the opinions of other Egyptians who were not the middle-class writers and reformers who usually analyzed bachelorhood and its causes. Readers were usually middle-class lawyers, doctors, teachers, academics, government employees, and students. Their correspondence demonstrates that marriage was not only a women's issue but also an issue that captured the attention of Egyptian politicians, religious leaders, social reformers, and other literate men and women.

Although these letter writers indicate that a wider spectrum of women and men from various literate classes were exposed to the notion of a marriage crisis, they still constituted part of a small literate minority of the Egyptian population. Likewise, those middle-class writers and reformers who wrote regular columns and articles about marriage were members of an even smaller segment of society. They constituted a particular social stratum within a specific context, but these writers and readers did not share similar perceptions of or reactions to the marriage crisis. To compare how different political parties, religious groups, social thinkers, and laypeople perceived and explained this crisis, I sampled journals, political newspapers, sociocultural magazines, and legal periodicals of various orientations from the male-run nationalist press, the religious press, the legal press, and the women's press for the period 1898–1936.

Precisely because press sources provide only a glimpse of how a small minority perceived and practiced marriage, I also consulted court records to gauge how Cairenes from all classes understood marriage and their marital rights and duties. An incorporation of the beliefs and practices of the urban lower, middle, and upper classes can help tell a more comprehensive story about marriage and the nation in early twentieth-century Egypt. My intention is not to assess whether middle-class writers who usually focused on themselves accurately reflected the ideas and habits of their peers, as well as their lower-class and elite counterparts in the courts, but merely to compare and contrast different class conceptions and practices of marriage if and where possible.

Legal scholars of other societies who use court records to demonstrate how couples devised inventive solutions to intimate disputes argue that the deepest insights into marriage can be gained by examining the margins of marital life, that is, when a husband and wife are in court.[47] The Egyptian Islamic court cases provide exceptionally rich insights into how litigants viewed marriage and their rights and duties. The registers from early twentieth-century Cairo contain a wide variety of testimonies by plaintiffs, defendants, and witnesses in addition to the verdicts and judicial opinions of judges. Handwritten court registers in their original form and legal petitions and appeals often record the direct voices of litigants, revealing perceptions and details that can rarely be found elsewhere in the historical record.

As invaluable as these sources are, however, they should not be treated as unfiltered mirrors of social reality and must be read critically and cautiously.[48] They do not capture empirical realities any more than press sources or census registers do, and they must be subject to the same rigorous interrogation and careful analysis. Like the press articles, however, court records can provide some insight into Egyptian understandings of marriage and the family. Individuals who brought divorce cases and custody battles to court did so because they had certain ideas about their duties and rights in marriage and divorce. How did litigants' perceptions of their marital rights and duties compare to those espoused by the middle class in the press? Court cases must be read in conjunction with press sources to answer this question. Telling moments of tension, conflict, and crisis in marriage can be discerned only through a detailed examination of legal registers along with press periodicals.

During the period of direct Ottoman rule in Egypt, which began in 1517, Muslims took a variety of civil, criminal, administrative, and personal status cases to the Islamic courts, which served as the central courts of the empire. Christians and Jews had their own religious court systems, but they also frequented the Islamic courts when a case involved Muslims or when the Islamic legal system provided them with more rights than their own laws did. During the nineteenth century, a variety of other nonreligious courts emerged that gradually assumed jurisdiction for all civil and criminal cases and reduced the power and authority of the Islamic courts.[49] By the onset of the British occupation in 1882, the jurisdiction of the Islamic courts had been limited mostly to issues of religious endowments and personal status. The Egyptian administration increasingly formalized the procedures of the Islamic courts and limited its jurisdiction through laws passed in 1880 and 1897 (which were further amended in 1909–1910, 1923, and 1931).[50] These five codes regulated the operations, procedures, and personnel of the Islamic courts. The 1897, 1923, and 1931 directives also dealt with the registration and documentation of marriage contracts, the minimum age of marriage for brides and grooms, and the documentary evidence necessary for certain divorce disputes to be heard in court.[51]

The 1880 code detailed the selection and appointment of judges, marriage notaries, scribes, and inspectors.[52] All court personnel were adult male government employees who were appointed, promoted, transferred, retired, and paid a fixed salary by the Egyptian administration. The court judges underwent the most training. They were drawn from the ranks of jurist-theologians who were trained in Islamic law at religious schools throughout Egypt.[53] During the early twentieth century, many Muslim judges (and court clerks and lawyers) were also educated in a professional training school that prepared them for the newly organized court system.[54] The 1880 code instructed the judges to implement the Hanafi school of law—one of four Sunni Islamic legal schools of thought that was the official school of the Ottoman Empire—despite the personal affiliation of the litigants. Although most Muslims in Lower Egypt adhered to the Shafi'i school of thought and most Muslims in Upper Egypt followed the Maliki legal school,[55] the Egyptian Ministry of Justice contracted Muhammad Pasha Qadri to codify the Hanafi Code of Personal Status Law, which it published in 1875.[56] This set of regulations was never officially promulgated and thus was not binding for the Islamic courts, but it served as the unofficial law of state and became a manual for judges and lawyers. Although legislative reformers made several attempts to amend the 1875 Egyptian Islamic Code of Personal Status, they did not succeed until they passed major legislation in 1920 and again in 1929.[57]

In this book I use the virtually untapped and only recently unearthed court records from the newly reorganized Islamic courts. The 1897 Code of the Organization and Procedure for Islamic Courts reorganized the courts into a clear hierarchy of lower-level and appellate courts: (1) Courts of Summary Justice (*Mahakim Juz'iyya*); (2) Courts of First Instance (*Mahakim Ibtida'iyya*); and in Cairo (3) the Supreme Court (*Mahkama 'Ulya*).[58] These courts lasted until 1955, when President Gamal Abdel Nasser abolished them and transferred their jurisdiction to the postcolonial state's civil courts.[59] During the early twentieth century, Egypt was divided into thirty-six provincial court districts, each headed by a Court of First Instance, and major Egyptian cities could have several subdistricts. Cairo, for example, had nineteen subdistricts, each with its own Court of Summary Justice.[60] Cases adjudicated in the Courts of Summary Justice could be appealed in the Courts of First Instance, where decisions, in turn, could be appealed in the Supreme Court.[61] I examine the three types of cases that litigants filed in the Cairo Islamic Court of First Instance: (1) summary verdicts (*al-ahkam al-juz'iyya*); (2) appellate verdicts (*al-ahkam al-isti'nafiyya*); and (3) detention verdicts (*al-ahkam al-habsiyya).* I sampled several hundred cases of the various marriage agreements, divorce settlements, child custody and support cases, obedience suits, spousal support agreements, inheritance disputes, and alimony suits that these three registers held.

Individuals brought cases to court because they held certain perceptions of their rights and duties in marriage and divorce. Although court transcripts do not divulge how women and men learned about their legal rights and duties or how to navigate the system, they indicate that knowledge of Islamic law was not determined by a litigant's social class, education level, or gender. The fact that the courts were frequented by thousands of Egyptians of all classes to record marriage contracts, file for divorce, and claim custody rights implies that most Cairenes were aware of their rights in marriage and divorce. Scholars of the nineteenth-century Egyptian courts have reached a consensus that rural and urban men and women of all classes frequented the courts.[62] Because early twentieth-century legislation mandated the registration of marriages and divorces, elite and nonelite Egyptians were forced to resort to the courts even more than their predecessors. Class was an ambiguous and evolving category in early twentieth-century Cairo, but the socioeconomic backgrounds of litigants were ascertained through their professions, honorary titles, and the financial amounts mentioned in their lawsuits.

Because the courts charged minimal costs for its various services, litigants from all financial backgrounds could afford to access the court, and impoverished litigants were eligible for exemption from court fees.[63] The standard fee for a marital-related legal decision in early twentieth-century cases was 5 piasters (1/20 of the Egyptian pound, which constituted roughly 1 percent of the average middle-class government employee's monthly salary of LE 5 in 1913).[64] The cost of hiring a lawyer also appears to have been minimal because men and women from various backgrounds increasingly employed lawyers over the course of the twentieth century as the latter became more professionalized. Furthermore, a court-appointed lawyer was obliged to represent a client for free if the client could not afford his fees.[65] Similarly, the court assigned a lawyer to represent a litigant who did not appear in court or send a representative. By the second decade of the twentieth century, most plaintiffs and defendants contracted lawyers, especially after Law 15 of 1916 organized the lawyers into a professional bar and expanded their rights and duties.[66] Undoubtedly, these lawyers helped Egyptians to navigate and better understand the Islamic legal system. As more Egyptians relied on lawyers over the early twentieth century, they likely neglected to educate themselves in the intricacies of the Islamic legal system as their predecessors had done. By the 1930s, few litigants stood before the court without legal representation.

Breaking Down the Marriage Crisis

I focus on a major explanation for the marriage crisis in each of the following chapters of this book. In Chapter 2, I analyze those press articles that blamed bachelorhood on the various economic crises that swept early twentieth-century Egypt. Inflation and unemployment made it financially nonviable for men to marry and afford the supposedly extravagant costs of the dower and maintenance that brides' fathers demanded. I also examine the arguments that accused middle-class men of not marrying so that they could indulge in idleness at the coffeehouse, prostitution, and alcohol instead. I demonstrate how writers and readers saw marriage as an institution that would discipline bachelors into responsible and moral national subjects. Court records reveal how the stagnant economy and financial demands of marriage affected men and their responsibilities in marriage. By comparing the arguments in the press with those in the courtrooms, I show how Egyptians used the marriage crisis to critique foreign economic domination, middle-class materialism, and bachelors themselves. I also illustrate how they used the crisis as a trope to define a new masculinity that would make men into husbands, despite the obstacles the occupation was placing before them.

The press debates that earmarked the customs of arranged marriage, female seclusion, and uneducated women as either the causes of or solutions to the marriage crisis are explored in Chapter 3. I survey Islamic court records to examine how the middle-class constructions of wifehood in the press reflected and affected the situations of wives from various classes in the Cairo courtrooms. Specifically, I look at the marriage of minors to understand the nature of arranged marriage and obedience orders to determine the extent of female seclusion and the

Islamic stipulations of a wife's duties. Although the prescriptions of obedient and secluded wifehood outlined in the press did not often mirror those displayed in the courtrooms, the courts and the press nevertheless worked together to construct a new, albeit confined, role of wifehood during a time of increased opportunities for women's education and gender integration.

In Chapter 4, I demonstrate how divorce served as a medium for Egyptians to articulate their anxieties over the reformation, modernization, and construction of their struggling nation. Legislators and reformers sought to restrict divorce in order to make marriage more permanent, or more modern, so that it would serve as a sturdy foundation for the emerging nation. To uncover what lay behind Egyptians' concerns, I analyze their lamentations of the supposedly soaring divorce rate by comparing them with court cases, statistics, and census registers. I also probe how and why the new divorce laws in early twentieth-century Egypt were proposed, legislated, and translated into practice in the courtrooms. Although their explanations and proposals often diverged, reformers and legislators shared a common hopeful vision that modern marriage would pave Egypt's path to independence, lower the divorce rate, and help alleviate the marriage crisis.

The press discussions that faulted women's inadequate maternal skills for the marriage crisis are the topic of Chapter 5. In contrast to the press, which emphasized the role of mothers in raising future citizens for the nation, the Islamic courts consistently awarded custody of minor children to fathers and accorded them sole responsibility for raising children. The silence in the press on fathers' roles in the nation reveals that when it came to parenting the future of the nation, women were to be active and men passive, at least within the household, but not according to Islamic laws. An analysis of press debates and custody battles in tandem helps explain the discrepancy between mothers and fathers in legal versus nationalist discourse to arrive at a better understanding of motherhood and fatherhood in early twentieth-century Egypt.

In Chapter 6, I conclude the book by comparing the early twentieth-century Egyptian marriage crisis to its early twenty-first-century counterpart and to marriage crises in other parts of the world during other periods of time. Although I acknowledge their similarities,

I argue for the uniqueness of the early twentieth-century Egyptian case. After summarizing the book's chapters, I attempt to explain why public debates over the Egyptian marriage crisis waned over the course of the twentieth century only to reappear in the early twenty-first century. I end by calling for future studies on the recently unearthed Islamic court records in the Egyptian National Archives and on marriage crises elsewhere to understand how various peoples from different eras deployed marriage to conceive of the problems and hopes of their families, nations, worlds, and futures.

2

The Grooming of Men

Marriage is the cornerstone of manhood and a principle of national
allegiance. A man who does not marry is like a deserter from the
army: Both betray their responsibility and duty to their nation.
Manhood can only be attained through marriage.

Mustafa Sadiq al-Rafi'i

MUSTAFA SADIQ AL-RAFI'I, a well-known conservative intellectual who regularly published short stories in the Islamic cultural weekly
al-Risala, viewed marriage as a prerequisite for manhood and nationhood, as noted in the epigraph.[1] For him, a real Egyptian man married
and provided for his female compatriot. Al-Rafi'i's concerns about the
marriage crisis were not new in 1934 Cairo. What was unique about his
tirade was the fact that he was so quick to emasculate bachelors and
question their national loyalty without bothering to examine their reasons for evading marriage.

The most common explanations that writers, reformers, and
bachelors offered to explain the purported male aversion to marriage
involved the economic challenges that early twentieth-century Egypt
faced. Foreign economic domination, the 1907 and 1921 economic crises,
the early 1930s Great Depression, the early 1930s unemployment crisis,

and periods of high inflationary prices but paltry government salaries were all blamed at one time or another for creating a financially nonviable climate that discouraged middle-class men from marriage. These men could no longer afford the reportedly extravagant costs of the wife's dower, food and clothing allowances, and domicile that were incumbent on a Muslim husband. A survey of Islamic court records provides exceptional insight into the economic conditions, financial obligations, and fiscal capabilities of various husbands of all classes during this period.

Another frequent explanation for the marriage crisis accused middle-class bachelors of wasting their time and money at the coffeehouse or, worse, on alcohol and prostitutes. Writers who criticized bachelors for such behavior saw marriage as an institution that would discipline bachelors into responsible and moral national subjects. Although observers might have disagreed over the reasons for bachelorhood, they were all defining a new notion of middle-class masculinity, one that would make men into husbands despite the various economic hardships of the early twentieth century. This emerging nationalist definition of manhood departed substantially from the Islamic legal one outlined in the 1875 Egyptian Islamic Code of Personal Status and upheld in the courtrooms. The marriage crisis was not just used to criticize the British colonial presence, the Egyptian economy, middle-class materialism, and bachelors' illicit behavior. It also served as a way to define a new middle-class masculinity.

Bankrupt Bachelors and Economic Emasculation

As early as 1898, middle-class men who earned low government salaries complained that they could not afford to marry.[2] Men who were already married during the 1907 economic crisis likewise wrote letters to the editor grumbling that their wives did not understand that the country's financial straits did not allow them to spend on them as they previously had.[3] Many husbands went to court to request reductions in the amount of support owed to their wives for the same reasons on the eve of this economic crisis.[4] Likewise, wives went to court to demand more money from their husbands because their existing allowances were "low compared to the [rising] prices of the country."[5] Because Islamic law recognized inflationary prices of basic commodities as a ground for redetermining a wife's allowance from her husband, these wives were granted increases.[6] The economic crisis of 1907 came to an end, but the grievances that men could not afford to marry because of the faltering economy and rising costs of living did not. In 1913, for example, *al-Ahram* reader Muhammad al-Bardisi was concerned enough about the economy that he wrote a letter to the editor in which he blamed measly fixed government salaries for middle-class bachelorhood. He argued, "Most young men earn no more than LE 5 a month, and it takes an extremely long time for them to set aside from this paltry sum sufficient funds for a dower and the costs of a wedding."[7]

Britain's involvement in World War I brought its Egyptian protectorate further economic debilitation. At various points between 1914 and 1918, Egyptian lower-class farmers and middle-class government employees on fixed salaries suffered widespread inflation as the price of foodstuffs rose and food, requisitioned for the British army stationed in Egypt, became scarce, even threatening some areas with famine. The price of cotton, which had constituted nearly 90 percent of Egyptian exports since 1910, plummeted, and its unstable postwar price created resultant financial crises.[8] The secular social reformer (but later Islamist martyr) Sayyid Qutb held the wartime devaluation of cotton responsible for endemic bachelorhood even years later, on the brink of the Great Depression, because its detrimental effects continued to make it fiscally impossible for men to marry.[9] Writers cited the "soaring" and "unbearable" costs of living, especially in proportion to insufficient salaries, as a major explanation for men's inability to marry in the 1920s and 1930s.[10] Although the average government salary would increase from LE 5 a month in 1913 to LE 8 a month in 1935, soaring food and clothing prices rendered the increase inconsequential. By 1933, real wages had fallen 50 percent and the annual per capita income had fallen from LE 12 in 1913 to LE 8 in 1930–1933.[11]

By the early 1930s, social commentators introduced a new economic factor as a chief deterrent to marriage: the unemployment crisis. The Great Depression coupled with the rapid expansion of education created a large pool of educated middle-class men without job prospects. Although the British administration in Egypt had spent only 1 percent of its budget on education in the late nineteenth and early twentieth centuries, education became a priority for the post-1922 semi-independent Egyptian government, which increased spending on education to nearly 11 percent of the total budget by 1931. A secondary-school degree was a passport to the prestigious bureaucratic service, which offered job security and a pension plan. By the mid-1930s, there were 7,500 university graduates, but nearly half of them were unemployed men.[12] Government employment was a mainstay of masculine respectability for the middle classes: "Without job prospects, these young men couldn't marry, and couldn't found a household which they would be responsible for financially supporting. In short, they were denied the status and position needed to be proper masculine national subjects."[13]

Several writers and readers echoed these concerns in the early 1930s. Their anxieties about the unemployment problem were steeped in anticolonial tones critical of the continued foreign economic domination. Although Egyptians had achieved a political independence of sorts in 1922, many nationalists believed that the struggling nation continued to suffer from European economic exploitation throughout the 1920s and early 1930s. Like their counterparts in colonial India, Egyptian nationalists viewed "colonialism's threat from the perspective of a territorially delimited economic collective" in which they saw "the deterritorialization of the national economy" as the result of British intrusion and its foreign capital.[14] Upon titular independence in 1922, nationalists unsuccessfully sought to create a local capitalist sector parallel to the foreign one that dominated the economy.[15] They succeeded in creating some nationally oriented and indigenously controlled economic institutions, such as Bank Misr, in which shareholding was limited to Egyptians. Foreign capitalists, however, continued to control the economy.[16] Because British policies had encouraged foreign firms to establish themselves in Egypt and these firms were not subject to local laws or taxes, many indigenous industries were doomed to fail in the post-1922 neocolonial economic regime.[17]

As a result, many nationalists blamed the British for Egypt's related marital and unemployment crises. One anonymous reader offered a stinging reproach of the Egyptian government and British domination, warning of the threat that educated unemployed men posed to national security. After condemning the state for not limiting European competition "so that you do not find [Egyptian] natives competing for jobs," he warned:

> If a young educated man graduates . . . with no capital . . . what are his prospects when . . . he is unable to find work? It is indisputable that the vast majority of young men are poor. Before they can think of marriage, they must think of making a living. If that is impossible then they are forced to neglect marriage. . . . Social experts agree that the educated unemployed man poses a greater danger to public security than the ignorant unemployed man because his knowledge enables him to realize his goals.[18]

This reader highlighted the threat that bachelors who had neither jobs nor wives to discipline them into responsible citizens could present to society. He deployed the common fear of regimes elsewhere that agonized over the danger of the single male subject who ostensibly bred crime and rebellion: "Such a man would be drawn to political action because there was no home life to contain him," unlike married men who "were fulfilled and complacent" because they "were restrained by marriage."[19] Yet this writer was not just conjuring images of threatening manly bachelors. His diatribe also underscored that unemployment emasculated single men in economic as well as sociopolitical terms. A bachelor's lack of professional and marital prospects would drive him to pose a threat to the already fragile nation.

This letter writer was not alone in using bachelorhood as a lens through which to criticize both the Egyptian government and British domination for Egypt's economic problems. The prominent Islamic reformer Muhammad Junaydi, who published a detailed study in 1933, *The Marriage Crisis in Egypt*, also asserted that unemployment caused by the lack of indigenous industries encouraged bachelorhood.[20] Junaydi proposed that young men should be trained to enter the business sector rather than government service because the government could not accommodate all of them. He also argued that bachelors wanted to enter commerce but did not have the courage or skills to do so because they had not been trained in school. Junaydi deployed economic nationalism as a means to end the unemployment crisis.

> We must teach each Egyptian that he who does not extend his help . . . is considered despicable. . . . We must appeal to each Egyptian's national pride

to purchase Egyptian products. . . . My dear compatriots, buy Egyptian-made products only . . . and do not buy foreign products . . . or else we only prolong our economic occupation.[21]

Economic nationalism, the favoring of local capital over foreign capital, was the solution to the entwined marital and unemployment crises for Junaydi. His use of the bachelorhood crisis enabled him to lament the unemployment problem and call for an end to foreign domination, proposing indigenous industrialization as the path to national progress and demanding state assistance to achieve these goals. Marriage did not merely reflect a union between a man and a woman; it signified a man's capacity to assert his full economic independence, individually and collectively as a member of an imagined nation. These writers were among those "Egyptians [who] finally came to the realization that true political independence could only come with economic independence. . . . All the frustrations of a society that was undergoing change and was in the throes of a recession were blamed on the influence of the Europeans. . . . The rejection of the British presence, the essence of the nationalist movement, was equated with a rejection of everything foreign."[22] Because Junaydi and the anonymous letter writer viewed financial security and confidence as vital ingredients for manhood, they held the foreign domination of the economy responsible for the emasculation of Egyptian men.

Dowers and Diamonds

Fathers' demands for extravagant dowers from their daughters' prospective suitors was the chief cause of bachelorhood for many of its observers. The dower (*mahr*) that the groom paid to the bride played a considerable role in Islamic marriage, and its amount was always noted in the marriage contract.[23] The dower typically consisted of two parts: the advanced amount (*muqaddam*), which had to be paid at the signing of the marriage contract before sexual consummation of the marriage, and the deferred portion (*mu'akhkhar*), which had to be paid at the termination of the marriage, either by divorce or death.[24]

In early twentieth-century Egypt, the advanced dower usually consisted of one-third to one-half of the total dower.[25] A larger portion, however, was paid in advance when the bride was from a wealthy or noble family to signify her family's elite status.[26] Although Islamic legislators did not provide figures, they noted that the dower should be determined according to the bride's social status.[27] The bride's family often insisted that the groom's obligation of the dower be fully observed because its amount was a reflection of their status and because it discouraged the husband from exercising his right to divorce, since he was required to pay its balance upon dissolution of the marriage.[28]

In the press debates over excessive dowers, only a few writers pointed out its dual justification: to protect the wife's economic position in the marriage and to deter her husband from divorcing her rashly. The renowned religiously conservative women's rights advocate Nabawiyya Musa, for example, argued in 1927 that significant dowers not only discouraged husbands from divorce but also encouraged bachelors to work hard to support a wife.[29] Certain readers of her women's issues column in *al-Balagh al-'Usbu'i* issued by the Wafd, the political party that led Egypt to semi-independence in the early 1920s, were not convinced. One male reader asked, "Do you think dowers are too low in Egypt today? Because reformers and everyone else are noticing the opposite."[30]

This man made a correct observation. Several writers, reformers, and readers condemned fathers who demanded excessive dowers, especially as the financial situation of middle-class bachelors deteriorated during the various economic crises of early twentieth-century Egypt. In 1913, for example, *al-Ahram* reader 'Abd al-'Aziz Isma'il observed that fathers "marry their daughters only to men with very high incomes who pay the highest dower. And this dower is too high for a [government] employee."[31] Commentators juxtaposed the rising costs of marriage with the declining purchasing power of government salaries. Many bachelors, such as M. A. Radwan, lamented their inability to marry.

> I am from a good family . . . found employment in a government agency . . . I presented myself to a family of equal stature to mine. What was my lot beyond their haggling and outrageous demands? Much shrugging of shoulders and mocking smiles on their faces, for no other reason than I am poor and unable to afford the price of their daughter [i.e., the dower] and the costs of a new home.[32]

Radwan's tragic tale was a common one in early twentieth-century Egypt.[33] Such bachelors did not blame the economic climate. Rather, they impugned fathers for demanding only rich men who could provide their daughters with a luxurious standard of living. Radwan's story was a stinging social commentary on the materialistic preoccupation plaguing middle-class families. It was not only bachelors who offered this censure of the growing materialistic fixation on a suitor's capital. Both Huda Sha'rawi, the founder of the Egyptian Feminist Union (EFU), and Mayy Ziyada, another prominent women's activist, asserted that the middle-class love of appearances, spending, and luxury, which manifested itself in outrageous dower demands, deterred men from marriage.[34]

The critique of materialism was directed at the middle class because, as one observer put it, "the poor do not demand high dowers and the rich can afford it."[35] It was the emerging middle class that became the most preoccupied with capital accumulation and consumption as Egypt became a market for European manufactured goods. Since the early 1900s, several commentators had bemoaned this situation, where money had become the "all and all."[36] In 1920, for example, the owner and editor of the women's monthly *al-Mar'a al-Misriyya*, Balsam 'Abd al-Malik, attributed bachelorhood to consumerism brought on by the incorporation of Egypt into the capitalist world market: "Europe blessed us all with the products of its factories and industries. . . . When young men see the amount of money spent, they become fearful of marriage . . . because they are unable to provide for the ladies of today."[37] For her, the mounting preoccupation with materialism was Europe's fault, not necessarily or only that of the Egyptian middle class.

Most critics blamed fathers, not brides, for making outrageous dower demands, even though Islamic law was clear that the dower was the wife's property alone in order to make her a party to the contract and ensure that the marriage would not be considered a sale.[38] Unlike historic Christian marriage, in which a woman's identity and property were subsumed into her husband's as a result of laws of comity and coverture, a Muslim wife retained her identity, name, and property.[39] Legally, the dower had to be paid in currency or anything that could be valued monetarily, such as jewelry and property.[40] In early twentieth-century Egypt, the dower was usually recorded in the contract as currency but was often used to pay for the diamond wedding ring, other gold jewelry, and/or the marital home's furniture.[41]

Nevertheless, male and female critics referred to fathers as "ignorant" or "greedy" for "haggling" over their daughters as if they were "commodities."[42] Their scorn focused on fathers because they were the ones who met with prospective grooms, inquired about their financial means, and set the amount of dowers. Rarely were women themselves blamed, although a few writers did speak to them. In 1933, "The Marriage Crisis" columnist 'A'isha 'Abd al-Rahman declared that middle-class fathers were not the ones to fault: "They want to use that money . . . to buy their daughters a huge trousseau. . . . We cannot fault them. . . . Every girl wants the nicest furniture and better than those before her."[43] This conservative female contributor to the Islamic journal *al-Nahda al-Nisa'iyya* called on women to reform their materialistic tastes to encourage men to marry them. When most bachelors who were interviewed by *al-Mar'a al-Jadida* in 1924 cited high dowers as the main obstacle to marriage, the magazine condemned women for "foolishly" thinking a high dower reflected their honor.[44] Writers warned women that they would end up as spinsters if they did not lower their expectations.[45] Most, however, impugned fathers and sympathized with insolvent bachelors who could not afford their demands during such economic times.[46]

How much exactly were these exorbitant dowers? Most writers did not provide specific numbers, but a few did. Throughout the 1920s and 1930s, writers occasionally provided an account of a father who shamelessly demanded a dower of LE 400 or LE 500. If the average middle-class government employee earned roughly LE 8 per month in 1935, then he would have had to spend more than five times his *annual* income to afford a dower of LE 500.[47] The moral of the story was usually that the modest bachelor could not afford the exorbitant amount and was thus forced to remain a bachelor or marry another, who was not his first choice and whom he would eventually divorce. Press accounts suggested that LE 100 was the average but still "outrageously high" dower demanded of a middle-class suitor in urban Egypt in the 1920s and 1930s.[48] One wealthy father explained his rationale for demanding LE 100 from his daughters' suitors: "I know that this amount is a lot for a government employee . . . but is it considered a lot for the dower of a girl who is accustomed to the income of her father?"[49] Despite demanding a sum that cost the average middle-class man more than twelve times his monthly salary, this father wanted to make sure that his daughters would not suffer a decline in their standard of living. Whereas critics considered such fathers materialistic, their desire to maintain their daughters' standard of living was religiously justified.

The Islamic doctrine of suitability (*kafa'a*) stated that a marriage was an appropriate union if the man was equal to the woman in lineage, financial standing, and profession.[50] Certain bachelors who wanted to marry complained that, although they were gainfully employed and could afford the dower, they could not support the standard of living of the potential bride.[51] A Muslim husband was obligated to cover his wife's food and clothing expenses, even if she had her own means, according to their standard of living.[52] This standard of living was determined by calculating the average between the husband's current economic status and the level to which the wife was accustomed in her father's home before her marriage.[53] If the husband refused to pay her expenses, then the wife had the right to sue him.[54]

According to the press, many early twentieth-century men aspired to marry women from a higher class. As one male writer explained, "An educated man wants to marry up to raise his social status. The son of an effendi wants to marry the daughter of a bey and the son of a bey wants to marry the daughter of a pasha."[55] Women writers also complained of the greedy aspirations of such men.[56] One fumed:

> When a man seeks to marry, he sets his mind on money above all else. It does not matter whether his bride-to-be is beautiful or ugly, educated or ignorant.. . . . For them [men], marriage is a form of commerce. I often come across letters to the newspapers from bachelors complaining of the prohibitive costs of marriage, when all the while there are beautiful, educated, and refined women . . . prepared to accept them for only a nominal sum of money solely to meet the needs of formality.[57]

This anonymous single woman did not disguise her resentment for bachelors who deceptively complained that they could not afford to marry while they coveted wealthy brides. Her observation that most women would accept negligible dowers contradicted the image painted by the press.

Because of its sensationalist nature, the press perhaps intentionally focused on exorbitant dowers as an example that society should *not* follow. Although it should not be doubted that some elite women did marry for a dower of LE 400 or LE 500, neither that amount nor LE 100 was the typical amount received by the vast majority of Egyptian brides who frequented the early twentieth-century Islamic courts. More significant than the sum is the fact that writers and readers used the dower as a trope to criticize the purportedly materialistic middle class, decry low government salaries, lament colonial economic domination and various economic crises, and lower society's financial expectations of middle-class suitors.

Nevertheless, critics continued to perceive the demand for a high dower as the main deterrent to marriage. Some observers reminded fathers that their excessive demands were contrary to Islamic law, which did not intend for dowers to be so high that they discouraged marriage.[58] The 1875 Egyptian Islamic Code of Personal Status stated that a husband should not be "gravely wronged by the payment of an excessive dower," but at the same time neither should a wife be "wronged by the inferiority of the dower assigned to her."[59] Reformers demanded that the state "intervene in this issue of such reproductive, moral, and national importance" by limiting dower amounts "to open the doors" to marriage for young men.[60]

So what were the limits on the dower that reformers suggested? Proposals ranged from half a piaster to LE 10 to LE 100, with the last amount limited to the wealthiest classes.[61] The most common suggestion, however, was 25 piasters (about 3 percent of the average middle-class man's monthly salary in 1935).[62] Although the nationalist press was attempting to devalue the role of the dower, the Islamic courts continued to uphold the importance of the husband's first matrimonial duty, which was to pay the full advanced portion before the marriage. According to Islamic law, a man could not and should not expect his marriage to be consummated before he paid the advanced dower in full.[63] The archival record shows that the courts upheld this principle for all classes. On 26 December 1898, for example, Zakiyya 'Amr al-Talib went to court to demand that her husband, a coffeehouse owner, pay the advanced portion of her dower. Her husband admitted that they were married but argued that he was not obliged to pay the amount because they had not consummated their marriage. The judge disagreed and upheld the Islamic principle for this upper lower-class couple that the advanced portion should have been paid in full at the signing of the marriage contract.[64]

Despite this law, many women apparently consummated their marriages without receiving their dowers and later came to court to demand that their husbands pay the sums that they had never received. Their husbands often claimed that they had paid the advanced dowers, but they did not bring evidence to corroborate their testimony.[65] If Islamic law was so clear that a husband was obliged to pay the advanced dower upon the signing of the marriage contract, how is it possible that some wives did not receive their dowers? Because many marriages were contracted beyond the state's legal system, especially before marriage contracts were legally mandated in 1931, women could be married without receiving their dowers.[66] Even in official marriage contracts many women—or their fathers who married them off—falsely claimed that they received a specified amount to show their faith in the man and marriage or to preserve the public image of a high dower, which was a symbol of prestige in a society where an individual's status was determined mainly by the wealth he possessed.[67] The press did make mention of these instances, but it preferred to focus on those fathers who refused to send their daughters home with their new husbands until the advanced dower was paid.[68] Its condemnation of such fathers was part of its campaign to remove financial barriers to marriage and construct a new notion of middle-class masculinity, one in which a bachelor's education and financial potential—and not his current status—determined his manhood.

In 1935, two well-known upper-class Egyptian women married upper middle-class men for an advanced dower of only 25 piasters each, which was highly publicized in the press. Huriyya Idris's aunt and guardian, Huda Sha'rawi, the leader of the EFU and daughter of the largest landowner in Egypt at the time, agreed on behalf of her niece to this amount. Ahmad al-Sawi Muhammad, the popular author of "Brief and to the Point," praised the gesture.[69] Later that year, when he married Duriyya Shafiq, a young feminist who would later found the Daughter of the Nile Union, at Huda Sha'rawi's summer home, she also agreed to a dower of 25 piasters. So significant was this new model of marriage to the middle-class press that a photograph of the couple appeared on the front pages of various newspapers; even the marriage of King Fu'ad (r. 1917–1936) had appeared only on the inside pages.[70]

Photographs of Duriyya Shafiq and al-Sawi and of Huriyya Idris and her groom appeared in the September 1935 issue of *L'Egyptienne* under the caption "a modern couple" with an article commending these couples for setting a positive example of minimal dowers.[71] Huda Sha'rawi's niece agreed to accept the paltry *advanced* dower as a point of honor to facilitate the marriage, but the groom fixed the *deferred* dower at LE 400 (about fifty times the average middle-class man's monthly salary of LE 8) to prove that he did not view her concession as an easy way to later dissolve the marriage. Although many lauded this initiative, the editor of *al-Usbu'* accused Huda Sha'rawi of deception: "But the delayed dower is 400 pounds and the wedding party by itself cost that much and on top of that the furniture of the bridal home cost no less than 2,000 pounds. Thus, the issue is heresy. It appears as reform. But it is really self-propaganda."[72]

For most, however, the revered public figure's endorsement of two marriages contracted with a negligible advanced dower signified an attempt to institute a new custom that would facilitate marriage during a purported marriage shortage. All the parties involved claimed that marriage should be about love, not money. The brides, however, did not make any claims that they would contribute to the household expenses or that they did not expect their husbands to support them after marriage. Rather, these women were telling society that a high dower did not necessarily prove a bachelor's manliness. Instead of judging a man by his income, fathers and women should inspect his other attributes.

Many writers asked fathers to consider a bachelor's potential based on his education and character. One female anonymous reader, for example, wrote:

> Many educated young men are of modest means. . . . When they go to propose to a girl they are asked only about their wealth and salary. Asking about their knowledge, virtue, or future is not important because fathers account for their daughter's happiness only through money, which is wrong and ignorant.[73]

For this woman, property and wealth should no longer count as criteria for middle-class manhood. Rather, a prospective husband's professional skill, knowledge, and ability to earn a living should be evaluated. Scholar Magda Baraka explains this new trend, which emerged in early twentieth-century Egypt: "Being of a good family could be reduced at will—for the sake of a professionally promising suitor—to mean a person whose parents though modest (but never working-class) were sufficiently 'respectable' and had given their son a good education and a proper upbringing."[74] Although a groom was usually valued according to the dower amount he was able to offer, urban fathers started to consider his education as an asset that compensated for a low dower in early twentieth-century Egypt.[75] Western-style education was a forcible catalyst of class mobility. It was the main factor responsible for the creation of the new middle class in early twentieth-century Egypt.[76] It also was an assurance of a man's future financial stability. Although a new notion of masculinity was emerging for middle-class men in the press, the legal and fiscal obligations that Islamic marriage placed on these men and the expectations many fathers continued to hold were not changing.

Home Sweet Home

In December 1932, the prominent young lawyer and magazine editor Fikri Abaza delivered a lecture about the marriage crisis at the American University in Cairo. He began his presentation by announcing his intention to remain a bachelor because four different fathers had rejected his marriage proposals for purely material reasons. It is noteworthy that Abaza, a member of one of Egypt's largest and wealthiest landowning families, was turned off by their materialism. His career as a lawyer and editor, however, earned him a modest middle-class salary. His narrative was the talk of the town, with many in the press expressing their astonishment that "a man of full manhood" who was "from one of the most honorable Egyptian families, holds an advanced degree, and has a noble profession" was rejected merely for financial reasons.[77]

Abaza's first marriage proposal was refused because the potential bride's father wanted the marital abode to be located in the more posh and closer Cairo neighborhood of Garden City or Heliopolis rather than in Zaqaziq, 53 miles away, where Abaza worked and could afford to establish a home.[78] The father had a religious right to demand a domicile from his daughter's suitor because the second obligation that Islamic law imposed on a Muslim husband was to provide and sustain an independent conjugal home.[79] As in the historic West, setting up a new household was an essential qualification for manhood.[80] In early twentieth-century Egypt, wives from all classes took their husbands to court if they were not fulfilling this obligation. It was not enough for a husband to provide a home such as his parents' home. Islamic law was clear that this home had to be independent of the husband's or his wife's parental home.[81] Tafida Mustafa 'Abd al-Raziq, for example, took her middle-class husband to court on 23 June 1898 to complain that "we are living with his parents in one home, which is not lawful, and I am harmed by that."[82] Her husband confessed, and the judge ordered him to establish a separate abode.

A wife whose husband left her without a home or money to pay rent for her home were entitled to borrow money in her husband's name if she could prove that her husband was absent or destitute.[83] If a husband was not financially capable or physically present to support his wife, then his paternal relatives were required to do so, and they had the right to recover the sums they paid from the husband when his economic situation improved or he returned.[84] On 2 February 1914 Biyada Shihata filed a claim to do just that.[85] Her lower-class husband, 'Abdu Shahata al-Jamil, a pastry chef, had failed to provide her with a home, despite a previous court order to do so. Because she brought two witnesses who confirmed her allegation, the judge deemed that she was entitled to borrow the amount of the monthly rent in his name from a relation, demonstrating that even lower-class men were not excused from this Islamic duty. Because this basic obligation was so clearly imposed on husbands of all classes (and so easily confirmed by witnesses or court inspectors), most men who were sued in court immediately confessed that they had not established homes for their wives.[86]

Husbands were not merely required to provide an independent home; the home had to be on a par with the couple's standard of living.[87] Wives often sued their husbands if they deemed that the home was unsuitable to their standard. On 28 October 1906, Hafiza 'Abd al-Qadir's lawyer alleged that the apartment her husband had provided was not lawful because it was within a building that was "occupied with the husband's relatives and that my client is from an honorable and wealthy family who deserves an isolated home yet the aforementioned apartment is connected to his relatives' apartment," which had a "roof terrace from which those on the fourth floor are able to watch her during her time of privacy."[88] In arguing that Hafiza was from a noble and wealthy family, her lawyer was referencing the Islamic doctrine that states, "When the spouses are well off, the husband should lodge his wife in a separate house. Otherwise he should furnish his wife with a separate apartment in proportion to their condition, having the necessary accessories and having neighbors."[89] This private residence was required to prevent the wife's exposure to neighbors and strangers so as not to endanger her chastity. It also needed to be surrounded by righteous neighbors who could come to her rescue in times of need and contain the appropriate household goods, such as furniture, bedding, and kitchen utensils.[90] Islamic law was class based: A lower-class wife was not legally entitled to the same amount of privacy and luxury. Although husbands of all classes were required to provide an independent home, this case shows that upper-class men faced additional obligations. It was incumbent upon Hafiza's husband to provide her with the privacy and luxury her status warranted. Doing so proved his upper-class manliness.

Returning to Abaza's plight in marriage, did the father who rejected Abaza's proposal because he objected to the marital dwelling being in Zaqaziq, some 53 miles from Cairo, have a religious right to do so? Although Abaza was critical of this father, court records reveal that a wife or her father could demand that her husband provide her with a home in the region in which she was raised and married because it was familiar territory where she enjoyed the protection of her paternal family. Islamic jurists agreed that "the husband was absolutely forbidden from insisting that his wife move" to a "distant place" if it entailed "undue hardship," evidenced by the 1898 ruling in Hasan Effendi Ghazi versus Habiba Ahmad Pasha 'Arabi.[91] Ghazi attempted to obtain a court ruling to force his unwilling wife to move from Cairo, her hometown in which they were married, to his home in Mansura, 87 miles away. Although Ghazi claimed that his wife had agreed to move with him before they married, the judge agreed with Habiba that the distance between Cairo and Mansura exceeded the legal limit, and thus Ghazi had no right to ask her to move with him.[92] Habiba, the independently wealthy daughter of a pasha, did not request that her husband provide her with a home in Cairo. Perhaps her husband, who was a mayor, had already established a marital residence for them in the country's capital. Or perhaps she either returned to her father's home or provided a home for herself; it is not clear from the court proceedings. Other less privileged wives also refused to accompany their husbands when they moved outside Cairo *and* demanded that their husbands provide them with a home in Cairo. On 27 November 1906, Bahiyya al-Shaykh Muhammad Hasan filed a claim demanding that her husband, who had moved to work as a merchant in Maghagha, an Upper Egyptian mill town located 153 miles south of Cairo, establish a home in the capital, where they had married. Because Maghagha was beyond the legal distance from her hometown, the judge ruled in her favor.[93]

Although the press was willing to accommodate the economic transformations that made it more difficult for men to fulfill their marital obligations, the Islamic courts were not when it came to a man's obligation to provide an independent home suitable to his wife's status and within reasonable distance to her hometown. Judges did not consider labor migration during periods of rampant unemployment as a reason to force a wife to move long distance with her husband, even if the job was his only opportunity to support her. Nor were they willing to excuse husbands who could not afford to sustain a home during the economic crises of the early twentieth century.

Boys Will Be Boys

When Ibrahim Fathi lamented "the reluctance of young men to marry" in 1913 as "a microbe that infects" bachelors, he did not empathize with their meager financial situation as many others did.[94] Although he also criticized foreign economic domination, he largely faulted Egyptian men: "The young men of today spend their time in coffeehouses and places of entertainment . . . squandering all their money, whereas if they economized, they could save great sums from the money they spend on coffee, water pipes, drink, and games."[95] Fathi called on bachelors to become more productive national subjects in order to rectify the crisis in marriage. Others agreed with him, arguing that young men could use the money they wasted in coffeehouses on a considerable dower.[96]

Over the next two decades, the coffeehouse continued to be perceived as a site of moral corruption that was to blame for bachelorhood.

During the early twentieth century, this locale was a predominantly male space omnipresent in Cairo's popular quarters. Men of all classes patronized coffeehouses, but the owners were widely believed to be criminals and vagrants who usually served as informants in police investigations.[97] Social reformers did not necessarily view the activities associated with coffeehouses—male bonding, drinking coffee, playing backgammon, and smoking water pipes—as morally bankrupt, but they blamed the men who frequented these venues for wasting time and money better spent at home or work. They argued that men who did not marry early would never learn fiscal and familial responsibility, instead preferring to preserve their freedom, independence, and money for themselves.[98]

Other places of entertainment, such as nightclubs, bars, and brothels, materialized in the late 1920s and early 1930s as dens of immorality that deterred men from marriage as these locales grew in number and popularity among middle-class Egyptians. These spaces were condemned because bachelors wasted their time and money "left and right" on alcohol and prostitutes in these sites of un-Islamic and illicit activities.[99] As these men retorted in 1935, "Marriage, why? Here we are happy and free to go out as we please. It will just hang us by our necks!"[100] The Egyptian media of the 1920s and 1930s was replete with images poking fun at the loss of freedom that marriage cost men.

Certain critics believed that middle-class men had enough money to marry but chose to spend their wages on prostitutes instead of wives. They blamed widespread bachelorhood on the existence of official prostitution because it made sex legally available without the responsibilities of marriage, a temptation many men purportedly could not resist.[101] Although these antiprostitution calls were most vociferous in the 1930s, reformers linked widespread bachelorhood to prostitution since the advent of the twentieth century. In 1902, Muhammad 'Abdu, the Islamic reformer and grand mufti of Egypt from 1899 to 1905, condemned educated middle-class bachelors for frequenting prostitutes instead of marrying honorable women. He held these men responsible for bachelorhood and the British occupation: "If moral upbringing existed among us, we would have had [real] men . . . there would be [national] wealth and there would be independence."[102] 'Abdu viewed morality as the defining characteristic of a real man. Morality and marriage would make the Egyptian bachelor into a

«يا عيني»

معناها قبل الزواج ، وبعده

The meaning of the expression ya 'aini *before and after marriage. (Figuratively, ya 'aini means "my dear," as in before marriage. Literally, it means "my eye," as in after marriage.)* Front cover of al-Fukaha, *no. 98 (10 October 1928).*

productive citizen who would confine his sexual desires to marriage, marry an honorable compatriot, contribute to the national economy, and lead the nation to independence. Like antiprostitution reformers elsewhere, 'Abdu believed marriage was the solution.[103] Egyptian prostitution abolitionists argued that marriage would be "morally and materially uplifting" because it would mitigate against the social perversions of prostitution and illicit sexual relations, "effectively normalizing middle-class sexuality."[104] Men's natural, even uncontrollable, sexual appetite itself did not compromise an Egyptian subject's moral manliness if it was contained within marriage, where nonreproductive sexuality was condoned and celebrated in Islam.[105]

Other writers called on the government to solve the marriage crisis through additional means. In 1914, a petition was submitted to the government demanding that it require its employees to marry and refuse to hire bachelors, who many feared were prone to licentiousness. Supporters argued that "it is the responsibility of the government to remain vigilant about the moral behavior of its employees" to ensure that they were "models of rectitude," thus revealing that they considered bachelorhood a national problem that fell under the jurisdiction of the government.[106] Although this proposal was never enacted into law, within a decade other calls demanding state involvement were made.

By the 1920s, for example, complaints about men "neglecting their duty" to marry multiplied to the point that many suggested a government tax, ranging from 25 percent to 50 percent, on financially independent and healthy bachelors who had reached the age of 25 but refused to marry.[107] Parliament members proposed such legislation in the late 1920s and again in the 1930s, but to no avail.[108] Many supporters of the bachelor tax acknowledged that marriage was costly, but they argued that if bachelors were forced to pay a tax, they would choose to marry rather than compensate the state. They believed that "the government alone is able to put an end to this crisis," which "is among the most dangerous crises that is no less dangerous than political or other crises" because marriage "is the source of nation formation."[109]

The marriage crisis often served as a lens through which to redefine the responsibilities of the government. Sayyid Mustafa, secretary general of the Association for Social Reform, also decried low government salaries, but only those of married employees "who might be the head of a family with children . . . exhausted with heavy costs."[110] He believed that bachelors with the same salary should be subjected to a special tax to make them take notice of their indifference to their duty to the nation. He was not convinced by bachelors' arguments that they could not afford to marry. If he had been, he would not have suggested a remedy that would defeat their attempts to save money for marriage. Mustafa also argued that the government should pay the married employee a higher salary than his single counterpart and "make him feel he is a favored citizen because he is raising the sons of the nation, and the soldiers who will shed blood defending its freedom and honor."[111] As elsewhere, campaigns for a family wage were gendered, exclusively demanded for male breadwinners who were obliged to support their families.[112] For Mustafa, the government was required to assist those married men who were fulfilling their national duty by marrying and fathering future citizens.

For Richer, For Poorer

In response to the new conceptualizations of middle-class masculinity, certain members of Egyptian society began to promote a new kind of marriage—one in which husbands and wives shared its costs—to alleviate the financial burdens on husbands. In 1932, for example, the schoolteacher and writer Nazli al-Hakim Sa'id and her middle-class husband spoke to *al-Ma'rifa* of their own new type of marriage, which they hoped would inspire others.[113] Rather than demand a high dower to pay for the furnishing of the marital abode, Nazli accepted a small amount and assisted her husband by contributing to the household income. Together they set aside money each month to buy the furniture one piece at a time, without burdening the husband to buy it all at once before the wedding, as was the custom. Some readers welcomed such examples of a modern marriage in which women and fathers lowered their expectations and provided suitors with some financial relief.[114]

Records from Cairo's Islamic courts, however, indicate that most of its lower-class, middle-class, and upper-class litigants continued to subscribe to the Islamic notion that the husband alone was responsible for his wife's financial support so long as she was obedient. If she was, then in addition to providing her with a dower and a dwelling, a Muslim husband was required to provide regular maintenance (*nafaqa*) to cover her food and clothing expenses. For a woman of the highest class, he was also mandated to provide a servant or two.[115] Judges and litigants did not seem affected by attempts in the press to lessen a husband's financial obligations or his wife's expectations. Although the press indicated that only wealthy men, who could afford high dowers and support, and poor peasants, who were not expected to pay dowers and maintenance above their means, had the luxury to marry, the courts reveal that men of all classes continued to marry and that husbands, regardless of their financial capabilities, did not always support their wives financially.

Marriage did not necessarily make men into responsible husbands. Early twentieth-century court registers reveal that the most common reason that wives of all classes frequented the Cairo courts was to claim support from husbands who either were not giving them enough or any at all. Occasionally, these cases were straightforward: The husband confessed that he was not providing for his wife and agreed to provide her with a set amount for food expenses on a daily or monthly basis and for clothing expenses every six months, as Islamic law stipulated.[116] The judge ensured that the amount was based on the husband's means, the couple's standard of living, and the cost of living, often confirmed by witnesses who knew the socioeconomic status of the spouses.[117]

More often than not, however, husbands did not attend the court hearing. If the wife could prove that her absent husband was not providing support, usually through the testimonies of the two witnesses that she brought with her, then the judge ordered her husband in absentia to pay her a specific amount, according to the prevailing costs of food and clothing for someone of her status.[118] When faced with a court order to pay, husbands who were absent from the specific court session sometimes went to court to appeal either the specified amount or the fact that they were ordered to pay. On 20 June 1923, for example, Salih Yusuf 'Ali opened a case in the appellate courts to contest the LE 3 per month for food and the LE 3 per half year for clothing awarded to his wife in his absence.[119] 'Ali did not argue that he could not afford the original amounts but that it was above their lower middle-class standard of living. Because he brought two witnesses who confirmed their status, the judge lowered the amount to LE 1.8 for each allowance.[120]

It was not only indigent husbands who neglected to support their wives. On 29 September 1906, for example, Bahiyya al-Hajj Muham-mad Bashat argued that her husband, a successful merchant, "unlawfully left her with no support, no clothing allowance, no lawful home, and no servants," even though he was "wealthy and capable of providing for her," and that her maintenance based on their standard of living should include the salaries for two servants.[121] Her husband countered that they "are among those who are not served," that is, they belonged to a social class that was not accustomed to hired help. Because neither spouse pro-vided witnesses who could confirm the couple's standard of living, the judge set an amount that included the salary for one servant, not two, as she desired, but not none, as he did. In such cases where the testimonies contradicted one another and witnesses could not corroborate one ac-count over the other, the judge set the amount as he saw fit based on "the means of the spouses and local custom."[122]

Regardless of financial ability, husbands attempted to avoid pro-viding support. Some argued that the case should not be tried in the Cairo Court of First Instance because they resided outside its jurisdic-tion. Others took advantage of the fact that marriage contracts were not always registered and argued that the women suing them were not their wives. Still others brought witnesses to lie on their behalf with claims that they already were supporting their wives or argued that they were not obliged to pay because their wives were disobedient.[123] None of these ploys worked if the husbands did not furnish proof, as was usually the case. More often, however, and probably because they knew that this was an enforced obligation, husbands claimed that they already were pro-viding support, which their wives denied. When the husband did not provide any proof to the contrary, the judge sided with the wife who provided evidence.[124] If husbands were absent or refused to pay, their wives could obtain their maintenance from their husbands' assets.[125] One cannot help but wonder, however, how many of these wives actually col-lected their due support if their husbands were determined not to sup-port them and found creative ways to hide their assets.

Marriage was assumed to make bachelors into responsible and pro-ductive husbands who would contribute to the national cause by taking care of the women of the nation. Although the courts clearly upheld the Islamic obligation on husbands to provide, the number of women who continued to sue their husbands indicates that marriage did not guarantee the transformation of Egyptian men into the dutiful providers that was so prevalent as a trope in the press. To resolve this dilemma, the Egyptian legal system created an institution designed to further enforce the male obligation of provision in 1910. Islamic doctrine stipulated that if a financially competent husband or his guarantor refused to support his wife, despite previous court orders, then his wife could request a judge to imprison either up to thirty days.[126] Although this principle was set forth in the 1875 Egyptian Islamic Code of Personal Status, the state did not codify it until Law 31 of 1910 was passed. This law established separate detention courts where such cases were to be tried.[127]

If a wife brought a copy of the original court ruling that ordered her husband to pay support, a copy of the announcement sent to him, and proof that her husband was capable of paying the amount he owed but had not paid her, then the judge would sentence her husband to imprisonment, whether he was present at the hearing or not.[128] Sentences ranged from a minimum of five days to a maximum of thirty days and were determined by the amount of accumulated money owed: the higher the amount, the longer the sentence.[129] Some husbands appeared to plead for a respite, claiming that they needed more time to obtain the money. Their pleas were refused if the wives, after proving their husbands' financial capability to pay, did not agree to the respite.[130] When the wife agreed to a reprieve, the case would be delayed to permit the husband an extension to pay. The occasional husband still would not come up with all or any of the money and was thus sentenced.[131] For the most part, however, the threat of imprisonment worked.[132] Most husbands did not wait for an official sentence: The detention records reveal that most of the cases consisted of couples coming to court together to close the case because the wife had received the due amount or they had devised a payment plan.[133]

Like late colonial Mexican legal culture, where women forged social weapons such as mobilizing outside male authority and turning to the legal system to win matrimonial disputes, early twentieth-century court cases reveal that the Egyptian husband also could fall victim to male-male hierarchies because of his spouse's use of the law.[134] His wife could take him to court and even send him to jail, and the judge nearly always sided with her if she could prove that her husband was not providing for her. Even in this patriarchal society, women did have some recourse to obtain their rights, and male judges, who held state-sponsored power, could force husbands to live up to their obligations in theory. In practice, however, countless wives failed to win settlements if they could not first prove that their husbands were not providing for them.[135]

Conclusion

Writers often chided bachelors for their refusal to marry, which was "among the biggest crimes against . . . the honor of the nation."[136] None, however, was as critical of men shirking this patriotic duty as al-Rafi'i. For him, the marriage crisis represented the deterioration of the nation and was caused by "the feminization of male temperament, the exaggerated inclination to comfort and meekness, and the retreat from shouldering responsibilities."[137] Al-Rafi'i urged his readers to emasculate bachelors by calling them "female widowers of the nation."[138] All the commentators who blamed bachelors were questioning their masculinity in one way or another. Bachelors could not be made into men until they were made into husbands. Writers saw marriage as an institution that would discipline bachelors into productive and moral national subjects.

These condemning voices, however, were the minority. Most viewed the bankrupt bachelor as a vulnerable victim of colonial economic control, periods of inflation, the unemployment problem, low salaries, and/or materialistic dower demands. In their emasculation of these bachelors, they too were offering a new definition of manhood to respond to the tumultuous times. Although this emerging definition stressed a man's moral character, it also advocated that men should be judged on their education level and future financial potential rather than on their current capabilities. Despite this definition of middle-class manhood in the press, court records reveal that the financial obligations continued to be upheld in the courtrooms for husbands of all classes. To fully comprehend the construction of Egyptian manhood, its simultaneous juxtaposition to womanhood, from which it is invariably defined, must be understood. For men to be made into husbands, women had to be turned into wives.

3

The Wedding of Women

The new generation of men prefer bachelorhood to marriage. . . .
They refuse to be committed to a wife whom they have never seen.
What they would like in a wife is a friend whom they can love . . .
[and who is] educated.

Qasim Amin, The Liberation of Women

IN HIS RENOWNED 1899 TREATISE *The Liberation of Women*, the prominent Islamic reformer and judge Qasim Amin noted the anomaly of educated urban middle-class bachelorhood. He blamed arranged marriage, female seclusion, and uneducated women—customs that no longer sufficed for the recent generation of middle-class men who either were educated in Egypt's new Western-style schools or had studied in Europe. Over the next three decades, the traditions of arranged marriage and female seclusion eroded rapidly as girls began attending school and marrying at a later age. Many in the press hailed the attrition of these traditions as a solution for bachelorhood. Yet the marriage crisis continued to grow in the Egyptian imaginary, leading many others to argue that it was the replacement of arranged marriage and female seclusion with gender integration and equal education for females, which led to their immoral behavior and inadequate domestic skills, that deterred men from marriage.

The marriage crisis debates over arranged early marriage, female seclusion, and female education provide rich insight into the discursive constructions of wifehood in the press. Islamic court records shed additional light on how the middle-class portrayals of wifehood in the press compared with the representations of wives from various classes in the Cairo courtrooms. Cases involving the marriage of minors reveal the nature of arranged marriage, and obedience orders indicate the extent of female seclusion and the sway of Islamic prescriptions in defining a wife's duties. Although the middle-class ideals of obedient and secluded wifehood outlined in the press were not always upheld by the minor brides and wayward wives in the courtrooms, the courts and the press nevertheless worked in tandem to construct a new, albeit restrictive, role for Egyptian wives that would wed them to the home during a tumultuous period of increased opportunities for women's education, employment, and integration outside the home. A new conceptualization of wifehood came into being in early twentieth-century Egypt because the disintegration of arranged marriage and female seclusion, the delay in marriage for women, the proliferation of girls' schools, and the supposed increase in bachelorhood threw many observers into a frenzy over the state of the emerging nation's female population.

The Rules of Engagement

Amin's concern lay with male bachelorhood, not female spinsterhood. For this reformer, the increasing number of cultured men was a waste for the Egyptian nation if they could not become acquainted with young women who could serve as skilled partners. Amin condemned the prevalence of female seclusion and arranged marriage, which justified young men's preference for bachelorhood. He called for the abolition of both practices, which did not entail "blindly adopting European values" but rather "a return to the religious principles and traditions of earlier Muslims" that would "support the young men and help them to achieve their aims."[1]

Amin did not discuss the fate of single Egyptian women if men continued to remain bachelors. He focused on men because women were passive and men were active in the contraction of marriages in Ot-

toman Egypt: Men *married*, whereas women were *married off* by their
male guardians. Before the early twentieth century, physical maturity
(determined by medieval Islamic jurists to be between 9 and 13 years of
age, when females appeared physically ready and sexually desirable for
intercourse) marked the turning point in the life of a middle-class or
upper-class girl. At this time she traditionally entered seclusion, became
veiled, and had her marriage arranged to a man she usually did not
know unless he was a relative.[2] Islamic law did not mandate arranged
marriage or seclusion, but both customs were widespread among Muslims as well as Christian and Jewish Egyptians who shared similar views
regarding women.[3]

Similar to the discourse on the separation of the spheres in various
Western nations, domestic confinement was seen as a tool to preserve the
honor and morality of Egyptian women. Western historic justifications
for secluding women to the home included their protection from male
sexual predators.[4] Egyptian women, however, were perceived to be in
need of protection from themselves because they were seen as sexual be-
ings whose more powerful libido threatened society because of the chaos
(*fitna*) it could unleash. Because women's sexual purity was linked to the
honor of the family, confining women to their homes and veiling them if
they went out were deemed necessary for the preservation of their purity
and the reputation of their families.[5]

Domestic confinement was limited to the women of the urban
middle and upper classes and rural gentry, who represented a minority of
the population, because they could afford not to work outside the home.
Women in seclusion constituted no more than 2 percent of Egypt's 5 million females at the end of the nineteenth century.[6] By this time, however,
even middle-class and upper-class women who observed female seclusion
began to permeate the public sphere through their published writings,
especially with the inception of the women's press in 1892.[7] Although the
vast majority of Egyptians may have accepted the principle of segregation in theory, they did not practice female seclusion in reality.[8] Because
the poverty of the bulk of the population mandated female laborers as
farmers in the fields, workers in the factories, and servants in the elite's
households, most women were not restricted to the home. They could
not afford to be. At the same time, however, even the visibility of these

women "served to justify control and supervision of all women" and their mobility in public space.[9]

Like Amin in 1899, later writers lamented the closely related practices of arranged marriage and female seclusion. A decade after Amin published his views, one mother decried her 25-year-old son's inability to marry because none of his prospects' parents would permit him to become acquainted with their daughters.[10] In 1909, she warned parents that this custom would result in an epidemic of bachelorhood. By 1920, 'Abdu al-Barquqi declared that arranged marriage was the leading cause of the marriage crisis and proposed that "the best method for alleviating this crisis is the liberation of women from seclusion."[11] Upon his 1931 return from studying in France, 28-year-old government employee M. Z. K. expressed his frustration with the seclusion of Egyptian women in a letter to Ahmad al-Sawi Muhammad, the author of the popular column "Brief and to the Point." Al-Sawi reprinted M. Z. K.'s letter because, he said, it spoke for him and hundreds of other bachelors.

> When I was in France, like other Egyptians I was always intermingling with the gentler sex for the good conversation and company. Then I returned to Egypt. I had high hopes of finding an Egyptian girl to be my partner in life . . . but . . . where are those Egyptian girls? Why are you hiding in your homes?[12]

For M. Z. K., the integration of the sexes was a positive Western custom that Egyptians should embrace so that men would marry. He represented the emblematic middle-class bachelor over whom Amin, the anonymous mother, and al-Barquqi fretted. Men who were exposed to Western education in Egypt or gender integration in Europe could no longer be expected to marry women with whom they were not permitted to interact before marriage.

Other writers also advocated the elimination of segregation and arranged marriage so that men could find suitable partners.[13] Even women rights' activists phrased their support for the dismantling of seclusion and the importance of premarital acquaintance for the welfare of men.[14] Male and female opponents of female seclusion and arranged marriage rarely advocated gender integration or premarital acquaintance for the sole benefit of women. At least among this handful of supposedly liberal writers, the notions that a woman had the same right to become acquainted with her future spouse or contribute to the public sphere of the nation other than through marriage and reproduction were not valid reasons for gender integration. What is even more striking is how similar their views on premarital acquaintance were to those who fervently supported seclusion. Most male and female supporters of seclusion did not oppose chaperoned meetings between a man and a prospective bride to ensure spousal compatibility.[15] These writers, who either wrote for religious journals or referred to themselves as Islamic reformers, argued that Islam sanctioned it.

Although advocates and critics differed in their views on whether female seclusion encouraged or reduced bachelorhood, they converged in their conception of Egyptian womanhood. Women's foremost purpose was to become marriageable and entice men out of bachelorhood. They also agreed, for the most part, that women did not have the right to choose their husbands freely. Even those who condemned arranged marriage were mostly upset by the inability of men to see or choose their wives, not vice versa. None of these writers even spoke of the possibility that women could contest their arranged marriages in court. Cases involving minor brides show that some actively challenged their arranged marriages upon reaching adulthood.

Whereas Islamic jurists decreed that an adult Muslim man had complete freedom to choose his spouse, they did not believe that an adult Muslim woman held this same right. Most agreed that she could not be forced to marry a man against her will but that she could not be trusted to make this decision alone without the input of her male guardian (usually her father).[16] Although nineteenth-century Egyptian court records reveal that judges invariably recognized an adult woman's ability to marry without the permission of her family so long as her groom was suitable to her in social standing, they also indicate that female minors were commonly married off without their consent.[17] A minor bride would typically remain with her family until she reached physical maturity, when she was expected to move into her husband's home and consummate the marriage. Upon reaching adulthood, however, she could successfully petition the court for a judicial divorce if she proved that a guardian other than her father or grandfather had married her to a suitor without her consent when she was a minor.[18]

Early twentieth-century Egyptian registers contain numerous suits involving minor brides filing for alimony or contesting some other marital issue,[19] but I found only two examples of wives who alleged that they were married against their will. Not surprisingly, few young women dared to stand up to familial and societal pressure that condoned arranged marriage and belittled a bride's say in the matter. Such cases were unusual precisely because the larger patriarchal cultural norms, regardless of what Islamic law dictated, made it difficult for a wife to prove she had been married against her will.

Take, for example, the case of Asiya Salih Nur al-Din.[20] On 13 February 1915, she appealed a ruling that had denied her request for a judicial divorce. Asiya alleged that her guardian (their relation was not divulged) had married her to his brother's son without her consent shortly after she had begun menstruating. Because she was an adult who did not consent to the marriage, she contended that it was invalid. Unfortunately for Asiya, it was her word against the testimony of several men: her middle-class guardian, her husband's upper-class father, and the two male witnesses to the contract who claimed that Asiya was a minor at the time of the marriage. Still, the judge granted her three separate extensions to bring witnesses who could testify that she had been an adult at the contraction of the marriage. Although Asiya was a woman of some stature as the daughter of an elite deceased landowner, she neither brought witnesses nor appeared in court at any of the sessions. The judge thus denied her petition in her absence.

It is not surprising that Asiya failed to win her appeals. How could a woman who had no medical evidence prove that she had reached physical maturity some years earlier? How could she demonstrate that she was married against her will when, as a minor, she was not permitted to sign the contract or even object to it? The guardians of the bride and the groom usually chose the two required males who would witness the marriage. These men rarely saw the bride, let alone discussed her opinion of the marriage with her, especially in a culture that did not value her opinion. Even if they had witnessed her express disapproval, they were unlikely to contradict her guardian's wishes, especially if she was a minor.

The court also failed to recognize Nabiha 'Uthman Kashif's claim that her marriage was invalid because she had been married against her will when she was a minor.[21] The middle-class Nabiha, however, made her allegations under different circumstances. Unlike her elite counterpart Asiya, she did not take the initiative to file for an annulment. Nor did she claim that she had been an adult at the time of her marriage. Rather, she chose to ignore her husband's repeated pleas to move into his home and consummate their marriage once she had reached physical maturity. On 19 December 1897, some nine years after their marriage contract had been signed, her husband demanded that the court force his unwilling wife to consummate the marriage. Nabiha repeatedly refused to appear in court, sending excuses that she was too ill to attend the hearings. The court even sent a doctor to examine her, but her mother and mother's husband refused to allow the doctor to see her. Finally, Nabiha sent a deputy on her behalf who testified that she did not recognize the marriage because it had been contracted by her middle-class uncle, who had married her to his son against her will when the bride and groom were both minors. Nabiha's husband and father-in-law countered that she had consented to the marriage before witnesses in 1888 and had not voiced any opposition to the marriage during the past nine years. Because she provided no evidence to the contrary, she was ordered to live with her husband and consummate the marriage.

Why didn't Nabiha file for an annulment upon reaching maturity? It is obvious she had the support of her mother and stepfather. Most likely, she knew she would not be able to prove her case in court. Despite the illegality of such a forced union in Islamic law and the occasional successful annulment, Nabiha, like Asiya, faced the insurmountable obstacle of finding two male witnesses to testify that she had been married against her will in a patriarchal culture where arranged marriage was the norm. In this sense, these cases confirm the press depiction of the deeply entrenched practice of arranged marriage and its disregard for a bride's consent. In contrast to the press portrayals, however, these cases reveal that some middle-class and upper-class women did attempt to control their marital destinies.

Girls Gone Wild

As the practices of female seclusion and arranged marriage began to wane in early twentieth-century Egypt, observers started to blame endemic bachelorhood on the existence of gender integration and the appearance of depraved women in public places. Whereas Amin and others advocated for the abolition of seclusion to encourage men to marry, some, such as "The Marriage Crisis" columnist 'A'isha 'Abd al-Rahman, viewed the integration of the sexes as the main cause of bachelorhood by the early 1930s.

> My mother says she married at age 13 . . . [when] the supervision of female seclusion was stricter. As for now, the age of marriage has been fixed at 16 as the minimum limit for girls and most girls advertise themselves scandalously and go out in the streets shamelessly unveiled to seduce men. . . . I do not approve of early marriage but I cite it as clear tangible evidence that seclusion was not a handicap to marriage . . . while [today] the marriage shortage grows.[22]

In 1933, this female contributor to the Islamic women's periodical *al-Nahda al-Nisa'iyya* saw a direct correlation between the decline in the marriage of minors and seclusion and the rise in bachelorhood. Despite Amin's arguments in 1899, 'A'isha 'Abd al-Rahman did not believe that bachelorhood was common during the days of women's domestic confinement: "When a woman was secluded in the past, she was far from public immorality and conspicuous unrestraint. There was no aversion to marriage."[23] Early twentieth-century Egyptian women were marrying at a later age than their predecessors, which contributed to the attrition of seclusion. Whereas the average marital age for females was 13.8 years in mid-nineteenth-century Egypt, the median was 18.6 years in mid-twentieth-century Egypt.[24] During the first two decades of the twentieth century, debates about the dangers of early marriage for girls led to growing social disapproval and to two laws, passed in 1923 and 1931, that set the minimum age for marriage at 16 for females (and 18 for males).[25]

A major motive for marrying off a female at a young age was the preservation of her chastity.[26] According to many observers, female seclusion and early marriage worked in tandem to protect society from the chaos that women alone could unleash. These mostly religious conservative male writers agreed that the rapid disintegration of seclusion was responsible not only for widespread bachelorhood but also for the decay of the fragile nation. As Yusuf 'Ali Yusuf explained in his 1934 lecture at the Society of Islamic Guidance headquarters, "Intermingling is an obstacle to marriage, not a facilitator of it."[27] For Muhammad 'Arafa, the marriage crisis, which "is a danger to the nation," was caused by "the lack of men's trust in women" who "adorn and expose themselves in the streets and public places to seduce them . . . and every time they do so men's doubt in women's virtues increases, they meet their needs without marriage, and they refuse marriage."[28] 'Arafa viewed single women who went out unrestricted and unveiled as active sexual aggressors who were attempting to seduce passive men into marriage, thus imperiling the active-passive dichotomy that nationalists attempted to assign men and women in order to maintain social order.[29] Like many of the contributors to Islamic reformer Muhammad Junaydi's 1933 *The Marriage Crisis in Egypt* who blamed bachelorhood on the social chaos engendered by female sexuality, 'Arafa, Yusuf, and 'A'isha 'Abd al-Rahman also reproached women alone for their active transgression into the so-called public sphere. They viewed men as vulnerable victims of women's sexuality.[30]

What exactly was so threatening about women penetrating traditionally male-dominated public spaces or attempting to lure men into marriage? Muharram Bey Fahim, a former chairman of the Islamic Lawyers' Association, elaborated in 1936 that men would have no need for marriage if they could mix with women outside the responsibilities of marriage and that the resulting moral depravity would corrupt the fledgling nation.[31] Fahim, like 'Arafa, Yusuf, and 'A'isha 'Abd al-Rahman, extolled seclusion as a way for women to attract marriage proposals from men who would not bother to wed them if they could mix freely with them beyond the bounds of marriage.[32] The *verbalized* concern behind these writers' panic over single women who were leaving seclusion, not getting married, and transgressing the public sphere was that bachelorhood would persist, the marriage crisis would escalate, and the nation would tumble into moral devastation. They blamed women alone because they equated women in public space with sexual and social disorder.

Interestingly enough, not one of these writers explained why a man could not be trusted to restrain himself, even if a woman was attempting to seduce him. Herein lies the *unspoken* concern: When it came to sexuality, men were passive and women were active. Women were not supposed to seduce men because only men should seek out women. These writers did not want to see any reversal of gendered roles. Women were to remain confined to the home, where they could not wreak havoc on the nation.

None of these writers dared to discuss the fate of the purported female aggressors if the crisis persisted. It was too terrifying to even entertain such a thought. Instead, they advocated seclusion in their reminiscences of a time when men married prepubescent women before they could unleash their sexuality or enter the public sphere and when there was no ostensible marriage shortage or moral decay.

In 1927, Muhammad Mas'ud asked, "Does the scandalous . . . woman exposed in the street make a man propose to her? Does . . . going out to the theaters and places of entertainment and dancing . . . in bars and dance halls make a young man seek to wed her? That is what our young girl . . . is doing today! Can she be reformed to become a wife . . . ?!?"[33] For Mas'ud, women who did not observe seclusion threatened the sanctity of the budding nation because they could not become virtuous wives who would preserve their husbands' honor. This view ironically placed women in a double bind. It allotted them the sacred role as custodians of morality in the nation-building process, but it also restricted them to the role of wifehood. Like Western colonialists, socialists, and nationalists, Egyptians also assigned women the burden of representing their nation's honor and morality.[34] In the Egyptian Islamic context, however, women were to be relegated to the home because they themselves posed a threat to the nation, not because their chastity needed protection from male predators.

The writers who supported seclusion were mostly middle-class professionals who belonged to organizations or contributed to publications with an explicitly Islamic orientation. Yet men and women who did not define themselves as explicitly religious or conservative also supported female seclusion.[35] More significantly, even self-identified liberal and secular writers who advocated the abolition of seclusion did not support women's unrestricted presence in public and shared nearly identical views on women's morality and wifehood with their religious counterparts. The editors of *al-Hilal*, the widely circulated secular journal that advocated Western reforms, for example, argued in 1898 that "complete seclusion is oppressive . . . and dangerous for men" but that unrestricted "freedom is more dangerous for young women so what is best is the middle ground."[36] Ibrahim 'Ali Salim, a secular lawyer who argued that Islam advocated premarital acquaintance, which would "annihilate the marriage crisis," described how the practice had evolved in 1931 Cairo: "Some narrow-minded people . . . hide their daughters from their fiancés but show them in theaters, amusement parks and . . . stores [practically] naked!!"[37] Salim responded to accusations that the abolition of seclusion was a modern invention by reiterating Amin's argument that Islam had never sanctioned seclusion. He also explained that abolitionists did not endorse women's unregulated presence in public.

To be sure, secular writers, such as Salim and the editors of *al-Hilal*, who accepted women's presence in public places so long as these women had a serious purpose and remained modest in dress and behavior, should not be blindly equated with seclusion proponents who did not want to see unveiled women without purpose outside the home. Like their religious counterparts, however, they too decried the purported immoral comportment and excess freedom of women. Even when advocates and adversaries of female seclusion differed in their views, they shared similar discontent with the supposed immoral behavior of Egyptian women in public places. This convergence by ideologues on both sides of the seclusion debate in the 1930s confirms that Egyptian nationalist discourse and public life witnessed a "return to Islam" that relegated Western influences to the margins beginning in the 1930s.[38] As early as 1899, however, Amin had insisted that Egypt retain its Islamic identity in his calls for abolishing seclusion within a discursive Islamic tradition, illustrating that Islam was completely compatible with modernity.[39] Most nationalists, whether secular or religious, opined that Egypt could modernize itself while retaining its Islamic identity. Although they greatly differed in their views on how this process should occur, they shared a general belief that a resuscitation of Islamic mores, most notably in relation to women, would resolve the marriage crisis.

Western Ways and Witless Wives

In 1899, Amin was the first to lament the increasing number of cultured bachelors who were disappointed by the paucity of educated women. He did not extol female education for the sake of women but for their husbands and sons. Women should be prepared so that they could properly execute their two primary roles as companionate wife and skilled mother.

The recent generations of middle-class men who were educated in Egypt's modern Western-style schools or in Europe required educated partners. At the same time, however, Amin insisted that equal education for women was unnecessary. Women merely needed primary schooling to bridge but not fully close the mental gap between them and their husbands, and they required domestic training to enable them to run households efficiently and provide a moral and educational upbringing for their children.[40]

From the early nineteenth century, a minority of Egyptian girls attended Qur'anic schools, private Coptic and Jewish schools, Western Christian missionary schools, and state-run secular European-style schools. The first government primary school for girls was founded in 1873, but religious and training schools for girls had been established in the 1830s. Although the first state secondary school for girls was not established until 1920, the previous two decades witnessed the opening of several primary state and foreign private schools in addition to a few foreign secondary schools, education missions to Europe, and teacher training schools for women. Despite the growing number of girls' schools, most Egyptian girls did not attend them before nominal independence in 1922. The lower classes, which constituted the bulk of the population, generally needed their daughters to work and contribute to the household income rather than attend school. Many middle-class and upper-class families also refrained from sending their daughters to school because they did not want to expose them to the men who taught in girls' schools before women began to replace them. Furthermore, because the British had set ceilings on state spending on education, expansion remained limited until Egyptians gained greater control over this domain with titular independence and set education as a national priority.

By 1929, the state sanctioned compulsory free elementary education for girls, opened several state secondary girls' schools and teacher training institutes for women, and matriculated female students into the university. The biggest beneficiaries of state education were middle-class girls because the upper echelons favored the private foreign schools, which still largely outnumbered these new state schools.[41] By 1937, there were 31 state primary schools with 4,000 girls and 7 state secondary schools with 2,000 girls versus 115 private elementary schools with 15,000 girls and 10 private secondary schools with 800 girls.[42]

Amin's condemnation of ignorant wives as a cause for bachelorhood resurfaced over the next three decades. When Amin published his views in 1899, only about 1,200 of Egypt's approximately 5 million girls attended state schools, but more than 25,000 girls attended state schools by 1912.[43] Whereas 0.2 percent of the female population was literate in 1897 (compared to an 8 percent male literacy rate), about 9.5 percent of the female population was literate in 1937 (compared to a 24.7 percent male literacy rate).[44] Because the gap between the numbers of educated men and women was still quite large, "the ignorance of women" continued to be chided as a "direct cause for the marriage recession" in 1926.[45] As female education became institutionalized and more accessible, particularly for the middle classes, whose members were the chief victims of the marriage crisis, the criticism of female ignorance turned to the curriculum offered in girls' schools and the newly educated women. Education advocates began to debate the type and extent of education that women should receive and the role it should play in preparing women for marriage.

Many commentators fiercely denounced the kind of instruction girls were receiving, particularly the secular education offered by Western female teachers, which often centered on foreign language and musical training. It had become increasingly prestigious and culturally acceptable for middle-class and upper-class families to send their daughters to foreign schools, where the objective was to turn a girl into a "Lady of the Salon" by teaching her French, piano, and dance.[46] Enrollment in these private schools was higher than it was in the state schools for girls, but even state schools were administered by Western teachers and based on a foreign curriculum with English or French as the main language of instruction.[47] Writers bewailed the fact that young Egyptian women were left in these "schools that corrupt them" because "they started imitating Western women in their dress and morals."[48]

Bachelors also blamed their aversion to marriage on Westernized women. In his 1924 letter to *al-Mar'a al-Jadida*, Muhammad Hijazi wrote:

> I have all the qualifications that permit me to ask for a girl's hand . . . but I have not . . . because . . . today's girls . . . imitate foreign women in everything: in the way they walk in the streets, in their clothes, in their hair cuts and hair

coloring, in going out with bare arms and chests. . . . I strongly commend
the renaissance of Egyptian women . . . [but] when they are . . . imitating
foreigners . . . their morals are corrupted and . . . [hence] many young men
abstain from marriage.[49]

For this bachelor, Egyptian women's imitation of the Western women
whom they encountered in their schools and streets, on the pages of
magazines and books, and on the screens of cinemas resulted in their immorality, which discouraged men from marriage. Eleven years later, 'Abd
al-Hamid al-Disuqi, a member of the Association for Social Reform, also
argued that the young Egyptian woman "imagines that the road to civilization is imitating the Western woman in everything despite the multiple
differences between them!"[50] This insistence on the vast disparities between Egyptian and Western women reveals that the incessant negative
use of terms such as *independence, freedom, immorality,* and *Western* stood
for the undesirability of female assertiveness. It also validated the quintes-
sentially anticolonial nationalist claim of being "different yet modern."[51]

As the 1930s progressed, countless male commentators increasingly echoed Hijazi's and al-Disuqi's unease with the Western ways of
foreign-educated Egyptian women.[52] Men could no longer guarantee the
sexual purity and moral rectitude of potential brides. Nor could they ensure that these women would preserve their honor. Although no specific
guidelines were suggested, many writers from secular liberal newspapers
as well as religious periodicals called on the government to return Egypt
to its Islamic heritage and reject the current Westernized female depravity
and gender integration.[53] In a 1930 lecture that Mahmud Hifni presented
at the headquarters of the Young Muslim Men's Association, the religious political organization whose rapid growth was rivaled only by the
Muslim Brotherhood, he explained that the Westernization of Egyptian
women was the real cause of the marriage crisis. Although this religious
activist acknowledged that Egypt could benefit from emulating the British in some regards, he made it clear that Egypt should not embrace their
women's behavior.[54]

Not all commentators, however, held Westernized women responsible for female immorality. Sayyid Hamdi, a government employee in
the Ministry of Islamic Endowments, argued that men were to blame

because they were the ones who had demanded educated wives but now were deterred by Western-educated women who were "disobedient, exceeding the limits of modesty, decency, and dignity, and exaggerated in their rights."[55] One might think that Hamdi opposed female education. Yet he demanded nothing short of the equal education of women in his 1928 letter. He encouraged the educated man to find a wife "who equals him in knowledge" but also insisted that schools teach its female students "that good morals and pleasing behavior are the basis of marital life."[56] Although the government required secondary state schools for girls to provide the same curriculum as its counterparts for boys in the early 1920s, Muhammad 'Ali 'Aluba continued to blame female ignorance for endemic bachelorhood in 1933 because men "desired wives with the same level of intelligence."[57] Although Hamdi and 'Aluba advocated equal education, they did not prescribe it for a woman's own benefit but so that she could serve as a better companion for her husband.

Their views on education were not that different from those writers who also blamed ignorant women for bachelorhood but did not champion their equal education. In recommending some sort of moral guidance in girls' schools, Hamdi and 'Aluba resembled religious nationalists who favored an Islamic component in a curriculum tailored for girls. Labiba Ahmad, an Islamic activist who founded the religious women's journal al-Nahda al-Nisa'iyya, Mahmud Hifni of the Young Muslim Men's Association, and Shaykh Muhammad Mustafa al-Maraghi, a leading drafter of Egypt's personal status laws who served as the rector of al-Azhar University in the 1930s, all cited the lack of religious instruction in girls' schools as a source of the marriage crisis.[58] Beginning in the early twentieth century, women writers and social reformers who were not officially affiliated with an Islamic organization also demanded increased religious indoctrination in girls' schools, whose curricula should not be akin to that in boys' schools, because women had different roles.[59] These writers, who represented the gamut of political and religious ideologies, deplored the dearth of religious guidance for women and believed that their moral depravity was the main reason men did not marry them. As Lisa Pollard explains, "Untrained, poorly educated women were held responsible both by Europeans and Egyptians for the decay that was found in Egyptian homes and that allegedly manifested itself in the political and economic behavior of Egyptian men. To remedy this, girls had to be subjected to moral training so that they could produce better men."[60]

The same writers who wanted to introduce Islamic study into girls' schools also wanted these schools to incorporate domestic management instruction. Many of them cited women's inadequacy as moral and efficient household managers as the reason men evaded marriage.[61] Even those who did not call for religious instruction in girls' schools condemned both Egyptian and foreign schools for failing to prepare women for wifehood. For example, Egyptian Feminist Union (EFU) members who had demanded equal education for girls in the early 1920s were blaming it by the 1930s for the alleged failure in their duties toward their families. As a result, some schools began to provide household management instruction, and the Ministry of Education established separate schools specifically geared toward domestic training in 1938.[62] Although some writers recommended such instruction from the beginning of the twentieth century, calls intensified and took on new meaning during the late 1920s and early 1930s apex of the marriage crisis, when more and more women were educated but supposedly remained ignorant about domestic affairs and hence became the scapegoats for bachelorhood.[63]

The vast support for female seclusion and limited education in the press reveals that many Egyptians were threatened by women's general presence in public spaces. The press extolled female seclusion and domestic education to wed women to the home, where women could not even imagine paid employment possibilities beyond its walls. The marriage crisis was not specifically about middle-class men's fear of women's competition for their jobs because its observers did not cite women's professional work as a cause for bachelorhood. Few middle-class women continued to work after marriage during this period. Rather, the marriage crisis largely reflected men's general unease about single women's rapid penetration into the so-called public sphere. In the first three decades of the twentieth century, girls began to attend (segregated) schools in growing numbers and enjoy new forms of entertainment and consumption, such as theaters, amusement parks, operas, and department stores, and transportation, including tramways, cars, and steamships, which helped further facilitate their mobility. By the 1930s, the institution of seclusion had crumbled. Middle-class and upper-class women were teaching in (segregated) schools, attending (integrated) universities, founding organizations and charities, and swimming on the beaches of Alexandria.[64] Yet it was not the mere presence of women in public places that troubled the middle-class press. It was what their presence supposedly signified. Single women would become accustomed to the freedom, independence, and immorality that they should never expect from their future husbands.

To Honor and Obey

In 1936, Jarmain Bumun attributed men's aversion of marriage to "the proclivity of women for freedom" and "independence" that "goes against a man's character and his desire to assume authority . . . and supervise the conduct of the woman who carries his name and represents his honor."[65] This non-Muslim female writer shed light on yet another concern about Westernized and educated women: Authentic Egyptian womanhood should not threaten Egyptian manhood, particularly during a turbulent period of British domination, economic crises, and a perceived erosion of Islamic traditions and values. A proper Egyptian woman was to be a virtuous and obedient wife who completely acquiesced to her husband. As the well-known conservative literary writer Mustafa Sadiq al-Rafi'i postulated the year before, it was a wife's duty to obey her husband in order to "preserve his manhood" or else it would "inevitably result in the destruction of the nation."[66]

Elsewhere al-Rafi'i suggested that overly erudite women could not make obedient wives. He argued that an educated woman remained virtuous only if her tutelage was directed and controlled by her male relatives.[67] In a 1927 issue of a secular weekly, the student 'Abd al-Rahman 'Ajiz blamed men's evasion of marriage on the educated woman who had no interest in "her natural role" as "the manager of a home" but instead in being "a stubborn wife."[68] The same year, Muhammad Mas'ud, a male contributor to the Islamic-oriented *al-Nahda al-Nisa'iyya* magazine, concurred that the educated woman had forgotten her "natural" role of wife and had become "a completely free girl who pleases herself, instead of pleasing us."[69] The new widespread image of independent and disobedient Egyptian women was supported by the many caricatures of overbearing wives bullying their husbands that frequently adorned the

Domestic flirtation. Husband: Wha—, wha—, wha—, what happened? Wife: Shut up. Another word and I'll make myself a widow. Front cover of al-Fukaha, *no. 90 (15 August 1928).*

1920s and 1930s press.

For these three men, education resulted in female mulishness and freedom instead of lifting women out of their persistent ignorance in domestic affairs. They were not, however, criticizing female education per se. Rather, they blamed learned women for thinking beyond their supposedly natural role of dutiful household manager. Education to train women to perform this role was completely acceptable; education for the sake of anything else was unnecessary and even threatening to the natural national order. For them, women's expectation to be educated and equal partners and public participants rather than subservient and nurturing wives was the main reason men were avoiding marriage.

These writers were likely influenced by Islamic prescriptions of wifehood. A proper Muslim wife was instructed to obey her husband fully, a principle called the house of obedience (*bayt al-taʿa*) that was legally upheld in the Islamic courts. A wife's obedience, however, was contingent on her husband's fulfillment of his financial duties toward her. Islamic law entitled a Muslim husband "to exercise his marital authority by restraining his wife's movements and preventing her from showing herself in public."[70] In return for her dower, maintenance, and home, the wife's sole legal obligation was to obey her husband. What specifically constituted wifely acquiescence in Islamic law was not clearly defined, but most jurists agreed that it entailed a wife providing conjugal rights and cohabiting with her husband in the marital domicile without demonstrating any aversion to him. If a wife displayed her hatred, refused sex, or abandoned the marital home against her husband's wishes, she was considered legally recalcitrant (*nashiz*) and lost her right to support.[71]

In early twentieth-century Egypt, judges usually ruled that a wife was disobedient only if she had moved out of her husband's home without his permission, perhaps because this was the only overt example of a wife's recalcitrance that easily could be proven in court. The 1875 Egyptian Islamic Code of Personal Status instructed: "The wife who leaves her husband's house without his permission and without legal reason renders herself disobedient and thus loses . . . any right to maintenance so long as she is in a state of disobedience."[72] Another article explicated that a wife's refusal to accede to sexual intercourse, guard her virtue, or preserve her husband's property also constituted disobedience.[73] How a woman should guard her virtue or preserve her husband's property was not clarified.

In Islamic law the burden of proof lay with the plaintiff, so the husband had to prove his wife's disobedience either through her admission in court or the corroboration of two male witnesses. Neighbors could easily verify a wife's blatant departure from her husband's home and assumption of a separate residence. But a wife's refusal to consent to intercourse, guard her virtue, or preserve her husband's property was difficult to prove unless she confessed. As a result, they rarely appeared as accusations in court.[74] Law 25 of 1920, as well as its 1929 amendment, which codified Egyptian personal status laws, did not even bother to list these conditions, or any others, as examples of a wife's transgression that forfeited her right to maintenance. Rather, the 1920 law obscurely stated that maintenance for the wife "who submits herself to her husband" was incumbent upon him.[75] Because the law provided no specific stipulations, its ambiguity expanded rather than restricted a man's unilateral prerogative over his wife in semi-independent Egypt.

Although many members of the middle-class press deemed a woman's secluded submission to her husband unconditional, numerous wives from all social backgrounds were aware that they could leave their husbands if they were not supporting them. Wives frequently abandoned husbands who were not providing for them, creatively manipulating the fact that husbands had to first fulfill their obligations to earn their compliance. The unsuitability of the marital domicile was the most common counterclaim of wives whose husbands accused them of disobedience. It was not enough for a husband to provide a home; it had to be an independent abode suitable for the couple's standard of living that did not require the wife to move beyond a reasonable distance from where she was married.[76] Wives made use of all these conditions to justify why they moved out of their husbands' home without permission. Some argued that the abode was unsuitable to their standard of living. Others countered that they were living with their in-laws and not in an independent home. Still others contended that the location of the dwelling exceeded the legal distance from the place of their marriage.[77] With the exception of one case, the judge ruled in all these cases that the wife was not required to obey her husband because he had not fulfilled his obligation, usually corroborated by the testimony of the court inspector who examined the home but occasionally confirmed by the confession of the husband.[78] Once a husband established the appropriate residence, however, he could return to obtain a court order to compel his wife to live with him.[79]

When a wife did not appear in court or send an agent to defend her husband's charge of disobedience, the court appointed a lawyer on her behalf and sent an inspector to verify the lawfulness of the marital abode.[80] Although provision of a lawful home was not the only obligation of a husband, the court's automatic appointment of a home inspector reveals the importance the court placed on this fundamental responsibility of husbands. Perhaps the court emphasized establishment of the household over payment of the dower and alimony because it was the easiest to confirm in the wife's absence. Those wives who did not appear may have chosen not to because they knew they had no *legal* excuse for their departure. A husband's abuse, marriage to a second wife (unless prohibited in her marriage contract), or her distaste for him were not valid reasons for a wife to disobey her husband.[81]

Other wives claimed that they left their husbands because they had not received their full advanced dowers.[82] When a husband confessed or could not prove that he had paid the dower, he was ordered to pay it and his wife was not obliged to return to him until he did.[83] If he were able to prove it, usually through a marriage contract that he brought as evidence, his request for an obedience order was granted.[84] Wives also attributed their departure to their husbands' failure to provide maintenance. Whereas judges did not find such wives to be disobedient, they ordered them to return to their husbands once they began to receive their allowances.[85] A cursory reading may give the impression that many obedience cases were strategic attempts of wives to negotiate financial deals with their husbands.[86] Although the legal language and manipulations sometimes concealed it, obedience suits more often than not indicated deep marital strife in which husbands were expressing their own domination in an attempt to enforce their wives' complete submission.

Perhaps no other cases exemplify the extent to which an obedience order could force an unwilling wife into submission than those that deal with spousal abuse. Although a husband's right to his wife's obedience was also theoretically conditional on his kind treatment of her, court records reveal that a wife's disobedience was excused only if her husband had not fulfilled his three material obligations.[87] It was difficult for a wife to prove unjust or excessive abuse, because Islamic law permitted a husband to beat a disobedient wife moderately. As a result, I did not find any cases in which a judge ruled that a battered wife was not required to obey her husband because of his maltreatment. Islamic judges were not inclined to deprive an abusive husband of his wife's submission because such a right was deemed to be inherent in the marriage contract and its removal was equivalent to annulment of the marriage.[88]

Battered wives appear to have been aware that judges would not excuse their flight based on abuse alone. Even when a wife did cite it as a cause for her departure, she also mentioned a material failure on her husband's part. Like their early twentieth-century American counterparts, Egyptian battered wives made the claim of spousal abuse "only when they had some reasonable expectation that they could win."[89] When Badr 'Abd al-Rahman and Zamzam Nuwayshi explained that they fled their homes because their husbands had beaten them, they also made sure to claim that these homes were unfit. In 1906, this strategic argument worked for the lower-class Badr but not for the middle-class Zamzam.[90] Likewise, Hanuba al-Rumayli asserted that she left her lower-class husband because "he hit her and threw her out on the one hand and on the other hand his mother lives with him in the home."[91] Knowing that her husband was obliged to provide her with an independent home, she remarked that she "has no objection to joining him if he prepares a lawful home independent of his parents' home," making it easy for the judge to rule in her favor.[92] That these three women mentioned that they left because of abuse suggests that they believed it was a legitimate excuse to leave their husbands. Their provision of additional reasons reveals that they also knew assault alone would not justify their extended absences from their husbands.

These cases underscore the potential for a husband's abuse of his right to his wife's submission. This wholly patriarchal privilege was further entrenched by an 1897 law that permitted a husband who had obtained an obedience injunction to seek police assistance in forcing his disobedient wife to return home.[93] Court cases made no reference to police assistance because such recourse occurred beyond its jurisdiction. Yet the increasing number of appeals over the next three decades to have an obedience injunction overturned suggests that wives attempted legal remedies not only to avoid returning home but also to show as evidence to an officer who could force her to do so.[94] Women's activists sought the abolition of this institution and its state-sanctioned police assistance.[95] Sayza Nabarawi, the disciple of EFU founder Huda al-Sha'rawi and editor of *L'Egyptienne*, wrote about this "barbaric" practice in 1927: "A wife is a companion to her husband, not his slave. . . . [She] should not be forced to remain with a tyrannical husband. . . . It is contrary to our modern idea of freedom."[96] The supposedly liberal columnist Ahmad al-Sawi Muhammad criticized such calls for the abolition of obedience orders in 1932: "Why does the woman refuse to obey when obedience is pleasant and peaceful? Obedience is one thing and slavery is another. . . . Even if . . . obedience is slavery . . . is not love the slavery of a lover to his beloved and vice versa?"[97] Al-Sawi attempted to reconcile the Islamic principle of wifely obedience with modern notions of companionate marriage. Feminists, however, were not criticizing mutual obedience and love between a husband and wife but rather the explicit abuse of power by husbands and policemen who forced a wife to return to a man who "can insult her and hit her and the courts will not consider this behavior to be outside his legal rights."[98]

State-sponsored obedience orders, which were not abolished until 1967, institutionalized "violence" and "marital incarceration" for many women.[99] Yet obedience cases were not always misogynist court orders for a victimized wife to return to an abusive husband. The courts endorsed a husband's absolute control over his wife, by which he could order her confinement to his home, only if he had fulfilled all his financial duties. Although some women undoubtedly fell victim to their husbands' abuse of obedience orders, many others creatively exploited this principle by withholding their own duties until they received what they wanted from their husbands. Once the husband had satisfied his duties, judges systematically upheld his exclusively male right to his wife's obedience, buttressing the patriarchal power a Muslim husband held over his wife. Their purpose was to preserve the institution of marriage in relation to male domination and female subordination, not to assist women in exploiting the system by accommodating their grievances.

Whereas Islamic jurists and Egyptian nationalists presumed that a husband should have complete control over his wife's movements, some court cases show that many husbands could not prevent their wives from leaving their homes and were forced to appeal to the external higher patriarchal power of the Islamic court or police station to enforce their wives' submission. How did this affect these husbands' sense of their own manhood? During a period in which many Egyptian men lacked total political and economic control in their public lives, their resort to public authority to coerce their wives' submission implied the lack of power that they held in their supposedly private homes. Obedience injunctions were not just requested by lower-class men, such as the parking attendants, cigarette rollers, coppersmiths, streetcar conductors, barbers, tailors, and taxi drivers who filed most of these cases.[100] Middle-class government employees, the chief proprietors of marriage crisis debates, also sought such orders.[101] Even landowners and high government officials with more public influence than their nonelite pendants had to resort to court to force their wives into submission.[102]

Take, for example, the case of Ahmad Bey Ghalib versus Amina Hanim ʿAli Pasha Hilmi. On 15 December 1906, Ghalib, a high official in the Ministry of Interior, summoned his wife to return to him. He claimed that her refusal to come home was illegal because he had paid her advanced dower in full and had provided a lawful home in which she had resided. His wife, Amina, the daughter of an elite landowner, countered that he was the one who left her "destitute and with . . . no support, no lawful home, and no food" and that she never lived with him in the "small" home that was "inappropriate" to her privileged status.[103] She testified that she had previously filed a claim for a proper home and maintenance in which the court inspector corroborated the unsuitability of the domicile. After responding that he could not afford the exorbitant LE 36.25 per month (which was more than seven times the average government employee's monthly salary) that she demanded, he conceded that he could pay LE 11.75 per month.[104] Because the inspector determined that the home was unlawful, the judge ruled that Ghalib had no right to demand his wife's obedience until he provided her with a suitable home and LE 17.67 in monthly maintenance.

This case illustrates that even women of the elite, the supposed bastions of female seclusion, also left their husbands and took their ostensibly private affairs to the public domain of the courtroom. Elite husbands did not have absolute control over their wives and were forced to resort to court to obtain a higher authority's enforcement of spousal obedience. Attending a court session once or twice with or without a male escort did not necessarily mean that Amina did not observe seclusion. That she did not send a deputy on her behalf but appeared in court on her own before the male judge, witnesses, scribe, other court personnel, and audience members and openly discussed her marriage, her financial needs, and the incapacities of her husband, who was a public figure, however, confirms that female seclusion did not necessarily imply total isolation or female naïveté.

Amina's insistence that she did not leave her husband may have been the truth, or it may reveal her awareness of larger social expectations that proper wifehood entailed complete obedience. At the same time, however, she took advantage of her husband's suit to reiterate that he did not provide her with support or a proper home. Although she denied leaving her husband, other wives admitted that they had left their husbands, promising that they would return home once their husbands provided support, a suitable home, or the rest of the advanced dower.[105] Some wives may have intentionally left their husbands to force them to resort to court where they would face cross-examination regarding their own marital duties. At the very least, these wives seemed aware that it was their right to leave husbands who were not upholding their end of the bargain.

If a husband was fulfilling his matrimonial duties, however, then a wife's departure from her home constituted disobedience and she could lose her right to maintenance. In such instances, the husband had the right to request legal authorization to cease financial support. Because a disobedient wife forfeited her right to maintenance, the judge agreed to the husband's request until she returned to her husband, thereby blackmailing wives into submission.[106] One wonders if this extortion worked, however, because rather than return home, many wives of all classes returned to court to contest such rulings or the original obedience injunctions.[107] Nearly all these appeals were either rejected or delayed because the wives did not provide sufficient evidence or did not appear. Husbands sometimes unsuccessfully attempted to manipulate this legal license to end payments even if they did not have a previous court order.[108] Others sought to stop payments by countering that their wives were recalcitrant when they were sued for support without success because judges used these opportunities to order the husband to provide support before he could request his wife's submission.[109] Other husbands failed to overturn alimony orders granted to their wives or court denials to stop payments by claiming that their wives were disobedient because they could not prove it.[110] In 1902, one middle-class husband, al-Sayyid Muhammad 'Abd al-Jalil, even demanded, albeit unsuccessfully, that the court oblige his wife to repay him the alimony he had paid her during her alleged period of disobedience.[111] A husband could receive relief from paying support only after he had sent his wife a copy of the court order of obedience, which did not prevent some husbands from deliberately not notifying their wives of obedience orders in order to avoid resuming alimony payments.[112]

Conclusion

The Islamic legal proscription that "a man was to provide; a woman was to consume. A man was to decide; a woman was to obey"[113] resembled the argument of Egyptian nationalists who insisted that women should remain secluded and passive and men public and active in the making of marriage and the nation. Cases from the early twentieth-century courts, however, complicate Islamic and Egyptian ideals of female obedience and seclusion, revealing that women frequently left their husbands and challenged their authority, thereby threatening their masculinity. They paint a different picture of early twentieth-century Cairo—one in which some women were asserting their (limited) independence and fighting for their rights in the public setting of a courtroom—than the one that nationalists portrayed in the press. Turning women into secluded, moral, and obedient wives was not an antiquated return to an idyllic Islamic past, as certain nationalists believed, but a modern response to the onslaught of changes that fostered women's presence in public arenas, which challenged many men who were already made to feel insecure by the political instability and economic domination of their nation.

The rapid transformations affecting women in early twentieth-century urban Egypt—the demise of seclusion, the increase in the marital age, and the spread of education—vexed reformers, writers, and readers, regardless of gender, political affiliation, or religious orientation, who were already worried about the fragile state of their nation. Disobedient, immoral, free, independent, or overly educated *single* women, traits negatively deemed Western, threatened not only men but also the entire Egyptian nation. If women were not turned into suitable potential wives, then men would not marry them, the marriage crisis would persist, and the nation would spiral into destruction. Although the press did not dare speculate what would happen to the nation if the supposed throngs of single women were not turned into wives, their diatribes about the unsuitability of women for wifehood revealed their underlying fear that bachelorettes were potentially more subversive than bachelors. Yet women's failure as wives was not the only factor that engendered bachelorhood. Divorce also turned men off marriage, endangering the family and, by extension, the nation.

4

Deterring Divorce, Modernizing Marriage

What we see in the Islamic courts is the greatest proof of . . . the
marriage crisis. When the bachelor sees the Islamic courts full of
disputing parties who are fed up with married life and want to
escape, he takes it as a warning and loathes marriage.

Muhammad 'Izz al-Din Hafiz

LAW STUDENT MUHAMMAD 'IZZ AL-DIN HAFIZ wrote to *al-
Nahda al-Nisa'iyya* magazine in 1935 to explain that middle-class urban men like himself were discouraged from entering into a union that
would inevitably disintegrate, given the supposedly skyrocketing divorce
rate plaguing Egypt in the 1920s and 1930s.[1] Many other marriage crisis
observers seconded Hafiz's argument. Although they offered different explanations for "the divorce problem," as they often called it, they agreed
that marriage was in an alarming state of disarray that reflected the social
decay of the nation and warranted immediate attention.

Like marriage, divorce served as a medium through which Egyptians voiced their anxieties over the social state of their struggling nation.
The ostensibly high divorce rate represented the fragility of their marital
ties, the unhappiness of their married partners, the frivolity and tempers
of their male subjects who abused their unilateral right to divorce, and,

most of all, the broken homes unsuitable for raising the future citizens of the nation. In other words, divorce symbolized the supposed backwardness of semicolonial Egypt. As a result, writers and readers called on legislators to restrict divorce in order to make marriage more permanent or, as they viewed it, more modern, so as to serve as the sturdy foundation for a flourishing nation-state. For these Egyptians, a modern nation enjoyed a low divorce rate, as in Western countries where divorce was illegal until the late nineteenth and early twentieth centuries. In contrast, Egyptian Islamic law provided men with the unfettered right to repudiate their wives at any time without reason until the 1920s legislation, and it also provided women with certain, albeit limited, access to divorce. As I have argued elsewhere, the government responded to its subjects' demands to legally limit divorce by passing in 1920 and 1929 personal status laws that placed certain restrictions on it.[2] Whether they blamed men's abuse of their right to divorce or women's overuse of the Islamic courts to seek redress, Egyptian legislators and writers were redefining what marriage meant and were debating how to make it modern, what kind of gendered access husbands and wives had to divorce, and what all this entailed for the nation. Legislators were responding to a divorce problem, but they shared with marriage crisis commentators a common hopeful vision that reforming divorce would pave Egypt's path to modernity, lower the divorce rate, and promote marriage.

Staggering Statistics and Vulnerable Victims

Historically and legally, Islamic marriage was not a permanent institution because a husband's mere declaration of divorce could end it at any time.[3] The 1875 Egyptian Islamic Code of Personal Status clearly stated that "the husband and not the wife has the right to break, by repudiation, the tie of a validly contracted marriage" whenever, wherever, and for whatever reason he wished.[4] He only had to verbalize his desire to divorce in or beyond his wife's presence by stating the oath of repudiation (*talaq*) three times before two male witnesses. An ex-husband was required to pay his repudiated wife her deferred dower and divorce alimony during the three-month waiting period (*'idda*) she had to observe before she could marry another.[5] Ideally, a man would divide the triple oath of divorce into three separate statements, each made at one-month intervals during his ex-wife's waiting period to permit him time to reconsider his decision before the divorce was finalized. The first two pronouncements of divorce were revocable because a man could take his repudiated wife back by words or resumed sexual intercourse with or without her consent. If he did not take her back verbally or sexually between his three declarations of divorce, then the third one served as the final and irrevocable dissolution of the marriage. Revocable divorces often served as temporary separations that did not result in permanent divorces. In contrast, irrevocable permanent divorces meant that the couple would have to sign a new marriage contract before two male witnesses and the husband would have to provide a new dower if the couple sought reconciliation.[6]

Observers perceived divorce as rampant in early twentieth-century Egypt. Western travelers and colonial officials were especially alarmed by divorce rates because their point of reference was their native countries, where divorce was mostly illegal at the time. The American traveler Elizabeth Cooper reported in 1914 an outrageously high 90 percent divorce rate based on hearsay.[7] Lord Cromer, the British consul-general in Egypt from 1883 to 1907, cited court registers that revealed a 30 percent divorce rate in 1903 as a result of the "great facility given to divorce," which permitted a Muslim man "when his passion is sated" to "throw off his wife like an old glove."[8] Given men's unfettered rights to divorce, it is not surprising that most commentators blamed men.[9]

Such stinging censures were not the sole domain of Westerners. From the emergence of the marriage crisis as a phenomenon in 1920, Egyptian commentators also deplored what they perceived as accelerating divorce rates throughout the 1920s and 1930s, claiming that it deterred single men from marriage. As they saw it, middle-class men who could barely afford the costs of marriage did not want to enter into a union that would likely end in divorce, for which they would have to pay as well. Just as they seldom cited figures on the number of bachelors, most commentators did not provide any real evidence of climbing divorce rates. The handful who did put forth divorce figures—such as 38 percent in 1925, 45.6 percent in 1930, and 52.5 percent in 1931—usually drew their numbers from the government's annual statistics.[10]

Egypt did in fact have the highest divorce rate of any state reporting such data during the first half of the twentieth century.[11] Both the West-erners' and the Egyptians' statistics are suspect, however, because when they were not based on hearsay, they were derived from government data. The government's numbers included revocable divorces, which explained the consistently higher rate of divorce. In addition, marriages and divorces that occurred outside the courts were not recorded at all.[12] Scholars who counted only irrevocable divorces found a much lower rate of 26.2 per-cent for the same general period.[13] A survey of divorce cases in the Islamic courts indicates that revocable divorces were common enough to explain this significant gap. Census registers also suggest that the number of di-vorced Cairenes climbed very slowly: 2.0 percent in 1917, 2.1 percent in 1927, and 2.7 percent in 1937.[14]

More relevant than whether or not the divorce rate was truly high is the widespread *perception* that it was and what that said about the state of the nation. The Egyptian press was largely responsible for fueling the notion of rampant divorce. Many dailies carried regular columns that reported various court cases in the late 1920s and early 1930s. Columns such as "In the Islamic Courts" and "In the Family," which were pub-lished in the most widely read daily, *al-Ahram*, often featured exceedingly woeful or particularly scandalous tales of divorce. Although the average column was based on a specific court case transcript, exaggerated descrip-tions and embellished details were often added for dramatic effect.[15] The average Egyptian reader who may have had no firsthand experience with divorce could easily have surmised that the country was in the middle of a divorce epidemic when he or she read these columns. Many who wrote letters to the editor about the divorce problem cited the news-paper reports of divorce cases as examples.[16] Social reformer Muhammad Junaydi, who considered "Egypt's disease of the frequency of divorce" as "among the important factors in young men's aversion to and hatred of marriage," wrote: "It is unfortunate that all the newspapers that report news of marital conflicts publish them only to attract readers. . . . [In-stead] they really should publish studies on how to solve this dangerous problem."[17] Junaydi did not believe that the press was exaggerating the extent of divorce, because he himself saw it as a main reason that men refrained from marriage. Rather, he condemned the press for sensation-alizing divorce to sell more papers instead of attempting to alleviate it.

Although the press did not heed Junaydi's advice, several readers and legislators did.

Many like Junaydi were quick to blame men for widespread divorce and held (divorced) men responsible for (single) men's aversion to marriage. 'Abdu al-Barquqi, for example, argued that Egypt's young men "tremble in the throes of marriage and flee from it as they would flee from prison" because of the climbing divorce rates that were the fault of men's unhindered right to divorce.[18] If men took marriage so lightly when they divorced so easily, then why did they hesitate to marry before serious contemplation? According to the few middle-class writers who tackled this question, divorce was a common problem among the poor masses, who did not take marriage seriously because it was not an expensive endeavor for them as it was for middle-class men. These middle-class writers who were quick to condemn their impoverished counterparts for unchecked divorce believed that they were immune from the same tendency.

Take, for example, Ahmad al-Sawi Muhammad, who penned the "Brief and to the Point" daily column in *al-Ahram*. He wrote a lapidary critique that explained what he saw as men's responsibility for the alleged high rates of divorce.

> Among the enlightened class now many hesitate about marriage and as a result divorce is less [common] among them. I look around me and I do not find, thank God, among my acquaintances one who divorced . . . so this frequency in divorce that we see is among the ignorant lower classes . . . [who] marry because it barely costs them a thing . . . but marriage for the educated is a serious psychological and costly endeavor . . . [so] they hesitate . . . [whereas] both the ignorant man and the poor man do not comprehend the responsibilities of family and children.[19]

Little did the enlightened and educated al-Sawi know that he would face divorce two years later. In 1935, his own wife, feminist Duriyya Shafiq, demanded that he repudiate her a mere month after they married because of his conservative views on women that he had kept well hidden from her before their wedding.[20]

Because other social commentators did not mention the class dimension of divorce, even when they were sure to note the middle-class nature of the marriage crisis, it is difficult to ascertain whether the observations of al-Sawi were representative. Census registers do not divulge the social class or financial status of divorced individuals, but a survey of the Islamic court records indicates that middle-class men in Cairo went, or were taken, to court for divorce dealings just as often as their lower-class and upper-class pendants in early twentieth-century Egypt. Other scholars have speculated that divorce was common across social classes and rural and urban regions during this period.[21] Al-Sawi's analysis resulted from the fact that his own class formed a minority of the population and, as a result, the number of his divorced counterparts did not match the number of divorced lower-class men even if the percentages of divorce in each class were similar.

Al-Sawi viewed the high divorce rate as a lower-class problem, but he argued that it still deterred middle-class men from marriage, thereby explaining the inconsistency that other writers did not. Al-Sawi never suggested that a middle-class bachelor could simply differentiate himself from his lower-class counterpart by refraining from divorce once he married, indicating that he perceived marriage as agonizing for men of all classes. Yet he failed to point out that lower-class peasants and urban workers who depended on the contributions of their wives and children to field labor and household incomes did not have the luxury to avoid marriage.

In some ways, al-Sawi's condescension toward the masses' purported predilection for divorce resembled Lord Cromer's disdain for Egyptian divorce. Al-Sawi's diatribe was merely classist, however, whereas the colonial critique was also racist because Cromer viewed Egyptian men's ostensible inclination to divorce as inextricably linked to their insatiable desire for new wives after they tired of their present ones.[22] Al-Sawi did not bother to provide evidence when he ascribed seeming pervasive divorce to the lower classes. In the class-segregated society of early twentieth-century Egypt, al-Sawi probably did not interact frequently enough with lower-class men to know firsthand if they were habitually divorcing. His statement reveals much less about the Egyptian masses than his perception of the emerging middle class, its efforts to dominate the nationalist movement and the Egyptian nation, and its Westernizing inclinations.

Al-Sawi may have appropriated colonial notions of Islamic divorce from his own years in Europe. Known for his "enlightened and progressive articles," he had studied journalism in Paris before graduating from the Sorbonne in 1927, and his Egyptian peers considered him "a European on the outside" who was "liberated in what he wrote."[23] France often served as al-Sawi's reference point: "If Parisians heard about what happens every day among us" in the Islamic courts, he wrote in another column about the high divorce rate, "their mouths would drop open in astonishment."[24] His concern about European perceptions of Egyptian divorce reveals his concerted effort to distinguish his Westernized social class from lower-class Egyptians, who purportedly abused divorce. Because many Westerners viewed divorce as a symbol of Egyptian backwardness, al-Sawi felt the need not only to condemn it but also to prove that such a barbaric practice was not common among his own class—the one that would lead the emerging nation to independence.

Why were men—whatever their class—divorcing in the first place? Some observers implied that the custom of arranged marriage was responsible because educated men could not bear to remain married to an incompatible partner.[25] Others, such as medical student Mahdi al-Din Sa'id, suggested that divorce was taken lightly by a lower-class "husband who tires of [his wife] and wants to enjoy another [woman]."[26] Why did a Muslim man not just marry another, given that polygamy was permissible in Egypt?[27] Egyptian and Western observers explained that divorce "substitutes for polygamy among the poor" because most men could not afford the costs of simultaneously supporting two or more wives.[28] That men did not commonly partake in polygamy in early twentieth-century Egypt is substantiated by the low incidence of polygamy, which became even more rare over the course of the twentieth century.[29] Marriage crisis writers rarely mentioned polygamy in their debates. The problem was that men were not marrying or not staying married, not that they were marrying too many women. The infrequency of polygamy, however, did not preclude nationalists and feminists from perceiving it as a backward custom that also stood in Egypt's path to independence and modernity, and one that they (unsuccessfully) attempted to outlaw in early twentieth-century Egypt.[30] Polygamy, however, did not even compete with the marriage crisis for the attention of Egyptians in the press, indicating that bachelorhood and divorce were perceived to be far more rife than polygamy. Nor did the possibility of polygamy detract from the numerous press inferences to the likelihood of men—regardless of their class—to commit adultery.

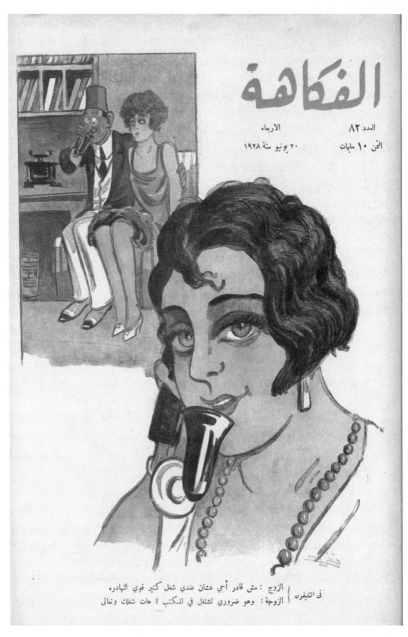

On the phone. Husband: I can't come home because I have a lot of work today. Wife: Do you have to work at the office? Bring your work home and come. Front cover of al-Fukaha, *no. 82 (20 June 1928).*

Most divorce commentators did not believe that arranged or monogamous marriage drove men to divorce. Instead, they blamed men's supposedly short tempers for causing them to divorce their wives in a fit of anger.[31] Like al-Sawi, they appropriated colonial notions about the inherently fickle nature of Egyptian men. Rather than analyze the reasons for men's ostensible impulsiveness, however, many of these writers focused on the immediate triple oath of divorce that enabled a man to hastily divorce his wife "with a word he can pronounce at any time in any place."[32] They regarded the facility of the triple oath, which permanently ended marriage, as a constant threat to "poor wives," who consequently "tremble with fear."[33]

Such sympathetic portrayals of wives were common in the press.[34] Women divorced by their husbands were not held responsible for encouraging bachelorhood, in contrast to their husbands. Although *single* women were often blamed for men not marrying, *divorced* women were not. Because divorced women had once been married, they must have done something right—that is, they were marriageable for a reason. Writers did not assume that divorced women were at fault because Islamic law did not require men to have a reason for divorce. Rather, they blamed men for abusing their privilege to divorce.

Minimizing Male-Initiated Divorce

Countless writers demanded that the government help resolve the divorce epidemic plaguing the nation. A certain A. F. went so far as to suggest that the triple divorce oath should be outlawed completely.[35] Because most commentators believed that the state should not completely prohibit a religiously sanctioned right of men, they did not endorse A. F.'s proposal.[36] Instead, between 1899 and 1945, various writers, legal reformers, and feminists recommended that a Muslim man be permitted to divorce his wife only before a judge after he first attempted to reconcile the couple.[37] The most vocal advocate of this proposal was the Egyptian Feminist Union (EFU), which launched a press campaign in the 1920s and 1930s to reform Islamic personal status law by drawing on minority legal opinions that were more favorable to women.[38] The proposal was never legislated, but it was highly publicized in the press.[39] Among those who made suggestions, few departed from this formula. Exceptions included a judge in the national courts who argued that marriage should not take place except in court with the permission of a judge who had determined that the couple was compatible.[40] Accountant Rashad Mahmud Nigm proposed that a couple should not be permitted to divorce during the first five years of marriage, and then only if they paid the government the value of half the dower.[41]

What all these reformers shared was an intrinsic belief that legislation restricting men's access to divorce would reduce Egypt's escalating divorce rate.[42] They also agreed that it was now the government's responsibility to involve itself in its subjects' marital lives—a supposedly private domain that had previously been largely beyond the gaze of the state. Although Egyptians had urged the government to address other marital issues, such as lowering the dower or taxing bachelors, the government actually responded to the demands to help resolve the divorce problem by passing Law 25 of 1929. The press was concerned with the marriage crisis as a whole, but legislators were only willing or able to respond to the divorce problem.

Legislators stated in the memorandum accompanying Law 25 of 1929 that to preserve the permanence of the family and society as a whole, they aimed to "cure [such] social diseases" as easy male divorce, which men were abusing contrary to Islamic prescriptions that divorce should be a last resort.[43] The concern of this cabinet-appointed personal status committee of secular ministers and religious scholars was the explicit problem of a man's unilateral right to divorce because, for them, it was simply incompatible with a healthy modern nation. If the family, which they referenced as the basic unit of the Egyptian nation, was self-destructing, then the nation itself would collapse.

To bypass Hanafi law—the authoritative school of Islamic law in Egypt for more than four centuries that considered the triple divorce oath so grave that it had made it valid under any circumstance—legislators ingeniously borrowed and combined principles from the other more liberal schools of Islamic law and minority legal opinions that more strictly regulated a man's right to divorce.[44] Law 25 of 1929 decreed that a husband's declaration of divorce was invalid if it was uttered in a state of intoxication or under duress, made as a threat to force his wife or a third party into a particular action, or implied rather than explicitly stated. It also ruled that only one divorce oath was accepted at any one time regardless of the number of oaths pronounced, so that three oaths must be voiced on three separate occasions for the divorce to be irrevocable.[45] Legislators also decided that every divorce would be considered revocable except a third divorce oath, a divorce that occurred before the sexual consummation of a marriage, or a divorce in exchange for money, in which a wife must surrender her financial rights in divorce.[46] Because a revocable divorce meant that the husband retained the right to bring back his wife during her three-month waiting period against her will without having to conclude a new marriage contract or pay a new dower, a revocable divorce preserved the institution of marriage in contrast to an irrevocable one.

Contemporary legal scholars view these legislative attempts as favorable to women.[47] A closer examination, however, reveals that the primary intention of legislators was not to protect wives from their husbands' hasty irrevocable utterances of divorce but to make marriage even more inescapable for husbands and wives who may have hoped for a quick divorce. The government appears to have achieved its goal to lower the divorce rate because its statistics indicate that the divorce rate declined steadily over the twentieth century.[48] Nevertheless, the common depiction of the victimized repudiated wife prevailed in the media because legislators did not completely curb male divorce. Although many wives may have feared repudiation by their husbands, court registers complicate the simplified portrayal of helpless divorcées. Even if wives had been devastated by divorce, many were aware that they were entitled to alimony and deferred dowers and were quick to get to court to demand them from their ex-husbands.[49]

Because men were not required to divorce their wives in their presence, let alone before a judge in court, Islamic ledgers rarely contain cases that are straightforward registrations of male-initiated divorces. They do, however, hold many examples of a wife who was unaware that her husband had divorced her.[50] Take, for example, the story of Sakina Hanim Muhammad al-Shazli. On 11 November 1914, this lady of high society went to court to demand maintenance and a home, clothing, and allowance for her, her servants, and her two young children from landowner Tahir Effendi 'Abd al-Rahman, her husband who had left them penniless.[51] It is interesting that Sakina claimed that she had been left destitute because her elite status likely meant she had capital of her own. Because Islamic law did not require a wife to spend her own money to support herself and her children, she was entitled to demand support from her husband. In response, 'Abd al-Rahman announced that he had divorced his wife a year and a half earlier, furnishing an official divorce certificate dated 21 May 1913. Therefore, he contended, her claims for support were invalid. Sakina retorted that she was not informed about the divorce until this moment and, as a result, she was only beginning her three-month waiting period during which he was required to provide divorce alimony. Her ex-husband immediately consented, and they settled on the alimony in court.[52]

That Sakina knew she was entitled to divorce alimony during her waiting period indicates that she was not a naive woman. The rationale of the waiting period was twofold: to allow an opportunity for reconciliation to occur and to ensure that no doubt would arise over the paternity of the child and his or her right to inherit if the ex-wife was pregnant.[53] In exchange for his ex-wife's observance, the ex-husband was required to provide all the allowances to which she was entitled before she was repudiated: food, clothing, and housing as well as servants if she was of an elite class.[54] Sakina's ex-husband was no fool either. Knowing that the waiting period lasted only three months for a nonpregnant divorcée, 'Abd al-Rahman returned to court almost exactly three months later to terminate his payments to her.[55] Whereas men did not need to resort to court to divorce their wives, they had to go to court to end or dispute alimony injunctions. Like 'Abd al-Rahman, some sought legal recognition of the end of their ex-wives' waiting period and their obligation to pay.[56] Others came to have the amount lowered because they claimed they could not afford it.[57] And still others sought permission to stop payment of alimony and/or deferred dowers because ex-wives were disobedient—that is, they had moved out of the marital home during the waiting period—among other reasons.[58] A few ex-husbands even sought court approval of not having to pay marital support because they had divorced their wives only to be told by the judge that they must pay divorce alimony.[59]

Far from the pathetic divorcées portrayed in the press, some women milked their ex-husbands for as long as they could, claiming their waiting period had not ended because their third menstrual cycle never arrived.

Nabawiyya al-Dahshuri countered that her third menstrual cycle still had not appeared on 21 October 1922, when her wealthy ex-husband argued that her waiting period must have ended by then because her second cycle had commenced nearly ten months earlier and she was neither pregnant nor breastfeeding.[60] The court accepted Nabawiyya's testimony and did not even require her to provide any sort of medical corroboration from a midwife or doctor. When her ex-husband filed a second appeal on 13 June 1923, nearly eighteen months after her second menstrual cycle began, and she still denied the arrival of her third cycle, the court sided with him and permitted him to end his alimony payments. The judge cited Law 25 of 1920, which stated that the waiting period of an ex-wife who was neither pregnant nor breastfeeding could not last more than one year, even if her menstrual cycle never returned.[61] Nabawiyya's strategy, whether or not she had been dishonest, must have been a common tactic among ex-wives if legislators deemed it necessary to set a limit to the waiting period in the 1920 law. Even that restriction, however, did not fully block all loopholes, as legislators observed nearly a decade later in their memorandum to the 1929 law: "Complaints have multiplied from husbands concerning the tricks and devices used by their divorced wives in order to obtain alimony to which they are not entitled."[62]

None of the writers and readers who sympathized with the wives who supposedly tiptoed around their husbands' rash inclinations to divorce considered that many wives may have viewed repudiation as a blessing, especially because their own access to divorce was so limited and often entailed forgoing their financial rights. Lower-class women such as Wasila al-'Issawi, Nabiha Mansur, and Amina Sulayman, among countless others, pleaded with the court to register their husbands' permanent triple oath of divorce.[63] Many women actively sought ratification of this permanent divorce because it meant that their husbands could not take them back against their will, a practice that the court registers and the press attested was fairly common.[64] If a woman could obtain a proof of divorce, then once her waiting period was completed, her ex-husband would have to remarry her with a new contract, another dower, and her permission to resume marital life with her.[65]

Few wives, however, managed to obtain a proof of divorce in court. Because their husbands denied uttering the divorce pledge and because they were unable to furnish two male witnesses to the utterance of divorce, their cases were dismissed.[66] A divorce oath made during a heated argument between a husband and a wife may not have occurred before an audience. Or, alternatively, it may have transpired before people who preferred not to be involved. Perhaps women lied about their husbands' divorce pronouncements to escape unwanted marriages. Occasionally, however, a witness or two did come forth at the wife's insistence. Amina Sayyid returned to court with two witnesses a week after she filed her proof of divorce case and managed to win, whereas Fatima Sulayman was not as successful because she could obtain only one witness.[67]

If a man uttered the divorce oath unintentionally in a fit of rage, rarely would he confess to this in the courtroom. An exception was Hasan Abu Zayd, who admitted that he continued to live with 'A'isha Ibrahim after divorcing her permanently, but only after she brought evidence that the divorce had been officially registered.[68] It is noteworthy that 'A'isha, a garbage collector's daughter who was most likely illiterate, unabashedly took her husband to court and knew to bring documentation to prove her case. Many other lower-class wives did not seem to know that they needed witnesses or documentation to prove their claims.

Women Who Walk

In stark opposition to the press image of wretched wives, women who actively pursued divorce were portrayed as untrustworthy troublemakers who beguiled the courts into granting them divorces from their harmless husbands.[69] So long as women were the submissive victims of divorce, they were to be pitied. If they initiated divorce, however, they were condemned, and much more harshly than their male counterparts were. Perhaps the middle-class members of the press denounced female-initiated divorce because they were influenced by Islamic law, which considered the right to initiate divorce an exclusively male prerogative. Even when writers and legislators censured men who abused their right to divorce, they rarely questioned their fundamental entitlement to this privilege with the exception of a few, such as A. F.

Before the introduction of Law 25 of 1920, which provided Egyptian women with three new official grounds for judicial divorce, an Egyptian

Muslim woman had three possible, but often unachievable, avenues to divorce: (1) She could ask her husband to stipulate her right to divorce in their marriage contract (*yad al-'isma*); (2) she could ask the judge to grant her a judicial divorce (*tatliq*); or (3) she could ask her husband to divorce her by mutual agreement (*khul'*). In the first two options, she maintained her financial rights in divorce, namely, her deferred dower and divorce alimony. In the third alternative, she usually but not always was forced to surrender these two material rights. Essentially, she had to buy her way out of the marriage. In all three options, however, she did not have the right to divorce. Rather, a divorce had to be given to her, either by her husband or by a judge, because Islamic law viewed her as a passive participant in the breaking of marriage.

The first option was the only instance in which a wife could initiate a divorce without providing a reason while retaining her financial rights, so long as her husband expressly granted her the prerogative to include the right to divorce in their marriage contract.[70] In practice, however, few Egyptian husbands gave their wives this right. If they did, it was usually only under a specific stipulation that they spelled out in the contract. In 1914, for example, Wasifa Mahmud 'Aliq, the elite granddaughter of a bey, exercised her right to divorce her husband, who had married a second wife, because they had stipulated in their marriage contract that she could be granted a divorce if he engaged in polygamy.[71] It is not unlikely that her middle-class husband had been pressured into granting his upper-class wife this right as a condition of their marriage. Marriage contracts in Ottoman Egypt only occasionally included the wife's right to an automatic divorce if her husband took another wife, and this stipulation continued to be rare in early twentieth-century conjugal contracts.[72]

Either few women knew that Islamic law conferred on them the right to divorce or, more likely, few were secure enough to ask their potential grooms to confer this right on them. Although a woman may merely have been seeking insurance, her future husband could interpret her demand as a sign that she and her family did not trust him. As a result, some men may have viewed it as a deal breaker in marital negotiations. Women who managed to obtain the right to divorce probably came from privileged backgrounds, such as Wasifa, with much family support or other marital prospects—that is, they were not impoverished women whose limited options in life made marriage a necessity.

The press display of shock and dismay at women who made such a stipulation in their marriage contracts further confirms that it was neither common nor accepted by the general public. In a report of a disgruntled wife who threatened to divorce her husband, *al-Ahram* explicated how the mere risk of being divorced by his wife threatened one husband's masculinity: "This husband had wanted after that to be a real man and have his masculinity awakened physically and tangibly near and far, witnessed by the blind and the seeing."[73] Even though press commentators often criticized husbands for irrationally divorcing their wives, they never questioned their manhood. On the contrary, these husbands were just being men. Wives who merely expressed a desire to divorce, however, were somehow unnatural aberrations whose intention threatened their husband's masculinity. When they sought the same right enjoyed by men, they were deemed not to be acting like proper women, and so their husbands could not remain real men. These writers viewed ideal manhood as contingent on proper womanhood, indicating how fragile the gendered roles of Egyptian men and women were.

The press was less judgmental of wives who had a religiously valid reason to seek a divorce. According to Hanafi doctrine, which provided the narrowest grounds for female-initiated divorce, a wife could be granted a judicial divorce and hence retain her financial rights only if her husband was impotent or an apostate from Islam or if a minor wife, upon reaching majority age, could prove that a guardian other than her father or grandfather had married her to a suitor without her consent.[74] Not only did a wife need grounds to file for a judicial divorce, but also her limited reasons were specific and quite atypical. Consequently, few examples of such judicial divorces are found in the early twentieth-century records. No examples of Muslim wives being granted a divorce because their husbands converted to another religion were found. Only one reference to a divorce as a result of impotence was found.[75] Nineteenth-century court registers likewise reveal that "women rarely succeeded in obtaining a decree" of judicial divorce.[76]

A woman could obtain a divorce without citing cause if her husband agreed, usually in exchange for forfeiting her deferred dower and/

or divorce alimony. Divorce by mutual agreement often but not always meant that a woman had to buy her way out of an unhappy marriage.[77] Giving up both the delayed dower and the divorce alimony was the norm among Egyptian women who sought this form of divorce in the nineteenth and early twentieth centuries.[78] In contrast to judicial divorce, this type of female-instigated divorce was contingent on a husband's express agreement.[79] Among the three divorce options for women, divorce by mutual agreement appears to have been the most common form of *successfully granted* female-initiated divorce in Ottoman and British-occupied Egypt.[80] It was also the least sensationalized in the middle-class press because it rested on the husband's consent and was a luxury of the wealthy female minority. An Egyptian woman who could afford to relinquish all her financial rights was rare because the vast majority were unable to support themselves independently. The few who could afford to do so must have had sufficient income, owned their own property, been able to claim support from male relatives, or planned to remarry as soon as their three-month waiting period ended.[81] Because legislators failed to reference this type of divorce in their 1920 and 1929 national codification of personal status laws, however, it nearly dropped out of practice over the course of the twentieth century.[82]

Additional Avenues or More Restraints?

Law 25 of 1920 provided Egyptian women with three additional grounds for judicial divorce.[83] Legislators drew on the more liberal Maliki and Shafi'i schools to grant a woman a divorce if her husband refused to provide financial support in general, if he failed to provide because of his absence or disappearance, or if he contracted an incurable or chronic defect that was unknown to the wife at the time of marriage or that developed after they were married.[84]

The first two grounds addressed the Islamic obligation of husbands to financially support their wives. If a husband could not or would not provide for his wife, then she had legal grounds for a divorce. Many in the Egyptian press were in favor of this new law.[85] Galal Husayn shed light on why so many nationalists welcomed this legislation. As he saw it, women whose absent husbands refused to divorce them ended up living as fugitives, without the legal possibilities of alimony or remarriage. The Egyptian nation would benefit only by allowing these desperate women to divorce and remarry.[86] At the same time, however, wives who divorced their husbands as soon as they fell on tough financial times were ridiculed and accused of exploiting this law.[87] Yet court records reveal that wives of deadbeat husbands who repeatedly failed to provide were the ones who attempted to take advantage of the new law.

Islamic registers indicate that judges did not easily grant this kind of divorce resulting from poverty (*tatliq li-l-faqr*) because the 1920 law carefully instructed them to confirm the financial circumstances of the husband before granting such a divorce.[88] Proving her husband's destitution was a difficult task for an Egyptian wife to accomplish. 'Aziza Radwan and Amina Ibrahim's attempts in 1930 were denied.[89] Fatima Hasan's first attempt was refused because her husband testified that he was able to support her, but her second attempt was successful because the court deemed that her husband was capable but "determined to not provide" for her. The divorce was not implemented, however, and she was back in court a year later for yet another attempt to obtain a divorce, which was also refused because her husband proved that he had a pension that could support her.[90] Among the handful of such suits found, only one succeeded: On 3 October 1922, Na'ima Muhammad was granted a divorce after she proved that her husband could not support her because his imprisonment had impoverished him.[91] This exception was made because she was able to prove her husband's imprisonment, which the court acknowledged deprived her husband of the opportunity to earn income.

These cases indicate that Law 25 of 1920 was not easily translated into practice. Na'ima, however, would not have won her case before the 1920 law was passed. In 1914, for example, Hanim Mursi could not file for divorce from her imprisoned husband, a farmer, on the basis of his extended absence, as post-1920 prisoners' wives such as Na'ima could. Hanim Mursi attempted to extract a proof of divorce from the court, testifying that her imprisoned husband had divorced her. Because he obviously could not appear in court to confirm this and because she did not provide acceptable witnesses, her case was denied.[92] The judge could not grant her a divorce on the basis of her husband's imprisonment, as judges would be able to after Law 25 of 1929 was passed. The 1920 law had stated that even if the whereabouts of an absent imprisoned husband were known, his wife could not file for judicial divorce so long as he continued to support her. The 1929 law, on the other hand, decreed that a woman whose husband was imprisoned for at least three years could, after a separation of at least one year, petition the court for divorce.[93] Many Egyptians applauded this new legislation, which sought to amend the legal injustice in which "we deny the woman [the right] to divorce her husband even if he is sentenced to life imprisonment, so that her life is destroyed and her reputation is smeared with the shame of a deed that she did not commit."[94]

Not all Egyptians, however, welcomed the introduction of this law. The prominent nationalist lawyer Muhammad Husayn Haykal, who in the 1940s would later serve as minister of education and Senate president, lambasted this clause because it would compel wives to claim potential infidelity if they remained married to their imprisoned husbands in order to convince judges to grant them a divorce. For Haykal, who called for the extensive Westernization of the Egyptian nation, a woman could not be entrusted with the right to divorce because it would threaten both public morality and the family unit.[95] 'Abd al-Hamid Hamdi, editor of the liberal weekly al-Sufur, responded that marriage should not be a forced bond that only a husband had the right to dissolve. In 1920, he condemned the 1875 Egyptian Islamic Code of Personal Status as ludicrous and outdated. Although Hamdi was critical of Islamic laws that did not afford women many grounds for divorce, he was careful not to directly criticize Islam. Rather, he believed that legislators could find elements in Islam to support the reform of marriage laws to recover its true original purpose and not its contemporary meaning, which translated into "a contract in which the husband owned his wife."[96] Another writer agreed with Hamdi, arguing that the high rates of suicides and spousal murders committed by miserable wives, publicized in the press as a phenomenon unique to desperate wives, would continue to increase if women were not permitted legal recourse to leave unbearable marriages. Although many of these male writers advocated female rights to divorce not in the name of gender equality but rather as a means to improve the social welfare of the nation, some were more adamant in their calls for marital reform than others. 'Abdu al-Barquqi called on the government to legislate equal rights to divorce for men and women, something that even the EFU did not demand. He argued that if marriage was not coupled with the right to divorce, then it was equivalent to bondage and slavery and that a nation which forbade divorce would cause its youth to fear marriage as they feared prison.[97] For al-Barquqi, both extremes—wholly unrestricted access to divorce *and* the abolition of divorce—contributed or would contribute to a marriage crisis.

Given the expanding role that the legal system assumed in monitoring marriage and divorce and the complicated process of female-initiated divorce, it is difficult to claim that these divorce laws constituted major new gains for women. The 1920 law, for example, enabled a wife whose husband was absent or missing to file for divorce only on the basis of his failure to provide financial support; that is, she had to prove that he was not sending her money or had not left her with a sufficient amount to sustain herself.[98] The divorce, however, was revocable if the husband returned and was willing to provide for her financially. If no information on the husband's whereabouts was known, then the wife had to wait four years from the date she filed the case until she could begin her waiting period, which the law set at four months and ten days (in contrast to the usual three-month period) after which the judge could issue a divorce. After the ex-wife completed her waiting period, she was free to marry another, but if her ex-husband reappeared before her marriage was consummated, she was forced to return to him.[99] Badr al-Zayn Mursi's divorce, for example, would not be finalized until four years, four months, and ten days after 5 March 1922, the day she filed for divorce from her missing husband.[100]

This law likely minimized the autonomy that judges enjoyed in Ottoman Egypt, where the four legal schools of Islam were available to them.[101] In nineteenth-century Egypt, for example, judges occasionally granted women permanent judicial divorces on the grounds of desertion or lack of material support.[102] In contrast, judges in twentieth-century Egypt were not supposed to draw on other legal interpretations, schools, or minority opinions as their predecessors had done because they were government employees, paid, promoted, transferred, and pensioned by a largely secular state that had adopted a monolithic understanding of

Islamic personal status law in the 1920s.[103] Unhappily married women were not necessarily better off in nineteenth-century Egypt, but those who relentlessly sought a divorce merely faced less state bureaucracy and perhaps were able to find more loopholes to the hegemonic interpretations that were codified by the 1920s nationwide legislation.

In addition to the three new grounds introduced in the 1920 law, the 1929 law introduced one additional ground for judicial divorce: the husband's maltreatment (*darar*).[104] The law did not explicitly define maltreatment; it merely stated that it contributed to marital discord and made reconciliation between the couple impossible, thus leaving the determination of whether or not harm occurred to individual male judges.[105] A survey of Islamic court records reveals only one instance of a successfully granted divorce on the grounds of maltreatment, indicating how difficult it was for women to obtain such a divorce.[106] *Al-Ahram*'s court case columns occasionally featured cases of this type of divorce, another indication that they were uncommon, because *al-Ahram* preferred the rare and juicy cases to the standard ones. Although they should be taken with a grain of salt, these press accounts can offer some insight into how judges chose to grant this form of divorce.

According to the newspaper's legal column, judges usually bestowed this type of divorce if there was concrete evidence that the husband had physically abused his wife.[107] *Al-Ahram*, however, almost always expressed shock that a husband could lose his wife because he beat her. In one account, the newspaper chided a wife who was awarded such a divorce because she had lied that her husband beat her to hide the fact that she no longer loved him.[108] In another account, *al-Ahram* condemned one wife for seeking (and winning) a judicial divorce because her husband had beat her after finding her with another man.[109] Whereas a wife's claim of her husband's verbal abuse alone did not warrant a divorce, a husband's lack of sexual intimacy could result in such a divorce, which also astounded *al-Ahram*.[110] The reporters of this nationalist daily held conservative views toward women and marriage, sometimes even more so than those found in Islamic legal discourse. Although it appears that these columnists were influenced by broader Islamic understandings of marriage and gender, they often did not support those Islamic laws that provided women with more access to divorce.

Conclusion

According to many writers and readers in the early twentieth-century press, divorce was not just a major source of the marriage crisis because it deterred men from marriage. Its incidence was supposedly so high that it constituted its own problem. Although the Egyptian government did not respond to other causes for rampant bachelorhood, it heeded its subjects' demands to reform divorce or, as they saw it, modernize marriage by deterring divorce through legislation in 1920 and 1929. Because Islamic law gave men unilateral rights to divorce, most social commentators held men responsible for the divorce rate. Yet most of them did not call for extensive curtailment of their right to divorce. Islamic legislators and Egyptian nationalists alike believed that men should not surrender this gendered privilege. Even those who deplored the victimization of wives or called for women's increased access to divorce did not advocate equal rights to divorce because they did not believe women should hold the same privilege as men. Why was divorce deemed so damaging to the fledgling nation? Some writers alluded to the havoc that hordes of destitute divorced women could wreak on the nation, but most were more concerned with the children of broken marriages—the future citizens who were to lead the nation to full independence.

5

Mentoring Mothers, Fettering Fathers

Many of the educated in Egypt who . . . have seen how organized
the European family and its methods for raising children into
proper men and women are complain about the Egyptian home
upbringing. Perhaps this is the reason the majority of young
educated men avoid marriage. . . . In other words, the ignorance of
the young Egyptian woman in the proper methods of upbringing is
the point of contention.

Anonymous writer in al-Siyasa al-Usbu'iyya

IN 1926, an unidentified writer to *al-Siyasa al-Usbu'iyya* offered
yet another reason to explain men's supposed aversion to marriage.[1] He
claimed that educated men did not want to marry Egyptian women who
could not raise proper citizens for the nation. Unlike other marriage ana-
lysts who blamed women's ignorance in general, this writer specified their
ignorance of proper child-rearing skills as a cause for bachelorhood. According to this anonymous writer, Egyptian women were not educated,
organized, hygienic, or well versed in child development and health, that
is, the child-rearing modes that modern civilized nations mandated.

Although nationalists in the press called for the reform of Egyptian
mothers so that these women could properly raise the future citizens of

the nation, they remained largely silent on the specific roles that Egyptian fathers should play in raising the next generation. In contrast, Islamic legal discourse assigned mothers the task of caring for dependent helpless children until they were old enough to receive the religious, moral, and professional guidance that their fathers were legally required to provide. Many in the press viewed Egyptian women as better moral guides and nationalist models than Egyptian fathers, but Islamic law did not accord mothers the same rights and responsibilities that nationalists did. The courts consistently awarded fathers child custody in disputes between divorced couples and gave them the primary responsibility for raising physically independent children.

The increased responsibilities that writers assigned the married mother in the nationalist family during the first three decades of the twentieth century coincided with a subtle, almost subversive, call for the curtailment of the absolute authority of the father with regard to one of his key duties within the family, namely, the arranging of his daughters' marriages. Press discussions and court cases that upheld a woman's right to choose her own partner reveal that fathers were becoming marginalized in the family. Similarly, Islamic judges began to extend slightly the custody rights of divorced mothers, indicating the influence of nationalist discourses that emphasized the significance of the mother in the best interest of the child. Although press discourses and legal practices often diverged, the legal practices of child custody were somewhat shaped by the nationalist discourses that promoted motherhood.

Active Mothers and Passive Fathers

Late nineteenth-century Egypt witnessed the emergence of a new nationalist ideology that accorded women the educational and moral responsibility of raising future citizens for the nascent nation. Nationalists encouraged female education to instruct mothers on how to instruct the next generation properly so that they could lead the emerging nation to full independence. The notion that to educate a mother was to educate the nation was embedded in the nationalist discourse when Egypt was intent on revitalization to liberate itself from colonial domination.[2] The mother as the central figure in shaping the child marked a new shift in focus and audience away from medieval Islamic literature on raising children (and even on nursing infants) that had been addressed to the father, who had been deemed the primary parental authority. This literature was mirroring the legal reality that children belonged to the father alone in Islamic marriage and divorce.[3]

According to patrilineal Islamic law, children assumed their father's religion, name, and identity. He alone was materially, legally, and morally responsible for the religious and educational upbringing of his sons until they gained economic independence and of his daughters until they married. Islamic law merely required a mother to care for her children during their period of dependence (*hadana*), which Hanafi jurists determined to be from birth until age 7 for boys and age 9 for girls.[4] Mothers did not assume formal guardianship of the child in cases of death or divorce, but they oversaw this stage because jurists deemed them emotionally and physically better equipped to care for a helpless child. If the biological mother was deceased or deemed unfit for motherhood, the child's female relatives supervised the child because a dependent child was seen to be in need of a woman's supposedly natural compassionate care.[5] Once the child's dependency ended, his or her educational and religious socialization, which only men were deemed qualified to provide, was assumed by the father or, in his absence, the child's paternal male relatives. In other words, women were assigned the actual labor of child care when the children were helplessly dependent, whereas men were in charge of the education of physically independent children who were ready to receive moral and educational guidance. This legal conception of fatherhood was not unique to the Islamic world. In most premodern Western contexts, fathers were considered the natural primary custodians of children and were responsible for their instruction and moral guidance.[6]

Despite Islamic laws that emphasized fatherhood, the new primacy of motherhood in nationalist discourses was reflected in the marriage crisis debates of early twentieth-century Egypt. In the construction of womanhood, the ideology of motherhood often took precedence over wifehood. Although a handful of male and female writers favored female education so that women could serve as intellectual companions for their husbands, the vast majority advocated education so that women would become better mothers. Women's ostensible incapacity to properly raise children was cited more frequently as a cause for bachelorhood than women's inability to provide intellectual companionship to their husbands, mirroring the privileging of motherhood over wifehood in the larger debates over women's issues.[7] By analyzing the women's press in the first three decades of twentieth-century Egypt, several scholars have shown how the press strategically exalted motherhood. Writers often emphasized maternal responsibilities over matrimonial ones and thus assigned women a higher but socially sanctioned role in the nation-building process that they could not join as equals. They framed their arguments for female education in terms of women's tasks as mothers, arguing that Egypt could not develop the educated male population essential for its progress without educating the women who raised them.[8]

Male writers in nationalist and religious journals also focused much of their attention on the need to educate women for motherhood in order to encourage men to marry.[9] Their religious or political affiliations did not affect their views on motherhood. Men who wrote in secular Westernizing periodicals shared with their counterparts who wrote in religious journals similar beliefs about the deficiency of Egyptian mothers as a cause for bachelorhood.[10] Both sides were influenced by colonial discourses that idealized Western conceptions of motherhood, and both sides took part in anticolonial nationalist discourses that simultaneously blamed Egyptian women for their country's backwardness while seeking to redefine proper methods of Egyptian motherhood, child rearing, and domesticity.[11]

At the same time, the early twentieth-century Egyptian press was glaringly silent about the role of fathers and did not regard them as a locus for resolving the marriage crisis or reforming the fledgling nation. It rarely advised men on how to be good fathers: "The father at home was an active observer" whose sole paternal-nationalist duty was "to control the wife as educator within the family."[12] The nationalists who led Egypt's three-year struggle for independence between 1919 and 1922 assumed a metaphorical maternal role as the reformers who were capable of leading the national Egyptian household into an independent era: "Male bourgeois nationalists were enjoined to behave outside the home in the same way that women had been asked to behave inside the home since the turn of the century."[13] The scholarly silence on the *actual* role that fathers were instructed to play *inside* the home reflects a lacuna in the press.

Although articles directed to fathers occasionally appeared in the early twentieth-century press beyond the framework of the marriage crisis, they usually materialized in simultaneous sermons to mothers and extolled the benefits of a stable efficient home under the loving guidance and watchful supervision of both parents for the proper upbringing of future citizens.[14] Even the few articles specifically devoted to fathers merely reminded them to serve as positive nationalist role models for their sons by working hard and behaving morally or advised them to show affection and refrain from excessive corporal discipline.[15] Fathers were not instructed on how to raise proper citizens or enjoined to learn child-rearing skills in school as women were. Similarly, their fathering skills were rarely criticized. Caricatures from this era, however, implied that the nationalist ideal of the picture perfect family under the father's tutelage was unattainable.

The neglect of fatherhood in the press was not inadvertent, and it invites two plausible interpretations. First, it served to consolidate further the new conceptions of the more active role mothers should play in the nation. Egyptian writers were clear about the nationalist formula for success: "The father-provider headed the household, and he worked diligently outside the home in order to materially support his family. He was aided by his partner, the mother-educator, who attended to the emotional and material needs of the household. . . . By advancing the moral and material level of the household, Egyptians could advance the nation."[16] The sharp division of labor between fathers and mothers in the Egyptian context mirrored the polarized demarcation of the positions of mothers and fathers in late nineteenth-century Western discourses.[17] Although nationalist writers began to confer on mothers many of the responsibilities traditionally assigned to fathers, they did not want to change the primary obligations of Muslim fathers. As the 1875 Egyptian Islamic Code of Personal Status set forth, men were obliged to provide their children with the same three kinds of support (food, clothing, and lodging) that they were required to render to their wives in addition to their educational and/or professional training.[18]

Second, fathers did not need to be instructed about their paternal duties because their knowledge and authority were fundamental and guaranteed givens. Historically and legally, Muslim men were granted unilateral

Realistic role play. Mother: What's wrong with the two of you, Ahmad? Why are you and your sister fighting? Ahmad: We're not fighting. We're playing Mother and Father. Mother: Play all you want but don't shout! Ahmad: How can we play Mother and Father without shouting? Why don't you and Dad stop shouting? Back cover of al-Fukaha, no. 67 (7 March 1928).

guardianship of and responsibility for their children. In contrast, women merely served as vessels for bringing men's children into the world and as caretakers for infants. Despite the Islamic notion of women as instinctively maternal toward small children, nationalists believed that women had to be taught good mothering. Thus women had to carve out places as mothers in the nation-building process because, in contrast to men, their participation and knowledge were not assumed. The growing nationalist favoring of motherhood over fatherhood in the press, however, did not imply that the mother replaced the father as the head of the household. Instead, nationalists allotted women a complementary but active position alongside their husbands within the household. If anything, fathers' threatened masculinity as colonial subjects perhaps heightened their need to express their authority over the household because most exercised little control in the political economic sphere dominated by the British.

Naive Nurturers and Moral Mothers

Marriage pundits—male or female, religious or secular—rarely elaborated on what was deficient in Egyptian mothers when they referred to their ignorant maternal skills as a cause for bachelorhood. They discussed the ostensible backwardness of Egyptian motherhood in vague terms and offered only general solutions, such as female education in child rearing, because their essays centered on the marriage crisis, not on specific modes of motherhood. Those writers who wrote about motherhood in general, however, did provide more detailed analyses of Egypt's so-called backward child-rearing practices. Some fulminated about the purported laziness and shamefulness of upper-class mothers who hired Egyptian servants or foreign nannies to raise their children. Most, however, condemned mothers of all classes. Some criticized women for spoiling their children instead of properly disciplining them. Others disparaged them for their lack of hygiene, which led to the high infant mortality rate. Still others ridiculed their ignorance of Arabic, Islam, and Egyptian history—subjects that their children were learning at school.[19]

Because most middle-class and upper-class children in the early twentieth century were being sent to school, mothers were expected to have some background knowledge to be able to keep abreast of their children's studies. When nationalists called for mothers to be educated, however, they were not demanding that mothers be educated in subjects other than domesticity, Islam, Arabic, and Egyptian history. As writer 'Aziza al-Hakim put it, the Egyptian mother was to learn "how to clean, iron, cook, manage the home, care for her children" and pursue "the study of national history and . . . heroes . . . to prepare her children . . . as young brave freedom fighters who will fight with courage for their rights and the homeland."[20] She was to provide the ideal home environment where her sons could excel in their studies and where she was to serve as a model of inspiration for her daughters, who would grow up and raise nationalist sons of their own.[21]

Like its Western counterparts, the Egyptian discourse on motherhood positioned women as the repositories of both the nation's progress and its backwardness. Although the Egyptian discourse often exalted Western women's skills in housekeeping, sewing, cooking, discipline, nursing, health, and hygiene, which were deemed necessary for properly raising children, it was not derivative of Western views on domesticity and motherhood. It also criticized certain Western methods, refused their wholesale adoption, and imbued them with local meanings.[22] The Egyptian discourse departed from its Western counterparts in remarkable ways. First, the Egyptian concern for motherhood was not couched in a colonialist imperative that underscored the necessity for the ascendancy of European motherhood and white superiority in the face of racial contamination through miscegenation or exposure to native nursemaids in the colonies.[23] Second, Egyptians did not criticize only lower-class mothers as unsanitary and backward. Although the Egyptian discourse was primarily a middle-class one, it criticized all classes of mothers and, if anything, was geared to the middle and upper classes, which formed the reading public.[24] Last, the Egyptian debates on motherhood were not guided by pronatalist policies steeped in colonialist, socialist, or nationalist fears over low reproduction rates in Europe for most of the twentieth century. In contrast, Egyptians remained unconcerned about family size until the 1930s, when a population control movement began to emerge in the face of an exploding populace.[25] By promoting Egyptian ideals and instructions, writers produced a localized modernity that validated the typical anticolonial nationalist claim of "different yet modern."[26]

Nationalists also began to confer on mothers the duty of providing their children with a moral upbringing in early twentieth-century Egypt. In his argument that men avoided marriage to Egyptian women because they were not skilled mothers, for example, one young bachelor commented, "It is not enough to send children to school. Rather, the mother must instill in them a moral upbringing because she is the first pillar of their formation."[27] Nationalists did not merely want mothers to serve as paragons of rectitude for future citizens. They also wanted them to nurture their children's ethical development by teaching them Egyptian values and Islamic morals in which they themselves should be schooled. Islamic jurists clearly emphasized that fathers were responsible for the moral upbringing of their children, but even they too required mothers to be principled. Whereas a father's guardianship of his children was unconditional in Islamic law, a divorced or widowed mother's right to custody during the first seven or nine years of her child's life was contingent on two stipulations: First, she had to be an adult free woman who was fit for motherhood, that is, sane, trustworthy, moral, and physically capable; and second, she could not remarry a man who was not an immediate relative of the child.[28] These conditions reveal how marginalized motherhood was in Islamic law.

Many ex-husbands tried to acquire custody of their children because their mothers were working outside the home, claiming that they were morally unfit for motherhood. Take, for example, the defense of Khalil Agha 'Ali al-Jawish, a lower middle-class employee in the Ministry of Finance. When his ex-wife, Zanuba Muhammad Effendi al-Rasim, sued him for the previous month's alimony for their 5-year-old daughter, despite a previous court order, he admitted that he had not paid but responded:

> Zanuba, the plaintiff, does not deserve custody of our aforementioned daughter because she leaves my aforementioned daughter, hungry and naked in the sun, at the neighbors while she goes out and sells scarves from house to house and, as a result, the girl is neglected, so I ask your honor to order her to hand over the aforementioned girl to me so that I can take care of her.[29]

Zanuba emphatically retorted, "I do not leave my aforementioned daughter with any of the neighbors or anyone else. I do not sell scarves in homes, and I do not work at all or leave my house."[30] Although Islamic law did not preclude a woman's right to work, even if she was caring for dependent children, the case was postponed to permit al-Jawish the opportunity to bring witnesses to corroborate his accusation of Zanuba's ineptitude.[31] When the litigants returned one week later, however, they informed the judge that they had come to an agreement: al-Jawish would pay his ex-wife the month of child alimony he owed, and Zanuba would retain custody of their daughter without any more child support from him.

Al-Jawish and Zanuba's custody case offers some insight into one lower middle-class couple's perceptions of moral motherhood. Al-Jawish did not merely accuse his ex-wife of working outside the home; he charged her with child neglect because she supposedly left their daughter hungry and naked. Zanuba's categorical denial that she left her child with others, or even left her home, indicates that she either agreed that a fit mother should not leave her child to work outside the home (and was perhaps defending her integrity by insisting that she observed female seclusion) or, more likely, that she believed that an Islamic judge would declare her incompetent for motherhood if she admitted to her ex-husband's allegations. Zanuba most likely did engage in paid employment because she did not permit her ex-husband the opportunity to return to court with witnesses and because she agreed to forgo her right to child alimony in order to keep their 5-year-old daughter for another four years.

Only rarely did a single mother agree to assume the costs of raising a child and absolve her ex-husband from alimony in return for keeping the child beyond his or her dependency years.[32] Yet she could neither assume legal guardianship nor prevent her ex-husband from demanding that she relinquish their child at a future date. Such cases were few and far between, however, because only a few financially independent women in early twentieth-century Egypt could afford to raise a child without financial support from their ex-husbands. Most mothers who wanted to keep their children did not have the legal option of remarriage, and most middle-class and upper-class mothers did not have the socially sanctioned or viable option of paid employment.

Al-Jawish, it seems, was less concerned about the welfare of his daughter than his own release from child support. He immediately consented to his ex-wife's continuance of custody so long as he did not have to provide for the child. The courts recorded the cases of many other fathers who accused their ex-wives of moral ineptness for tutelage, usually because they worked and left the child unattended, and demanded fiscal absolution when they were sued for child alimony.[33] That these fathers used their ex-wives' employment to argue that they were morally unqualified for motherhood either revealed their genuine belief that women should devote themselves solely to motherhood or served as a convenient argument in court to end their ex-wives' custody and hence their obligation to pay child alimony. Court records disclose a number of fathers who initiated child custody cases because their ex-wives were working and supposedly not caring for the child. In all such cases, the father's request was denied because he could not prove child neglect, revealing that a mother's employment did not disqualify her from custody in the eyes of the court.[34] These cases signify a marked departure from nineteenth-century rural Egypt, which witnessed many "painful custody cases, where women were deprived of custody because they were independent working mothers" because judges refused to accept a changing reality in which the countryside's economic transformations robbed peasant women of former support networks as members of the production/consumption family.[35] By the early twentieth century, however, judges no longer penalized employed urban mothers, suggesting that they were willing to adapt to socioeconomic changes and that they may have been affected by nationalist discourses that emphasized the significance of motherhood in the newspapers they were likely reading.

Interestingly, the middle-class press rarely discussed working mothers, whether divorced or married, in debates over marriage. This silence probably reflected the journalists' own milieu. Most middle-class and upper-class mothers did not work for wages in early twentieth-century Egypt. It also may indicate that there was no room for divorced and widowed mothers in their neat equations of the married nationalist family in which the mother raised the children within the home while the father provided for them by working outside the home. Al-Ahram, which regularly reported scandalous court cases, was stupefied by a court's refusal in 1932 of a lower-class father's plea for custody of his son on the basis that his ex-wife was an unfit mother because she had opened a coffeehouse that engaged her night and day. As if to explain such an idiosyncratic ruling to its middle-class readers, *al-Ahram* reported:

> Islamic law does not prevent a woman from a profession to obtain support especially if she is divorced or has no provider. Also, there is nothing that prevents a mother from caring for her son while she is a professional to earn support, even if [it] . . . is incompatible with the decency of Islamic ethics as long as the son is protected, not neglected, and not exposed to corruption.[36]

Because the child was still dependent, the judge denied the father's request. Yet a father could wrest custody of a dependent child from his ex-wife if he proved that she was unscrupulous. Muhammad 'Ali, for example, was awarded custody of his 6-year-old daughter in 1930 when he proved that his ex-wife was sexually promiscuous, which disqualified her for custody because it could risk the virtues of their daughter.[37]

Even liberal male intellectuals who depicted European women as paragons of progress insisted that Egyptian women "be 'modern but modest,' to emulate the European woman, the prototype of the modern liberal world in every way, but at the same time . . . hold on to traditional conduct and behavior."[38] Other than avoiding the moral laxity and promiscuity attributed to European women, what exactly defined moral conduct and behavior? Unfortunately, neither male nor female writers specified, but they made sure to label this morality an Islamic one.[39] Writers vaguely defined Islamic moral mothers as those who were religiously devout and regarded skilled mothers as those who were versed in Islamic history, rituals, and customs as well as domestic management.

In the marriage crisis debates of the 1920s and 1930s, however, writers were more concerned about mothers' Egyptian identity than their Islamic faith because they emphasized national unity over religious unity during the national struggle for full independence.[40] Nationalists did not depart that drastically from medieval Islamic jurists on the view of a mother's religion: Neither saw it as a cause for serious concern. According to Islamic law, the children of an Islamic marriage acquired the religious identity of the father.[41] Because a child's religious socialization did not begin until the child reached the age of religious understanding (after dependency), a non-Muslim divorced or widowed mother was entitled to oversee her child's dependency stage like her Muslim counterparts. Her religion became a concern only if she took her child to live with non-Muslims or if she tried to raise the child in her religion.[42] In 1906, for example, Dr. 'Uthman Bey Ghalib successfully petitioned the court for custody of his 6-year-old son when he proved that his Italian Christian ex-wife was raising the child as a Christian.[43]

Although Islamic jurists assigned to fathers the religious training of their sons and daughters, Egyptian nationalists assigned to mothers the patriotic socialization of their children. Between the 1890s and 1920s, the various journals of the Egyptian women's press posited women as "mothers of the nation" whose job was to inculcate nationalism in their sons and daughters.[44] Most writers did not explain why only an Egyptian mother could impart her children with a sense of national identity, but writers often underscored women's unique ability to do so. According to Iskandar Bulus, a Coptic man writing in a church journal in 1909, women alone ensured that their children were socialized in Egyptian values, manners, and customs.[45] Islamic scholars also emphasized that only Egyptian women could raise loyal Egyptians. In his 1920 lecture to a male audience at the Egyptian Democratic Party's headquarters, Shaykh 'Ali Surur al-Zankaluni underscored a mother's influence over her child, who would assume her "tendency to love her race" because "the mother is the child's first school."[46] Although Egyptian law deemed that the father established the religion and citizenship of his child, these nationalists were claiming that the mother determined the child's true national identity.[47] By emphasizing the influence a mother wielded over her children, they implied that the Egyptian patriarch commanded little power in his home, subtly questioning his significance as a father.

Fettering Fathers Who Arrange and Annul

Nowhere is the historical assumption of a father's unchallenged position as head of the household more evident than in the press debates over dowers, arranged marriage, and female education in early twentieth-century Egypt. Whether positive feedback or stern disparagement, these discussions were usually addressed to fathers, rarely to mothers or even the daughters themselves. The assumed and intended audience indicates that fathers ultimately oversaw their households and children. Fathers

were the ones who sent their daughters to school, chose their spouses, ne-
gotiated their dowers, contracted their marriages, and represented their
minor daughters in court. Fathers often influenced their sons' marriages
as well, but most early twentieth-century Egyptian men theoretically
chose their own brides because a man did not need a guardian to marry
under Islamic law, whereas a bride usually did. If a bride's father was
deceased, then her grandfather, brother, or paternal uncle acted as her
deputy in marriage. Neither her mother nor any of her maternal male
relatives could act as her guardian. If she had no paternal male relatives,
then she had to ask an Islamic judge for permission to marry.[48] The arranging of marriage occurred between two men: the bride's father and her
future husband. The breaking of her marriage also was often the result of
a decision by either man: Her husband could divorce her, or her father
could have her marriage annulled.

During the first three decades of the twentieth century, however,
many brides and writers would begin to challenge a father's absolute authority in the arranging and annulling of his daughter's marriage. The
case that largely inaugurated this trend was a cause célèbre that garnered
the attention of the middle-class press, Egyptian elites, and even Egypt's
nominal ruler, Khedive 'Abbas Hilmi II, during the late summer of 1904.
Earlier that summer Safiyya al-Sadat, the daughter of Ahmad 'Abd al-
Khaliq al-Sadat, a wealthy notable and descendant of Prophet Muhammad, had married Shaykh 'Ali Yusuf, a man of humble origins. In 1889,
Yusuf had founded *al-Mu'ayyad*, an Islamic anti-British newspaper that
he owned and edited until his death in 1913; the paper backed and received support from Khedive 'Abbas Hilmi II. Yusuf's stellar career in
journalism and close ties to the Egyptian dynasty catapulted him to national prominence and permitted him to become a member of the General Assembly and to amass considerable wealth. He was rumored to have
wanted to marry an educated woman from a noble household to help
him attain the status of a notable. After he had met the teenaged Safiyya
at a literary salon, her father agreed to the match and accepted his dower,
but the wedding was postponed repeatedly because Safiyya's father ultimately decided not to accept Yusuf because of his inferior social class.[49]

After four years, Safiyya and Yusuf decided to marry nonetheless.
Because she was an adult by then, Islamic law did not require the permis-

sion of her father or a male guardian. An adult Muslim woman could contract her own marriage so long as her suitor and dower were worthy of her status, which was determined by the two male witnesses to the marriage. The Islamic doctrine of suitability (*kafa'a*) stated that a marriage was an appropriate legal union if the man was equal in status to the woman in a number of respects, among them lineage, financial standing, and profession.[50] When al-Sadat learned what his daughter had done, he petitioned the Islamic court for an annulment of their marriage. He argued that the marriage was void on the basis of the lack of suitability between the spouses because Yusuf's humble origins and lowly profession as a journalist were socially inferior to Safiyya's noble lineage. After widely publicized proceedings, al-Sadat won the case and his daughter's marriage was annulled. Once his paternal authority and pride had been restored, and after much mediation and reconciliation, however, al-Sadat later consented to his daughter's remarriage to Yusuf in his presence.[51]

Contemporary scholars see this case as an exceptionally unusual one in which the vast majority of early twentieth-century reporters believed in al-Sadat's right to exercise absolute authority over his daughter.[52] Situating this case in its broader context, however, provides another reading. For example, a survey of the Islamic court records and *al-Ahram*'s court case column provides an increasing number of examples of Egyptian women marrying without their fathers' permission during the first three decades of the twentieth century, indicating that the 'Ali Yusuf case would not remain uncommon. A review of these suitability cases shows that most fathers did not win their suits, in contrast to Safiyya's father, revealing that the notion that fathers should have unilateral rights over their daughters was starting to unravel. If anything, the press viewed the 'Ali Yusuf case as a showdown between two famous men, Safiyya's father versus her husband, rather than as a conflict between a father and his daughter. Al-Sadat probably won public support because of his noble lineage and because his opponent was the highly controversial Yusuf, who had made many enemies in the press and the courts, not because most believed that a father had the right to dissolve his daughter's marriage that had already taken place.[53]

In 1906, for example, the middle-class daughters of Ahmad al-Sadat, Hasan 'Amr al-Dalal, Husayn Muhammad al-Farash, and Ahmad Harun al-Fiqi all married men whom their fathers deemed unsuitable without the fathers' permission.[54] In all these cases, except for that of Muhammad al-Farash, the judge upheld the validity of the marriage in dispute, indicating that he did not believe the bride's father had a right to dissolve his daughter's marriage.[55] These cases demonstrate that the early twentieth-century courts recognized a woman's right to choose her partner and marry without her father's consent. Judges sought to uphold a woman's right to choose her spouse for the sake of preserving the institution of marriage, which took precedence over the pride of a father who felt wronged by the lack of consultation and disrespect from his daughter and her husband.

At the same time, however, if the father could prove the inferior social status of his son-in-law, then he could easily have his daughter's marriage annulled. A wealthy landowner and Senate member effortlessly won his case seeking the annulment of his daughter's marriage to their driver when he provided the court with a letter from the Ministry of Interior certifying his own Senate membership and documentation confirming that his son-in-law had worked as his driver for five years.[56] This well-known and respected public figure, however, won his case because his daughter's husband was socially inferior, not because he—as her father—had a right to single-handedly undo his daughter's marriage. *Al-Ahram* and *al-Usbu'*, two supposedly secular and liberal newspapers, took special interest in such interclass unions between elite women and working-class men, expressing shock and disgust that educated and cultured daughters of wealthy landowners and professionals would marry drivers and servants against the will of their fathers, the dictums of Islam, and the mores of Egyptian society.[57]

All these cases highlight a number of debates in early twentieth-century Egypt regarding the social standing of various professions in a class-based society, interclass marriage, a woman's right to choose her spouse, and the extent of a father's authority over his daughter. The considerable attention these cases attracted illustrates that interclass unions were not all that common in early twentieth-century Egypt and that most Egyptians were not ready to accept such unions, especially when an elite woman was marrying a working-class man. The doctrine of suitability was another gendered Islamic stipulation. It typically caused concern over the man's status because a woman's status was raised to her husband's position through marriage.[58] The near absence in the press of articles berating interclass unions between elite men and working-class women indicates that such marriages were not regarded as problematic.

Most writers who criticized the custom of arranged marriage were more concerned with men's right to choose their future partners, not women's. A vocal minority, however, advocated a woman's right to pick her own spouse, beginning in 1904 with a handful of commentators on the 'Ali Yusuf case.[59] Over the next three decades, calls for a woman's right to select her husband grew. Like Safiyya's supporters, these writers—who were both male and female contributors to largely secular journals—directed their criticism of arranged marriage to fathers. Their demands represent the initial unraveling of one of the father's few remaining responsibilities within the home and confirm the slight marginalization of his role in early twentieth-century Egypt. In 1909, for example, one female writer reproached fathers who still married their daughters off to men against their will in "this era of light and knowledge, this era of civilization and culture, this era of freedom and equality."[60] Several women wrote heart-wrenching letters to the editor bemoaning their own "forced" marriages, which ended in misery or divorce, begging fathers not to marry off their daughters against their will.[61] Men writing in secular journals also advised members of their own sex to permit their daughters to participate in choosing their husbands.[62] Yet the vast majority of advocates—men and women alike—merely asked fathers to consult their daughters regarding the husbands they chose for them. Few called for a woman's unilateral right to select her spouse.[63]

These calls for a woman's right to choose or at least participate in choosing her spouse provide evidence of the questioning of Egyptian fathers' authority. They also indicate that many middle-class journalists and readers were ready for fathers to hand over some of their unilateral power. In a heartfelt letter titled "Marriage and Its Victims," a woman using the moniker Armanusa related the story of her own arranged marriage, explaining why fathers wielded this power: "The father wholeheartedly believes that he possesses his children and controls all their affairs. . . . It is the father who engages his daughter and she has no right to refuse even if the fiancé is not someone she loves."[64] Writing in 1920, Armanusa painted a portrait of early twentieth-century Egyptian fathers who exercised complete ownership of their daughters. In the emerging nation that was ringing with calls for political independence, equality, and freedom for Egyptian men, many nationalists were prepared to extend some of these rights to other family members as well. The archetype patriarchal household master with arbitrary and complete control no longer befitted the emerging Egypt. With the spread of constitutionalist notions in which Egyptians began to demand that the power of the head of the nation be limited, some nationalists extended such calls to the head of the family. Because they viewed the family as a microcosm of their nation, it is not surprising that nationalists no longer wanted its head to have unfettered control over it.

This advocacy for a curtailment of a father's power and an extension of his daughter's participation was not for the sake of women per se. Rather, the goal was the encouragement and preservation of happy healthy marriages that would bind the nation tightly together. For them, the couple, not the extended family, determined the success of the nation. Most writers believed that a woman had the right to at least participate in contracting her own marriage to ensure its success. A rare exception was 'A'isha 'Abd al-Rahman, the author of "The Marriage Crisis" column in the Islamic journal *al-Nahda al-Nisa'iyya*. She condemned the majority who argued that women should have a say in whom they marry because she believed women could not be trusted with such a monumental decision. She knew she held a minority view in the Egypt of 1933: "I know that many of the dear readers will become furious when they read my words."[65]

More liberal voices also believed that a father's authority still reigned supreme over his daughter, but only until she was married. Once a daughter shifted her economic subordination from her father to her husband in a suitable and consummated marriage, her sole authority was her husband. The case of Ahmad al-Shurbagi versus Muhammad Ahmad Khalil highlights the clout a husband could exert over his wife's father as well as the new emphasis on the nuclear family with the modern couple at its center.[66] In 1922, al-Shurbagi filed a suit against his son-in-law for denying him the right to visit his daughter. Khalil said his father-in-law could visit on Fridays, the only time he could be present because he was a government employee who worked the other days of the week. Although the plaintiff pleaded for any other day, the court sided with Khalil.[67] Al-Shurbagi was not even permitted to visit his daughter, let alone exercise any rights over her, without the presence or permission of her husband.

This case underscores the transfer of authority from a woman's father to her husband upon her marriage. It also underlines different generational conceptions of the family in early twentieth-century Egypt. The older al-Shurbagi clearly viewed the extended family as the norm. He expected his daughter to maintain ties with her agnatic family and carry them into her new family. The younger Khalil, on the other hand, favored the new ideal of the nuclear family. He wanted to create with his wife a new modern family founded on their marriage. The courts defined the married woman through her husband rather than her father. Although fathers could exert unrestricted authority over their daughters, this entitlement was short-lived. The basic unit of the nation had become the marital couple (and their underage children). It was a man's role as breadwinner that inevitably gave him this power over his children and wife. But what happened when fathers did not provide for their children? Were they still entitled to paternal authority? How did nationalists account for those fathers who did not support the future citizens of the nation?

Marginalized Moms and Deadbeat Dads

Both Egyptian nationalist and Islamic legal discourses dictated that a father's primary responsibility to his children was financial. The nationalist view expanded a mother's obligations to her children, but neither discourse reflected or accounted for the realities of deadbeat fathers and single mothers in the child support and child custody cases that the early twentieth-century Islamic courts witnessed.[68] Because the wife oversaw the dependency years, she received her children's support payments on their behalf. The abundance of wives' petitions for increases in child support and husband's appeals for reductions because of their paltry salaries or unemployed status confirms that many men were not fulfilling their paternal obligations. It also reveals that many lower-class and middle-class men had to struggle to support their families in early twentieth-century Cairo.[69] If a father proved that he could not afford child support because he was destitute, then the obligation fell on the child's paternal relatives.[70] Yet even wealthy patricians, such as the landowner Mahmud Effendi

Ibrahim and the mayor Ahmad Bey ʿAbd al-Rahman Hamd Allah, whose wives proved they were not afflicted by economic troubles, refused to support their children.[71] The nationalist vision in the press did not make provisions for capable fathers who neglected to support their children or for poor men who could not afford to provide for their children.

Like nationalists, Islamic jurists did not excuse fathers who tried to escape providing for their children. In 1914, Ahmad Effendi Riyad, a lower middle-class court scribe, asked the judge whether his mother could assume custody of his son from his ex-wife to whom he could no longer afford to pay child support. His mother testified that she would assume custody at her own cost because her son's measly salary did not suffice for child support. Their creative ploy to absolve him of paying support failed, however, as the judge refused their plea. Because Riyad did not prove that his ex-wife was unfit for custody, the judge upheld that the young child's best interests lay with his mother and reminded Riyad of his fundamental obligation.[72] Many other divorced fathers proved reluctant to pay child support.[73] In cases of divorce, women could retain custody of their dependent children, but the father remained the child's sole legal guardian and financial provider. As the custodial caretaker, a divorced mother was entitled to receive a caretaker fee, housing allowance, nursing wage, and child support.[74] During her child's dependency years, a single woman was essentially paid to mother her child, which perhaps explains why fathers such as al-Jawish did not believe that their ex-wives who retained custody were entitled to work outside the home for additional income. In return for the father's financial support, the mother was forbidden from moving their children beyond a reasonable distance from the town in which the couple had lived before the divorce because the father had to be able to visit his children and return home within the same day if he chose.[75]

Once the child matured, the father or the child's male paternal relative who assumed guardianship in the father's absence had the right to demand that the child leave the mother to come live with him. Although not particularly large, the number of cases opened by fathers to demand that their ex-wives hand over their children indicates that some mothers were reluctant to relinquish custody.[76] Because this rule was explicit, mothers often immediately confessed that the child was no longer dependent and agreed to surrender the child.[77] Others, however, tried a variety of ploys to avoid doing so. Because the Egyptian state did not require the registration of births until 1912 (thus births usually went unrecorded before this date), some mothers manipulated the child's birth date to argue that he or she had not yet completed dependency.[78] Others hid their children and repeatedly evaded court hearings or denied that the children were still in their custody.[79] Only rarely did a mother blatantly refuse to hand over her child in court or attempt to appeal a ruling that awarded her ex-husband custody because she had no legal right to custody once the child's dependency ended.[80]

A Muslim father's right to custody was considered absolute in contrast to a mother's restricted right, which was conditional on her moral and physical state. It was also predicated on the stipulation that she did not marry a man who was not a blood relative forbidden to the child in marriage. This gendered precondition assumed that a mother's remarriage to a stranger would cause her to neglect her child because her new husband would not feel a bond to the child. If she married her child's relative, for example, the child's paternal uncle, who would supposedly show the child compassion because they were already related, then her remarriage did not abrogate her right to custody.[81] Mothers, however, rarely married their child's blood relatives, and fathers took advantage of their ex-wives' remarriages to file for custody.[82] Some lower-class fathers apparently did not mind leaving their children in their mothers' hands long after their period of dependency had ended so long as their ex-wives did not remarry. The lower-class tailor Sayyid Mubarak's son was 10 years old, three years beyond dependency, and the lower-class peasant Ga'far Ahmad's oldest daughter was 15 years old, six years past dependency, when they sought custody immediately upon their ex-wives' remarriages.[83] Some lower-class mothers, such as Husna Muhammad 'Uthman and Khadija Muhammad 'Atabi, remarried quickly upon divorce when their infants were 1 year old and 5 months old, respectively, and they consequently lost custody of their infants to their ex-husbands, although Islamic law deemed dependent children in need of a woman's care.[84] It is impossible to know how many ex-husbands permitted their children to remain with their remarried mothers if they came to agreements among themselves outside the courts. Within the legal system, however, only rarely did a father permit his ex-wife to retain custody after her remarriage, but he still capitalized on it to cease paying child support.[85]

A father's remarriage, on the other hand, or his polygamous marriage was not assumed to hinder his faculty for custody. After Law 25 of 1929 extended a mother's custody if it was in her child's best interest, however, some divorced mothers began to apply this gendered bias to their remarried ex-husbands who sought custody.[86] Al-Ahram recounted a case that highlighted the argument one such mother advanced in court. After her ex-husband was awarded custody of their 7-year-old son, she successfully appealed on the grounds that her ex-husband's remarriage and subsequent children with his new wife who would never care for their son as she cared for her own offspring was not in their son's interest.[87] Al-Ahram reported that she won the appeal on the basis of Article 30 of the 1929 law, but it did not explain what that article actually stated. This omission may have led readers to believe that a father could lose permanent custody as a result of his remarriage. But the case actually relied on a law that merely authorized a judge to prolong a divorced mother's custody for an additional two years (until age 9 for males and age 11 for females), if he found that a child's welfare warranted this extension.[88] If the judge deemed it in the child's best interest, he could grant his or her divorced mother two extra years of custody. A father's remarriage did not revoke his right to custody after the two-year extension; it merely could prolong his ex-wife's custody by two years.

Other divorced mothers capitalized on the 1929 revision to argue that their child's welfare lay in remaining with them for the additional two years because their fathers had remarried.[89] When the middle-class government employee 'Abd al-Karim Ibrahim appealed a ruling that had awarded his ex-wife, Fa'iqa Darwish Mustafa, custody of their 8-year-old son, her lawyer contended that "the plaintiff has married a stranger to him [the son] and his interest lies in remaining with his mother until he reaches age 9."[90] Her lawyer also argued that the father worked in the Ministry of Health from 7:30 in the morning until 1:30 in the afternoon, during which the child would be under his new wife's tutelage rather than his own. In a remarkable reversal of the two main arguments about remarriage and employment, Fa'iqa and her lawyer turned these same tactics against a father. To demonstrate that his new wife was not a stranger to his son, however, Ibrahim countered that he had married his second wife four years *before* he divorced Fa'iqa. Indeed, he made a strategic point. A polygamous father, as Ibrahim claimed to have been, was legally permitted to raise his children from all wives in one household. Nevertheless, the court rejected Ibrahim's creative plea because it deemed that the dependent child's best interest lay with his birth mother.

The middle-class Hasan Salim endeavored an equally clever appeal. In his 25 August 1930 appeal to overturn a 23 June 1930 decision that extended his ex-wife's custody of their son until age 9 because he had remarried, he told the court that he had since divorced his wife, showing the court their divorce certificate dated 25 July 1930. The appellate judges, however, were not impressed. "It appears that the divorce occurred for the sake of deception so that the father could obtain custody," they stated, and as a result, "the interest of the young boy lies in remaining with his mother."[91] Even though Salim was no longer remarried, these judges upheld the mother's custody extension on the basis of Article 30 of Law 25 of 1929.

The drafters of the 1929 law explained in their memorandum that they had revised the law in response to "the large number of complaints of women" seeking custody by arguing that their children were still too young to be cared for by the father, "especially if he were married to a woman who is not their mother."[92] Lawmakers and judges were likely influenced by nationalist discourses that extolled the importance of mothers in the development of future citizens. Because they could not fundamentally alter Islamic law to accommodate these new nationalist visions, they were restricted to religious prescriptions that marginalized mothers and favored fathers. But they could find loopholes, such as locating minority views, that slightly prolonged a mother's tutelage to accommodate nationalist prescriptions for the sake of Egypt's future citizens. Whether or not they intended to protect motherhood, the legislators' extension of a mother's custody (and the financial support it entailed) did translate into practice in the Islamic courtrooms.

Conclusion

Mostly motivated by the welfare of future citizens, nationalist writers sought to carve out a place for educated motherhood that would simultaneously elevate women's position in the nation but contradictorily keep them wedded to the domestic sphere of the family without disturbing male privilege. Few, if any, pointed out that these goals were in tension with one another or explained why an educated mother would want to remain in the domestic sphere. Various press discourses positioned the Egyptian mother as the site of educational and moral reform so that she could properly prepare the nation's next generation. So long as she remained married to her children's father, she was not a mere babysitter of helpless toddlers; she also was the moral educator and nationalizer of her sons and daughters. By the early twentieth century, nationalists had transferred to mothers the duties of religious and educational rearing of older children that Islamic discourse had traditionally accorded fathers. At the same time, however, they maintained the patriarch's traditional duty of breadwinner.

In contrast, Islamic law marginalized single and remarried mothers and continued to uphold a father's unilateral guardianship of his children. By the 1930s, however, Islamic lawmakers and judges appear to have been influenced by the nationalist discourses that exalted motherhood. After the passage of the 1929 law, child custody cases demonstrate a greater recognition of the importance of motherhood. These records also show that notions of a nation composed of happily wedded families in which the division of labor between mothers and fathers could be neatly maintained neither represented nor made allowances for the realities of many Egyptian families that were stricken by divorce, death, and poverty. Middle-class nationalists presupposed that the nuclear family was the bedrock of the nation, bounded by a stable marriage in which educated moral mothers inculcated the future generation with the necessary patriotic and religious values within the home while fathers provided for the family by toiling outside the home. As the court records reveal, however, this neat nationalist ideal was not the prototype for many Egyptian families. Yet the press did not want to make allowances for divorced mothers and deadbeat fathers who did not fit into its formula.

6

Conclusion

Marriage, long the centerpiece of Middle Eastern life, is in crisis. The reason: A new generation of young men cannot afford to marry. . . . While marriage costs have risen with inflation over the years, incomes have been largely stagnant [and] youth unemployment exceed[s] 30 percent. . . . Dowries increasingly involve long lists of consumer goods. Newlyweds want homes of their own, instead of living with their parents. Western media dangles the good life before them, but most have no means of realizing it. . . . Financial independence and marriage remain the mark of manhood and social standing, yet it is increasingly difficult to attain.

Navtej Singh Dhillon, "The Wedding Shortage"

This passage captures many of the explanations for the Egyptian marriage crisis that writers and readers advanced in the previous chapters. Yet Navtej Singh Dhillon, director of the Middle East Youth Initiative at the Brookings Institution, did not pen this article for an Egyptian audience in the early twentieth century but for a Western audience in the early twenty-first century. This most recent Egyptian marriage crisis garnered considerable attention in the international and local media from journalists, bloggers, and laypeople as well as from Western and Egyptian economists, academics, and policy experts.[1] Its causes, effects, and meanings merit their own academic study.

The marriage crisis that was the subject of this book, however, had its own reasons, which were unique to the social, political, legal, and economic circumstances of early twentieth-century Egypt's semicolonial status. As I showed in Chapter 2, the marriage crisis served as a means through which to criticize British domination and create a new middle-class masculinity to combat the financial obstacles and sexual temptations engendered by the various economic depressions, cycles of inflation, low and stagnant salaries, unemployment problems, and legal status of prostitution in the early twentieth century. In Chapter 3, I highlighted how other writers and readers used the crisis to construct a new formulation of wifehood to combat the rapid dissolution of arranged marriage and female seclusion in the face of increased opportunities in female education and gender integration. In Chapter 4, I demonstrated how the early twentieth century's supposedly explosive divorce rate resulting from men's unilateral Islamic right of repudiation discouraged bachelors from entering into an institution that they would likely later dissolve. Like marriage, divorce was also deployed as a trope to analyze the destruction and reformation of the struggling Egyptian nation. In Chapter 5, I revealed how bachelorhood served as a medium for Egyptians to articulate their anxieties over the ostensible inabilities of women to raise proper citizens, and to create new responsibilities for mothers that slightly marginalized those of fathers in the making of the nation.

When Egyptians gained fuller independence from the British in 1936, most believed that they were on their way to complete political and economic independence, and their fears of a marriage crisis largely waned over the late 1930s and 1940s. By the late 1950s, after President Gamal Abdel Nasser liberated Egypt from the pro-British monarchy, expelled the final military and political vestiges of foreign influence, established a socialist state, nationalized university education, enfranchised women, and guaranteed employment for all college graduates, many Egyptians were more confident about the future state of their independent nation. The political, social, and economic anxieties of the semicolonial era had largely dissipated, and the literate minority no longer perceived their nation or marriage to be in crisis.

Personal status legislation remained virtually unchanged for the remainder of the twentieth century, which also explains the abatement of the Egyptian discourse on the marriage crisis that was so intimately tied to the new Islamic legislation and court reorganization of the early twentieth century. Law 78 of 1931 was the last major piece of legislation that affected marriage and divorce in the twentieth century, with the exception of a 1979 presidential decree by President Anwar Sadat that offered women minor gains in divorce rights, which were revoked a few years later.[2]

Nasser's abolition of the Islamic courts in 1955 also empowered the postcolonial state to exert more control over the marital lives of its citizens. Nasser transferred the jurisdiction of the Islamic courts, which oversaw all issues of personal status, to the largely secular national courts so that all Egyptians would be subjected "to a single juridical jurisdiction."[3] Despite the attempts of socialist feminists in the 1950s and 1960s to reform personal status law, the legal rules governing marriage, divorce, custody, and inheritance remain the only remnants of religious law in a largely secular state and legal system.[4] As a result, Egyptian marriages and families have become even more constrained by state bureaucracy and monolithic understandings of Islamic law. Although some articles of the personal status laws of the 1920s were slightly revised by Law 1 of 2000,[5] most women (and some men) find it more difficult to divorce their spouses, collect alimony and child support, and win child custody than many of their predecessors did—not that the latter had it all that easy either.

Despite the particularities of the Egyptian marriage crisis, the press was aware that Egyptians were not the only ones to suffer from marital problems and bachelorhood epidemics. Many writers and reformers referenced the marriage shortage in other Arab and Western nations, realizing that these places had their own reasons for the problem.[6] They argued, for example, that in various European nations the shortage stemmed from surpluses of women as a result of the heavy wartime male casualties from World War I. Europeans fretted over the future of single women, whereas Egyptians were anxious about the large number of middle-class men who were supposedly evading marriage. Egyptians did not want to even speculate about the fate of a nation full of unwed women.

A comparative study of the marriage crisis, which has ostensibly occurred in many parts of the world at one time or another, can help us to understand how various peoples in different eras deployed marriage as a metaphor to talk about their nation and its problems. At the same time, however, each period and nation has had reasons wholly its own for prolonged bachelorhood, real or imagined. What perhaps unites these different case studies—regardless of how secular, liberal, religious, or conservative their societies—is a belief that heterosexual marriage is the foundation of a modern nation and that this institution is responsible for the next generation: If people do not marry, they will not reproduce children in legal and socially acceptable unions who will grow up healthy, secure, and capable of leading the nation in the future.

The Islamic registers of early twentieth-century Egypt also warrant future studies of all kinds. Although Egyptian courts of earlier times have been studied extensively by scholars, the Islamic records of the early twentieth century have only recently been unearthed by the staff of the Egyptian National Archives and thus have been largely untapped by scholars. These sources demand scholarly attention because the extensive Islamic legal reforms that the Egyptian administration initiated from the late nineteenth century into the early twentieth century—whose significance colonial officials, Egyptian nationalists, and scholars have either criticized or downplayed—resulted in a completely reorganized and a more bureaucratized and hierarchical legal system that enlarged and formalized the state-sponsored role of these courts in the lives of Egyptians. These largely overlooked reforms constituted a major rupture in court practices and procedures. They also assigned the state an unprecedented role in monitoring Egyptian women and men, drastically changing the very nature and role of the Islamic courts in early twentieth-century Egypt. Future scholarship can help uncover the ways in which the state and these courts assumed a much larger role in the lives of men and women who married, divorced, and wrestled over child custody before the courts, as well as the roles of the scribes, judges, ushers, and lawyers who worked in the courts. Undoubtedly, these court records can be used to study a number of phenomena, processes, and practices in early twentieth-century Egypt.

Most Egyptians and foreigners do not realize that many of Egypt's contemporary marital issues have historical precedents. Similarly, many Egyptians are not fully aware of their Islamic rights in marriage and divorce because the semicolonial state adopted, centralized, and promoted its own hegemonic conceptions of marriage, gender, and law that prevail to this day. By using both press articles and court records from the semicolonial period, I have attempted in this book to provide insight into the historical origins of contemporary controversies, beliefs, and practices surrounding marriage and the family in order to offer alternative understandings to the state-sponsored portrayals and dominant practices.

Reference Matter

Notes

In general, I have used short titles and authors' last names to cite sources in the notes, except for Arabic-language primary source periodicals, which I cite in full. Complete citations of all other works are provided in the bibliography. Documentation of the primary court records uses the following abbreviations, which are followed in the notes by the register number, serial case number, and the date the case was first filed.

Court Registers

J   Mahkamat Misr al-Ibtida'iyya al-Shar'iyya: al-Ahkam al-Juz'iyya [Cairo Islamic Court of First Instance: Summary Verdicts]

I   Mahkamat Misr al-Ibtida'iyya al-Shar'iyya: al-Ahkam al-Isti'nafiyya [Cairo Islamic Court of First Instance: Appellate Verdicts]

H   Mahkamat Misr al-Ibtida'iyya al-Shar'iyya: al-Ahkam al-Habsiyya [Cairo Islamic Court of First Instance: Detention Verdicts]

Chapter 1

1. Gayyid's letter to the editor is William Gayyid, "Mushkilat al-Zawaj," *al-Mar'a al-Misriyya* 10, no. 10 (December 1929), 399. Most writers referred to endemic bachelorhood in the singular as "the marriage crisis," but some, like Gayyid, called it "the marriage problem." For consistency's sake, I use the more common term.

2. Although the capital was Egypt's largest and fastest growing city in the early twentieth century, it still represented only a minority of the country's population: 5.9 percent of Egypt's 9.72 million lived in Cairo in 1897 (Ministry of Finance, *Census of Egypt Taken in 1907*, 23, 27), and 8.2 percent of Egypt's 15.92 million lived in Cairo in 1937 (Ministry of Finance, *Population Census of Egypt, 1937*, 8, 56).

3. Badran, *Feminists, Islam, and Nation*, 61; and Baron, *Women's Awakening*, 36.

4. Amin, *Liberation of Women*. This book and Amin's 1900 rejoinder, *New Woman*, reaped more than thirty furious reviews in the press. See Abdel Kader, *Egyptian Women*, 58.

5. Abdel Kader, *Egyptian Women*, 8; Cole, "Feminism, Class, and Islam," 401; Haddad, "Islam, Women, and Revolution," 160; and Tignor, *Modernization*, 341. For critiques of Amin, see Abu-Lughod, "Marriage of Feminism and Islamism," and Ahmed, *Women and Gender in Islam*, 162–163.

6. In my survey of several hundred daily, weekly, and monthly issues from more than thirty-five different periodicals between 1898 and 1940, I found that the first use of the term *marriage crisis* to refer to widespread bachelorhood was 'Abdu al-Barquqi, "Azmat al-Zawaj," *al-Mar'a al-Misriyya* 1, no. 2 (February 1920), 53–57.

7. Marsot, *Short History*, 81.

8. Brown, *Rule of Law*, 38–39.

9. It should be noted, however, that the larger process in which the multiple Egyptian legal systems were reformed, Western laws were introduced, and religion was privatized was part of a larger Westernizing reform movement that was partly responding to colonialism, even if it was undertaken solely by Egyptians. Laws pertaining to women, the family, and sexuality, however, were to remain Islamic in semicolonial and postcolonial Egypt. See Asad, *Formations of the Secular*, 205–256.

10. Chakrabarty, "Difference-Deferral"; Chatterjee, *Nation and Its Fragments*; Chatterjee, *Nationalist Thought*; Sinha, *Colonial Masculinity*; Stoler, *Carnal Knowledge*; and Stoler, *Race and the Education of Desire*.

11. Chatterjee, *Nation and Its Fragments*, 116–134.

12. Sinha, "Lineage of the 'Indian' Modern."

13. Rabinow, *French Modern*, 9.

14. Nolan, "Housework Made Easy," 552. See also Nolan, *Visions of Modernity*.

15. Heineman, *What Difference Does a Husband Make?*

16. Abdel-Malek, *Egypt*, 57–61.

17. Lockman, "Imagining the Working Class," 161n3.

18. Jacob, "Working Out Egypt," 99.

19. Gershoni, *Emergence of Pan-Arabism*; Gershoni and Jankowski, *Redefining the Egyptian Nation*; and Jankowski, *Egypt's Young Rebels*.

20. Ahmad al-Sawi Muhammad, "Ma Qilla wa-Dalla," *al-Ahram* 57, no. 16673 (11 May 1931), 1.

21. The fez, a red felted wool cap with a flat circular top and tassel, was mandated as official headgear for Muslim men in the Ottoman Empire as

part of a broader clothing reform decreed by Sultan Mahmud II in 1829. In early twentieth-century Egypt, it was worn mainly by middle-class and upper-class men.

22. Mahmud Abu al-ʿAyun, "Man al-Masʾul ʿan Azmat al-Zawaj," *al-Ahram* 60, no. 17662 (8 February 1934), 1; and al-Sawi Muhammad, "Ma Qilla wa-Dalla."

23. On the unreliability of the marriage statistics and the 1931 law, see Baron, "Making and Breaking of Marital Bonds," 282, 286n54.

24. Ministry of Finance, *Population Census of Egypt, 1927*, 64; and Ministry of Finance, *Population Census of Egypt, 1937*, 108.

25. On the problems of the Egyptian censuses, see Baron, *Women's Awakening*, 82; and Owen, "Population Census of 1917."

26. Badran, *Feminists, Islam, and Nation*, 136.

27. Dunne, "Sexuality," 269; and Bier, "Prostitution," 6.

28. Badran, *Feminists, Islam, and Nation*, 206.

29. See Balibar, "Nation Form," 101–102; and Eley and Suny, "Introduction," 26.

30. Baron, *Egypt as a Woman*, 31–34; and Booth, *May Her Likes Be Multiplied*.

31. Pollard, *Nurturing the Nation*, 166–204.

32. Also see Badran, *Feminists, Islam, and Nation*; Russell, *Creating the New Egyptian Woman*; and El Shakry, "Schooled Mothers."

33. To be sure, I am not the first to recognize the centrality of marriage. Beth Baron, Ron Shaham, Amira Sonbol, and Judith E. Tucker have made significant contributions to the portrayals and practices of Islamic marriage in nineteenth-century and early twentieth-century Egypt without which my own study would not have been possible. However, they have not used marriage as an analytical category for studying nationalism.

34. Cott, *Public Vows*, 3.

35. Scott, *Gender*.

36. Eley and Suny, "Introduction," 27.

37. Blewett, "Manhood and the Market," 92.

38. Badran, *Feminists, Islam, and Nation*, 91–92, 95, 111, 125, 142, 165, 192, and 207. For the premier study of the EFU, see Badran, *Feminists, Islam, and Nation*.

39. Ayalon, *Press in the Arab Middle East*, 143; and Baron, *Women's Awakening*, 81. Both scholars take these figures from the 1897 Egyptian census.

40. Safran, *Egypt in Search of a Political Community*, 59.

41. For the pioneering study on the early Egyptian women's press, see

Baron, *Women's Awakening.* On women's journals published between the 1920s and 1940s, see Badran, *Feminists, Islam, and Nation*; and Booth, *May Her Likes Be Multiplied.*

42. Baron, *Women's Awakening*, 91; and Ayalon, *Press in the Arab Middle East*, 81, 150.

43. Ministry of Finance, *Population Census of Egypt, 1937*, 246–247; and Ayalon, *Press in the Arab Middle East*, 75, respectively.

44. Ayalon, *Press in the Arab Middle East*, 138–165; and Baron, *Women's Awakening*, 91–92.

45. Cited by Ayalon, *Press in the Arab Middle East*, 157; and Baron, *Women's Awakening*, 92.

46. Baron, *Women's Awakening*, 92.

47. Hartog, *Man and Wife*; and Stern, *Secret History.*

48. Agmon, *Family and Court*, 41–46; Peirce, *Morality Tales*, 8–9; and Ze'evi, "Use of Ottoman Shari'a Court Records."

49. Fahmy and Peters, "Legal History," 131–134.

50. Anderson, "Law Reform," 222. For the actual codes, see *La'ihat al-Mahakim al-Shar'iyya bi-l-Aqtar al-Misriyya*; and *La'ihat Tartib al-Mahakim al-Shar'iyya wa-l-Ijra'at al-Muta'alliqa bi-ha.*

51. Anderson, "Law Reform," 225; and Esposito, *Women in Muslim Family Law*, 51–52.

52. See *La'ihat al-Mahakim al-Shar'iyya bi-l-Aqtar al-Misriyya.*

53. Tucker, *Women in Nineteenth-Century Egypt*, 10–12.

54. Ziadeh, *Lawyers*, 56–57.

55. Shaham, *Family and the Courts*, 12–13.

56. Qadri, *Kitab al-Ahkam al-Shar'iyya fi al-Ahwal al-Shakhsiyya.*

57. Ahmad Muhammad Shakir, Muhammad 'Abdu, and Qasim Amin each made such proposals in the 1890s. See Amin, *Liberation of Women*, 99; 'Imara, *al-Islam wa-l-Mar'a fi Ra'y al-Imam Muhammad 'Abdu*, 25–31, 78–95; and Shakir, *Nizam al-Talaq fi al-Islam*, 9–11.

58. Section 1, in *La'ihat Tartib al-Mahakim al-Shar'iyya wa-l-Ijra'at al-Muta'alliqa bi-ha*, 1. See also Shaham, *Family and the Courts*, 12.

59. Anderson, "Law Reform," 222; and Shaham, *Family and the Courts*, 11–12.

60. Tucker, *Women in Nineteenth-Century Egypt*, 10–12.

61. Shaham, *Family and the Courts*, 12.

62. Cuno, *Pasha's Peasants*; Sonbol, *Women, the Family, and Divorce Laws*; Toledano, *State and Society*; and Tucker, *Women in Nineteenth-Century Egypt.*

63. Section 16, in *La'ihat al-Wukala' Amama al-Mahakim al-Shar'iyya*, 8.

64. Section 68, in *Ta'rifat al-Rusum al-Muqarrara bi-l-Mahakim al-Shar'iyya*, 8. For the average salary in 1913, see Muhammad al-Bardisi, "I'rad al-Shubban 'an al-Zawaj," *al-Ahram* 38, no. 10881 (15 December 1913), 1; and 'Abd al-'Aziz Isma'il, "I'rad al-Shubban 'an al-Zawaj," *al-Ahram* 38, no. 10893 (27 December 1913), 2.

65. Section 16, in *La'ihat al-Wukala' Amama al-Mahakim al-Shar'iyya*, 8.

66. Shaham, *Family and the Courts*, 15; and Ziadeh, *Lawyers*, 57–58.

Chapter 2

1. Mustafa Sadiq al-Rafi'i, "Istanwaqa al-Jamal," *al-Risala* 2, no. 64 (24 September 1934), 1564.

2. Baron, "Making and Breaking of Marital Bonds," 279.

3. See 'A. Y. 'A., "Zawjati," *al-Jins al-Latif* 1, no. 4 (October 1908), 124–127.

4. J91, 151 (27 January 1906). During the early 1930s economic crisis, most similar requests were denied because of insufficient evidence: I47, 465 (8 January 1930); I47, 466 (8 January 1930); I50, 1551 (19 June 1930); I50, 1617 (2 July 1930); and I50, 1754 (28 July 1930).

5. J97, 1313 (18 July 1906). Also see J97, 1253 (10 July 1906); J100, 1660 (17 October 1906); and J100, 1748 (3 November 1906). For unsuccessful men's appeals to increases in support owed their wives during the 1930s economic crisis, see I47, 465 (8 January 1930); I47, 466 (8 January 1930); I50, 1551 (19 June 1930); and I50, 1754 (28 July 1930).

6. Shaham, *Family and the Courts*, 69.

7. Muhammad al-Bardisi, "I'rad al-Shubban 'an al-Zawaj," *al-Ahram* 38, no. 10881 (15 December 1913), 1.

8. Marsot, *Short History*, 79–80, 86–87.

9. Sayyid Qutb, "al-Azma al-Zawjiyya," *al-Balagh al-Usbu'i* 3, no. 108 (10 April 1929), 28. On Qutb's transformation from a pro-Western intellectual to an Islamist activist, whose 1966 execution turned him into a revered martyr, see Haddad, "Sayyid Qutb."

10. Husayn 'Afif, "Azmat al-Zawaj," *al-Ahram* 38, no. 10893 (14 June 1932), 2; Balsam 'Abd al-Malik, "al-Zawaj," *al-Mar'a al-Misriyya* 1, no. 4 (April 1920), 113–117; and "Sa'a ma' Za'imat al-Nahda al-Nisa'iyya," *al-Usbu'* 5, no. 4 (31 January 1938), 7–8.

11. Marsot, *Short History*, 87. The average 1913 salary comes from al-Bardisi, "I'rad al-Shubban 'an al-Zawaj," 1; and 'Abd al-'Aziz Isma'il, "I'rad al-Shubban 'an al-Zawaj," *al-Ahram* 38, no. 10893 (27 December 1913), 2. The average 1935 salary comes from Walid al-Sitt Banat, "Ma Qilla wa-Dalla," *al-Ahram* 61, no. 18003 (21 January 1935), 1.

12. Marsot, *Short History*, 94–95.

13. Bier, "Prostitution," 8.

14. Goswami, *Producing India*, 226.

15. Gershoni and Jankowski, *Egypt, Islam, and the Arabs*, 40.

16. Deeb, "Bank Misr"; and Tignor, *State, Private Enterprise, and Economic Change*, 251.

17. Marsot, *Short History*, 92.

18. M. F., "Mushkilat al-'Atilin bi-Misr," *Misr al-Haditha al-Musawwara* 3, no. 50 (18 June 1930), 31.

19. White, "Matrimony and Rebellion," 178.

20. Junaydi, *Azmat al-Zawaj fi Misr*, 111–118. See also 'Abd Allah 'Allam, "Mas'alat al-Zawaj," *al-Nahda al-Nisa'iyya* 11, no. 1 (January 1933), 17; Mahmud Abu al-'Ayun, "Shababna wa-Azmat al-Zawaj," *al-Ahram* 60, no. 17653 (30 January 1934), 1; and Sabri Hamdi, "Azmat al-Zawaj," *al-Nahda al-Nisa'iyya* 6, no. 63 (March 1928), 88.

21. Junaydi, *Azmat al-Zawaj fi Misr*, 122–123.

22. Marsot, *Short History*, 89–90, 91.

23. Abdal-Rehim, "Family and Gender Laws."

24. Tucker, *Women in Nineteenth-Century Egypt*, 45, 54.

25. Shaham, *Family and the Courts*, 29; and Huda Sha'rawi, "al-Hay'a al-Nisa'iyya fi al-'Alam," *Fatat al-Sharq* 20, no. 2 (15 November 1925), 75.

26. Abdal-Rehim, "Family and Gender Laws," 103.

27. Section 77, in Qadri, *Code of Mohammedan Personal Law*, 18.

28. Esposito, *Women in Muslim Family Law*, 23.

29. Nabawiyya Musa, "al-Afrah wa-l-Muhur," *al-Balagh al-Usbu'i* 1, no. 40 (26 August 1927), 31–32.

30. Katib, "al-Mughala fi al-Muhur," *al-Balagh al-Usbu'i* 1, no. 42 (9 September 1927), 31.

31. Isma'il, "I'rad al-Shubban 'an al-Zawaj."

32. M. A. Radwan, "Mushkilat al-Zawaj," *al-Ahram* 57, no. 16666 (10 May 1931), 9.

33. T. M. R., "Mushkilat al-Zawaj," *al-Ahram* 57, no. 16672 (16 May 1931), 9.

34. "Sa'a," 7–8; and "Hawla Mashakil al-Zawaj fi Misr," *Misr al-Haditha al-Musawwara* 3, no. 41 (17 April 1930), 17.

35. Ahmad al-Sawi Muhammad, "Ma Qilla wa-Dalla," *al-Ahram* 57, no. 16651 (18 April 1931), 1.

36. Baron, "Making and Breaking of Marital Bonds," 279.

37. Balsam 'Abd al-Malik, "al-Zawaj," 114.

38. Tucker, *House of the Law*, 52.

39. Tucker, "Marriage and Family," 168–169.

40. Section 71, in Qadri, *Code of Mohammedan Personal Law*, 17.

41. "Al-Ahkam," *al-Shara'i'* 1, no. 1 (31 October 1913), 10.

42. Abu 'Abdun al-'Adrusi, "Azmat al-Zawaj bi-Misr," *al-Ahram* 56, no. 16455 (28 September 1930), 3; 'Abd al-Hamid Hamdi Ibrahim, "Mushkilat al-Zawaj wa-Kayfa Tahull? Hajatuna ila Tashri'," *al-Balagh al-Usbu'i* 3, no. 131 (18 September 1929), 29–30; "Mahr al-Zawaj," *al-Ahram* no. 58, 17159 (14 September 1933), 8; "Mawani' al-Zawaj," *al-Mar'a al-Misriyya* 3, no. 4 (April 1922), 186; "al-Mughala fi al-Muhur," *al-Mar'a al-Misriyya* 11, no. 5–6 (May–June 1930), 207; Ahmad Salah al-Din Nadim, "Azmat al-Zawaj fi Biladina," *al-Mar'a al-Misriyya* 6, no. 7 (15 September 1925), 372; al-Sawi Muhammad, "Ma Qilla wa-Dalla," *al-Ahram* 57, 1; and "al-Zawjiyya," 758.

43. 'A'isha 'Abd al-Rahman, "Mushkilat al-Zawaj: 4," *al-Nahda al-Nisa'iyya* 11, no. 3 (March 1933), 91.

44. "Li-Madha La Tatazawwaj?" *al-Mar'a al-Jadida* 1, no. 8 (30 October 1924), 66

45. "Li-Madha La Tatazawwaj?" 66; al-'Adrusi, "Azmat al-Zawaj bi-Misr," 3; Ibrahim, "Mushkilat al-Zawaj wa-Kayfa Tahull?" 29; and M. A. Lashin, "Hall Azmat al-Zawaj," *al-Ahram* 59, no. 17608 (13 December 1933), 1.

46. Sadiq 'Abd al-'Alim, "al-Idrab 'an al-Zawaj: Asbab wa-Nata'ij," *al-Nahda al-Nisa'iyya* 5, no. 55 (July 1927), 246; Sadiq 'Abd al-'Alim, "al-Idrab 'an al-Zawaj: Asbabihi wa-Nata'ijihi," *al-Nahda al-Nisa'iyya* 4, no. 42 (May 1926), 199; Husni, "'Aqabat al-Zawaj fi Misr wa-l-Sabil ila Tadhlilha," *al-Siyasa al-Usbu'iyya* 1, no. 14 (12 June 1926), 10; Ibrahim, "Mushkilat al-Zawaj wa-Kayfa Tahull?" 29–30; Katib, "al-Mughala fi al-Murhur," 207–208; "Li-Madha La Tatazawwaj?" 66; Ibn Malik, "Wasiya Ghariba," *al-Jins al-Latif* 13, no. 2 (February 1921), 65–69; "Mawani' al-Zawaj," 186–188; Nadim, "Azmat al-Zawaj fi Biladina," 372–373; and Mikha'il Thabit, "al-Zawaj fi al-Sharq 'Ammatan wa-Misr Khassatan," *al-Ahram* 55, no. 15915 (9 March 1929), 1.

47. Walid, "Ma Qilla wa-Dalla," 1, claimed that LE 8 was the average salary of the four government employees who proposed to his daughters in 1935.

48. Ibrahim, "Mushkilat al-Zawaj wa-Kayfa Tahull?" 29–30; Ahmad al-Sawi Muhammad, "Ma Qilla wa-Dalla," *al-Ahram* 58, no. 17240 (4 December 1932), 1; "Sadaq al-Zawja," *al-Ahram* 59, no. 17417 (5 June 1933), 7; and Walid, "Ma Qilla wa-Dalla," 1.

49. Walid, "Ma Qilla wa-Dalla," 1.

50. Esposito, *Women in Muslim Family Law*, 21, 155.

51. "Al-Mughala fi al-Murhur," 207–208; al-Sawi Muhammad, "Ma Qilla wa-Dalla," *al-Ahram* 58, 1; and Thabit, "al-Zawaj fi al-Sharq 'Ammatan wa-Misr Khassatan," 1.

52. Sections 160–205, in Qadri, *Code of Mohammedan Personal Law*, 43–51.

53. Shaham, *Family and the Courts*, 68.

54. Esposito, *Women in Muslim Family Law*, 25–26.

55. 'Allam, "Mas'alat al-Zawaj," 16.

56. Hanim Muhammad al-'Asqalani, "Azmat al-Zawaj," *Fatat Misr* 1, no. 5 (15 April 1930), 1; "Li-Madha Tamtana'una 'an al-Zawaj?!" *al-Usbu'* 3, no. 37 (5 September 1936), 15; and al-Manqiyadi, "Ahjam al-Shubban al-Misriyyin 'an al-Zawaj," *al-Mar'a al-Misriyya* 9, no. 5–6 (May–June 1928), 220–221.

57. Anisa, "Mushkilat al-Zawaj," *al-Ahram* 57, no. 16671 (9 May 1931), 9.

58. 'Abd al-'Alim, "al-Idrab 'an al-Zawaj: Asbab," 246; 'Abd al-'Alim, "al-Idrab 'an al-Zawaj: Asbabihi," 199; and "al-Mughala fi al-Murhur," 207–208.

59. Section 45, in Qadri, *Code of Mohammedan Personal Law*, 10.

60. Ibrahim, "Mushkilat al-Zawaj wa-Kayfa Tahull?" 30. See also 'Abd al-'Alim, "al-Idrab 'an al-Zawaj: Asbabihi," 199; and al-'Adrusi, "Azmat al-Zawaj bi-Misr," 3.

61. Mahmud 'Ali, "Azmat al-Zawaj," *al-Usbu'* 2, no. 86 (24 October 1935), 11; and Lashin, "Hall Azmat al-Zawaj," 1. See also Rizk, "Diwan of Contemporary Life (490)."

62. Nelson, *Doria Shafik*, 63. The average salary comes from Walid, "Ma Qilla wa-Dalla," 1.

63. Section 17, in Qadri, *Code of Mohammedan Personal Law*, 4.

64. J8, 1750 (26 December 1898). Also see J3, 496 (6 April 1898), for a similar case.

65. J2, 301 (14 March 1898).

66. Anderson, "Law Reform," 225.

67. Shaham, *Family and the Courts*, 29–30.

68. See "Sadaq al-Zawja," 7; and "Yuhtall li-l-Zawaj," *al-Ahram* 60, no. 17635 (11 January 1934), 9.

69. Ahmad al-Sawi Muhammad, "Ma Qilla wa-Dalla," *al-Ahram* 61, no. 17843 (13 August 1935), 1. See also Badran, *Feminists, Islam, and Nation*, 81.

70. Nelson, *Doria Shafik*, 62–63. See also Badran, *Feminists, Islam, and Nation*, 82.

71. Nelson, *Doria Shafik*, 63.

72. Adwar 'Abdu Sa'd, "Mas'alat al-Muhur," *al-Usbu'* 2, no. 87 (31 October 1935), 1.

73. "Mawani' al-Zawaj," 186. See also al-'Adrusi, "Azmat al-Zawaj bi-Misr," 3.

74. Baraka, *Egyptian Upper Class*, 216–217.

75. Shaham, *Family and the Courts*, 29.

76. Baraka, *Egyptian Upper Class*, 129.

77. Al-Sawi Muhammad, "Ma Qilla wa-Dalla," *al-Ahram* 58, 1. Also see 'A'isha 'Abd al-Rahman, "Mushkilat al-Zawaj: 6," *al-Nahda al-Nisa'iyya* 11, no. 5 (May 1933), 166–167.

78. Al-Sawi Muhammad, "Ma Qilla wa-Dalla," *al-Ahram* 58, 1.

79. Sections 184 and 185, in Qadri, *Code of Mohammedan Personal Law*, 47.

80. Tosh, *Manliness*, 36.

81. Sections 184 and 185, in Qadri, *Code of Mohammedan Personal Law*, 47.

82. J5, 866 (23 June 1898).

83. Section 177, in Qadri, *Code of Mohammedan Personal Law*, 46.

84. Shaham, *Family and the Courts*, 68.

85. J185, 1389 (2 February 1914). For a similar case, see J100, 1894 (1 December 1906).

86. J6, 924 (9 July 1898); J7, 1215 (14 September 1898); J92, 60 (13 January 1906); J92, 62 (13 January 1906); and J92, 72 (14 January 1906). Only rarely would a husband deny his wife's allegation and win the case if he was able to furnish evidence that he had established a home. See I47, 495 (13 January 1930), which refers to a wife's futile appeal to such a case.

87. Section 184, in Qadri, *Code of Mohammedan Personal Law*, 47.

88. J99, 1721 (28 October 1906). See also I2, 31 (7 December 1915).

89. Section 184, in Qadri, *Code of Mohammedan Personal Law*, 47.

90. Shaham, *Family and the Courts*, 77–78.

91. Tucker, *House of the Law*, 64. The Egyptian Personal Status Code determined that a move that incurred undue hardship entailed a distance that required more than three days' travel by camel. See Section 208, in Qadri, *Code of Mohammedan Personal Law*, 53. See also Shaham, *Family and the Courts*, 92.

92. J2, 356 (22 March 1898).

93. J100, 1868 (27 November 1906).

94. Ibrahim Fathi, "I'rad al-Shubban 'an al-Zawaj," *al-Ahram* 38, no. 10885 (19 December 1913), 1–2.

95. Fathi, "I'rad al-Shubban 'an al-Zawaj," 1–2.

96. For Fathi's supporters, see their views summarized in Isma'il, "I'rad al-Shubban 'an al-Zawaj," 2. Also see Muhammad 'Izz al-Din Hafiz, "Mushkilatna al-Ijtima'iyya wa-Kaifa Yumkin Hallha," *al-Nahda al-Nisa'iyya* 13, no. 12 (December 1935), 405.

97. Jacob, "Working Out Egypt," 423.

98. Al-'Asqalani, "Azmat al-Zawaj," 1–2; "Azmat al-Zawaj," *al-Hilal* 38,

no. 10 (August 1930), 1270; and al-Firdaws, "Taqaʿ Masʾuliyyat al-Iʿrad ʿan al-Zawaj ʿala ʿAtiq al-Shubban La al-Fatiyat," *al-Marʾa al-Misriyya* 15, no. 1–2 (January–February 1934), 24–26.

99. Al-Banafsaja, "Fi Mushkilat al-Zawaj," *al-Marʾa al-Misriyya* 11, nos. 1–2 (January–February 1930), 18; "Mushkilat al-Zawaj," *al-Nahda al-Nisaʾiyya* 13, no. 9 (September 1935), 296; Sayyid Mustafa, "Azmat al-Zawaj wa-l-Hulul al-Muqtaraha li-Tafrigha," *al-Usbuʿ* 2, no. 80 (12 September 1935), 17–18; and ʿAbd al-Salam al-Nalmisi, "Mashakil al-Zawaj fi Misr," *Misr al-Haditha al-Musawwara* 3, no. 41 (17 April 1930), 41.

100. "Mushkilat al-Zawaj," 296.

101. Bier, "Prostitution," 2.

102. Muhammad ʿAbdu, "al-Zawaj wa-Shubban Misr wa-Shawabuha," *al-Manar* 5, no. 9 (5 August 1902), 343.

103. Ullman, *Sex Seen*, 86.

104. El Shakry, *Great Social Laboratory*, 190.

105. Musallam, *Sex and Society*.

106. "Zawaj al-Muwazzafin," *al-Ahram* 39, no. 11038 (17 June 1914), 5.

107. ʿAʾisha ʿAbd al-Rahman, "Mushkilat al-Zawaj: 1," *al-Nahda al-Nisaʾiyya* 10, no. 12 (December 1932), 416–417; ʿAfif, "Azmat al-Zawaj," 8; ʿAllam, "Masʾalat al-Zawaj," 15–18; N. J., "Mushkilat al-Zawaj," *al-Marʾa al-Misriyya* 11, no. 1–2 (January–February 1930), 21; Junaydi, *Azmat al-Zawaj fi Misr*, 72; "Mushkilat al-Zawaj," *al-Nahda al-Nisaʾiyya* 13, no. 9 (September 1935), 296; Mustafa, "Azmat," 17–18; Sayyid Mustafa, "Daribat al-ʿAzuba?" *al-Usbuʿ* 3, no. 37 (5 September 1936), 15; Rashid Rashid, "Azmat al-Zawaj," *al-Ahram* 59, no. 17609 (14 December 1933), 2.

108. ʿAbd al-ʿAlim, "al-Idrab ʿan al-Zawaj: Asbab," 246; and Badran, *Feminists, Islam, and Nation*, 140.

109. Rashid, "Azmat al-Zawaj," 2.

110. Mustafa, "Azmat," 18.

111. Mustafa, "Azmat," 17–18.

112. Kessler-Harris, *Woman's Wage*.

113. "Al-Zawjiyya," 759. See Saʿid's views on the marriage crisis in Junaydi, *Azmat al-Zawaj fi Misr*, 200–209.

114. Husni, "ʿAqabat al-Zawaj," 10. See also a review of supporters in Rizk, "Diwan of Contemporary Life (490)."

115. Section 165, in Qadri, *Code of Mohammedan Personal Law*, 43–44.

116. Sections 173–184, in Qadri, *Code of Mohammedan Personal Law*, 45–47.

117. J1, 63 (12 January 1898); J1, 111 (19 January 1898); J2, 440 (5 April 1898);

J259, 2344 (24 July 1922); and I51, 101 (19 November 1930). Also see Shaham, *Family and the Courts*, 68.

118. J92, 162 (28 January 1906); J184, 928 (4 January 1914); J185, 1395 (2 February 1922); J264, 29 (6 November 1922); and J265, 126 (14 November 1922).

119. I21, 917 (20 June 1923); and the original case, J265, 126 (14 November 1922).

120. I21, 917 (20 June 1923). Husbands who did not bring witnesses usually lost their appeals. See J93, 731 (18 April 1906); J97, 1187 (27 June 1906); J99, 1765 (4 November 1906); J99, 1889 (15 December 1906); and J185, 1455 (9 February 1914).

121. J97, 1608 (19 September 1906).

122. Section 181, in Qadri, *Code of Mohammedan Personal Law*, 47.

123. For a husband's argument that he resided outside the court's jurisdiction, see J185, 1701 (23 February 1914). For a husband's claim that the plaintiff was not his wife, see I50, 2215 (29 October 1930). For a husband's lying witness, see I50, 2105 (16 October 1930). For husbands who countered that their wives were disobedient, see I20, 778 (9 May 1923); I50, 1857 (18 August 1930); and I51, 74 (17 November 1930). For other various tactics that husbands used to avoid paying spousal support, see I1, 92 (13 February 1915); I21, 945 (27 June 1923); I21, 961 (3 July 1923); I22, 1240 (15 October 1923); I47, 456 (8 January 1930); I50, 1555 (19 June 1930); I50, 1564 (23 June 1930); and I51, 98 (19 November 1930).

124. J257, 1196 (7 March 1922); J257, 1280 (19 March 1922); J264, 45 (7 November 1922); I50, 1546 (19 June 1930); and I51, 143 (24 November 1930).

125. State authorities assigned to execute such court orders first distrained a portion of the husband's salary, then his movable property, and finally his lands, if he had any. After the seized property was sold, the proceeds were given to the wife. See Sections 176, 189, and 195, in Qadri, *Code of Mohammedan Personal Law*, 47–49; and "Qanun Nimrat 25 li-Sanat 1920," 37.

126. Section 176, in Qadri, *Code of Mohammedan Personal Law*, 46. See H44, 170 (9 January 1923); and H44, 302 (19 February 1923), in which the wife sued her husband's guarantor for failure to pay her.

127. Shaham, *Family and the Courts*, 71–72.

128. H19, 756 (29 April 1915); H44, 175 (11 January 1923); H44, 192 (17 January 1923); H44, 213 (23 January 1923); H45, 388 (22 March 1923); and H45, 502 (9 May 1923).

129. The husband was sentenced to five days for 50 piasters in H19, 756 (29 April 1915), and for 80 piasters in H45, 502 (9 May 1923); fifteen days for LE 3.90 in H44, 175 (11 January 1923); and thirty days for LE 9 in H44, 213 (23 January 1923), and for LE 19.60 in H44, 192 (17 January 1923). Rarely a wife was unable

to obtain a sentence because she did not bring sufficient evidence. See H21, 1223 (7 October 1915); and H44, 302 (19 February 1923).

130. H20, 994 (8 July 1915); H44, 289 (15 February 1923); and H45, 388 (22 March 1923).

131. H19, 833 (22 May 1915); H21, 1241 (14 October 1915); H45, 519 (14 May 1923); and H46, 678 (18 July 1923).

132. H19, 831 (20 May 1915); H20, 985 (6 July 1915); H20, 1011 (15 July 1915); H20, 1019 (19 July 1915); H20, 1111 (29 August 1915); and H46, 908 (29 October 1923).

133. H19, 843 (25 May 1915); H19, 911 (1 June 1915); H20, 1066 (5 August 1915); H21, 1220 (7 October 1915); H21, 1221 (7 October 1915); H21, 1233 (11 October 1915); H44, 146 (1 January 1923); H45, 414 (3 April 1923); H45, 439 (15 April 1923); and H46, 905 (29 October 1923).

134. Stern, *Secret History of Gender*, 98–100.

135. I22, 1265 (24 October 1922); I51, 113 (19 November 1930); and I51, 125 (30 November 1930).

136. Al-Manqiyadi, "Ahjam al-Shubban," 220.

137. Mustafa Sadiq al-Rafi'i, "Armalat Hukuma," *al-Risala* 2, no. 66 (8 October 1934), 1643–1644.

138. Elsadda, "Imaging the New Man," 46.

Chapter 3

1. Amin, *Liberation of Women*, 82.

2. Badran, *Feminists, Islam, and Nation*, 5.

3. Badran, *Feminists, Islam, and Nation*, 5; and Baron, *Women's Awakening*, 47.

4. Clark, *Women's Silence*; and Walkowitz, *City of Dreadful Delight*.

5. Badran, *Feminists, Islam, and Nation*, 5.

6. Abdel Kader, *Egyptian Women*, 17.

7. Baron, *Women's Awakening*, 1.

8. Badran, *Feminists, Islam, and Nation*, 4; and Baron, *Women's Awakening*, 39.

9. Kozma, "Women on the Margins," 192.

10. 'A. Y. 'A., "Intiqa' al-'Arus," *al-Jins al-Latif* 2, no. 1 (May 1909), 7–9.

11. 'Abdu al-Barquqi, "Azmat al-Zawaj," *al-Mar'a al-Misriyya* 1, no. 2 (February 1920), 53.

12. Ahmad al-Sawi Muhammad, "Ma Qilla wa-Dalla," *al-Ahram* 57, no. 16803 (17 September 1931), 1.

13. "Ihtijab al-Khatiba," *al-Hilal* 6, no. 11 (February 1898), 417–418; Ibrahim

'Ali Salim, "Mushkilat al-Zawaj," *al-Ahram* 57, no. 16730 (7 July 1931), 10; and "al-Zawaj Ams wa-l-Yawm," *al-Hilal* 10, no. 5 (December 1901), 152–153.

14. Su'ad Shahin, "Shakawi al-Zawaj," *al-Siyasa al-Usbu'iyya* 3, no. 144 (8 December 1928), 26; "al-Zawaj," *al-Mar'a al-Jadida* 1, no. 17 (8 January 1925), 176; and Zakiyya's views as cited by M. A., "al-Tashri' al-Jadid aw al-Zawaj al-Qahri," *al-Sharq al-Jadid* 1, no. 12 (30 October 1924), 2.

15. Junaydi, *Azmat al-Zawaj fi Misr*, 51–55; Sa'diyya, "Azmat al-Zawaj," *al-Mar'a al-Misriyya* 1, no. 3 (March 1920), 96; and Yusuf 'Ali Yusuf, "Mushkilat al-Zawaj fi Misr," *al-Hidaya al-Islamiyya* 7, no. 1 (October 1934), 89.

16. Khadduri and Liebesny, *Law in the Middle East*, 137.

17. Tucker, *Women in Nineteenth-Century Egypt*, 52–53.

18. Sections 137 and 139, in Qadri, *Code of Mohammedan Personal Law*, 36–37. For examples, see Sonbol, "Adults and Minors," 241–246.

19. J91, 161 (28 January 1906); J91, 249 (17 February 1906); J91, 325 (3 March 1906); J91, 349 (6 March 1906); J92, 134 (24 January 1906); J92, 330 (3 March 1906); J93, 409 (13 March 1906); J97, 1501 (5 September 1906); J100, 1802 (10 November 1906); J184, 1008 (10 January 1914); J185, 1675 (21 February 1914); J185, 1695 (23 February 1914); J185, 1971 (15 March 1914); J185, 1975 (15 March 1914); J195, 70 (11 November 1914); J195, 146 (18 November 1914); J195, 207 (25 November 1914); J195, 246 (30 November 1914); H20, 947 (22 June 1915); J261, 2146 (23 October 1922); J261, 2520 (17 August 1922); I19, 280 (15 January 1923); I20, 504 (7 March 1923); H45, 387 (22 March 1923); I20, 672 (16 April 1923); I20, 683 (18 April 1923); H45, 501 (9 May 1923); I21, 876 (11 June 1923); I21, 1057 (15 August 1923); and I21, 1172 (24 September 1923).

20. I1, 98 (13 February 1915). For a similar case, see I1, 184 (13 May 1915).

21. J1, 36 (19 December 1897).

22. 'A'isha 'Abd al-Rahman, "Mushkilat al-Zawaj," *al-Nahda al-Nisa'iyya* 11, no. 1 (January 1933), 22.

23. 'Abd al-Rahman, "Mushkilat al-Zawaj," 23. See also Sayyid Hamdi, "Azmat al-Zawaj: 1," *al-Nahda al-Nisa'iyya* 6, no. 62 (February 1928), 47.

24. Fargues, "Family and Household," 41; and Fargues, "Terminating Marriage," 250n3, 262–263.

25. Kholoussy, "Nationalization of Marriage," 320–324; and Kholoussy, "Talking About a Revolution," 30–32.

26. Shaham, *Family and the Courts*, 45.

27. Yusuf, "Mushkilat al-Zawaj fi Misr," 89.

28. Muhammad 'Arafa, "Azmat al-Zawaj," *al-Hidaya al-Islamiyya* 8, no. 1 (October 1935), 10–11.

29. Mosse, *Nationalism and Sexuality*, 16.

30. Dunne, "Sexuality," 269; and Junaydi, *Azmat al-Zawaj fi Misr.*

31. Muharram Bey Fahim, "Azmat al-Zawaj," *al-Usbu'* 3, no. 37 (5 September 1936), 5.

32. 'Abd al-Rahman, "Mushkilat al-Zawaj," 23; 'Arafa, "Azmat al-Zawaj," 11; Fahim, "Azmat al-Zawaj," 5; and Yusuf, "Mushkilat al-Zawaj fi Misr," 89.

33. Muhammad Mas'ud, "al-Idrab 'an al-Zawaj," *al-Nahda al-Nisa'iyya* 5, no. 53 (May 1927), 176.

34. Wildenthal, "Race, Gender, and Citizenship"; Wood, *The Baba and the Comrade*; and Heineman, *What Difference Does a Husband Make?*

35. M. A., "al-Tashri' al-Jadid aw al-Zawaj al-Qahri," 2; and Sa'diyya, "Azmat al-Zawaj," 97.

36. "Ihtijab al-Khatiba," 418.

37. Salim, "Mushkilat al-Zawaj," 10.

38. Gershoni and Jankowski, *Redefining the Egyptian Nation*, 54–55.

39. El Shakry, "Schooled Mothers," 148.

40. Amin, *Liberation of Women*, 11–34.

41. Badran, *Feminists, Islam, and Nation*, 8–9, 58, 142–144, 148; and Baron, *Women's Awakening*, 123–124, 127–129, 131, 134, 143.

42. Rizk, "Diwan of Contemporary Life (609)."

43. Pollard, *Nurturing the Nation*, 122.

44. Ayalon (*Press in the Arab Middle East*, 143) and Baron (*Women's Awakening*, 81) take the 1897 figures from the Egyptian census. For the 1937 ratios, see Ministry of Finance, *Population Census of Egypt, 1937*, 246–247.

45. "Mashakil Ijtima'iyya Khatira," *al-Afkar* 23, no. 7 (18 September 1926), 3.

46. Nelson, *Doria Shafik*, 13.

47. Badran, *Feminists, Islam, and Nation*, 42, 64.

48. Sayyid Hamdi, "Azmat al-Zawaj: 3," *al-Nahda al-Nisa'iyya* 6, no. 64 (April 1928), 118. See also Sa'diyya, "Azmat al-Zawaj," 96.

49. Muhammad Hijazi, "Li-Madha La Tatazawwaj," *al-Mar'a al-Jadida* 1, no. 9 (6 November 1924), 77.

50. 'Abd al-Hamid al-Disuqi, "Azmat al-Zawaj fi Misr," *al-Usbu'* 2, no. 53 (17 March 1935), 10.

51. Chakrabarty, "Difference-Deferral," 51, 64.

52. Abu 'Abd Allah, "al-Sa'ada fi al-Zawaj," *al-Nahda al-Nisa'iyya* 12, no. 8 (September 1934), 264–266; al-Disuqi, "Azmat al-Zawaj fi Misr," 10; "Hall Mushkilat al-Zawaj," *al-Nahda al-Nisa'iyya* 13, no. 11 (November 1935), 370–371; Sabri Hamdi, "Azmat al-Zawaj," *al-Nahda al-Nisa'iyya* 6, no. 63 (March 1928), 88; Mahmud Hifni, "Azmat al-Zawaj: 2," *al-Shubban al-Muslimin* 2, no. 2 (November 1930), 145–149; "Idrab al-Shubban 'an al-Zawaj," *al-Thaghr* 2,

no. 326 (17 May 1930), 1; Junaydi, *Azmat al-Zawaj fi Misr*, 26–34; and Mustafa al-Maraghi, "I'rad al-Shubban 'an al-Zawaj: 1," *al-Hidaya al-Islamiyya* 4, no. 6 (March 1932), 319–326.

53. Abu 'Abd Allah, "al-Sa'ada fi al-Zawaj," 264–266; Hifni, "Azmat al-Zawaj: 2," 145–149; and "Idrab al-Shubban 'an al-Zawaj," 1.

54. Mahmud Hifni, "Azmat al-Zawaj: 1," *al-Shubban al-Muslimin* 2, no. 1 (October 1930), 75–78.

55. Sayyid Hamdi, "Azmat al-Zawaj: 4," *al-Nahda al-Nisa'iyya* 6, no. 69 (September 1928), 306.

56. Hamdi, "Azmat al-Zawaj: 4," 306.

57. As quoted by Fikri Abaza, "Mushkilat al-Zawaj fi Misr," *al-Hilal* 41, no. 4 (February 1933), 463. Also see Badran, *Feminists, Islam, and Nation*, 142–143.

58. Labiba Ahmad, "Azmat al-Zawaj al-Hadira fi Misr," *al-Nahda al-Nisa'iyya* 10, no. 11 (November 1932), 362; Mahmud Hifni, "Azmat al-Zawaj: 3," *al-Shubban al-Muslimin* 2, no. 3 (December 1930), 208–213; al-Maraghi, "I'rad al-Shubban 'an al-Zawaj: 1," 319–326; and Mustafa al-Maraghi, "I'rad al-Shubban 'an al-Zawaj: 2," *al-Hidaya al-Islamiyya* 4, nos. 7–8 (April–May 1932), 319–324.

59. Mustafa Gad Abu al-'Ila, "Kayfa Nu'adu al-Fata li-l-Zawaj?" *al-Ma'rifa* 2, no. 16 (August 1932), 468–470, 480; Ahmad, "Azmat al-Zawaj al-Hadira fi Misr," 361–363; Jarmain Bumun, "Akhlaq al-Fata al-'Asriyya," *al-Nahda al-Nisa'iyya* 14, no. 5 (May 1936), 151–152; "Hall Mushkilat al-Zawaj," 370–371; "al-Haya al-Zawjiyya: 2," *al-Manar* 8, no. 4 (21 April 1905), 141–147; and "Wazifat al-Mar'a," *al-Jins al-Latif* 1, no. 5 (November 1908), 151–153.

60. Pollard, *Nurturing the Nation*, 123.

61. Abu al-'Ila, "Kayfa Nu'adu," 468–470, 480; Ahmad, "Azmat al-Zawaj al-Hadira," 361–363; Bumun, "Akhlaq al-Fata al-'Asriyya," 151–152; 'Aziza al-Hakim, "Manahij al-Ta'lim La Takhluq Zawaj," *al-Isha'a* 4, no. 1 (20 January 1936), 13; "Hal al-Lughat wa-l-Biyano wa-l-Raqs am Tadbir al-Manzil wa-l-Tabkh wa-l-Khiyata Ta'mal Zawja?" *al-Sayyidat wa-l-Rijal* 8, no. 7 (May–June 1927), 472–478; "Hall Mushkilat al-Zawaj," 370–371; Hifni, "Azmat al-Zawaj: 3," 208–213; Junaydi, *Azmat al-Zawaj fi Misr*, 87–98, 128–132; al-Maraghi, "I'rad al-Shubban 'an al-Zawaj: 1," 319–326; al-Maraghi, "I'rad al-Shubban 'an al-Zawaj: 2," 319–324; and "Wazifat," 151–153.

62. Badran, *Feminists, Islam, and Nation*, 143, 147. Also see Saniyya Zahir, "al-Fata al-Muta'allima Khayr Zawja," *al-Mar'a al-Misriyya* 15, nos. 9–10 (December 1934), 389–391.

63. On Malik Hifni Nasif's suggestions, see El Shakry, "Schooled Mothers," 145–148.

64. Badran, *Feminists, Islam, and Nation*, 8, 47–69, 159–164, 170; and Baron, *Women's Awakening*, 50. Also see Russell, *Creating the New Egyptian Woman*.

65. Bumun, "Akhlaq al-Fata al-'Asriyya," 151.

66. Mustafa Sadiq al-Rafi'i, "Zawjat Imam," *al-Risala* 3, no. 85 (8 March 1935), 283.

67. See Elsadda, "Imaging the New Man," 48.

68. 'Abd al-Rahman 'Ajiz, "al-Zawaj," *al-Siyasa al-Usbu'iyya* 1, no. 53 (12 March 1927), 7.

69. Mas'ud, "al-Idrab 'an al-Zawaj," 176.

70. Esposito, *Women in Muslim Family Law*, 22.

71. Fluehr-Lobban and Bardsley-Sirois, "Obedience," 40, 45.

72. Section 171, in Qadri, *Code of Mohammedan Personal Law*, 44–45.

73. Section 212, in Qadri, *Code of Mohammedan Personal Law*, 54. Also see sections 207 and 215–216, in Qadri, *Code of Mohammedan Personal Law*, 52, 55.

74. I found no such examples, but I did locate cases in which husbands demanded that their resistant wives inhabit their homes so they could consummate the marriage: J93, 581 (3 April 1906); and J93, 683 (14 April 1906).

75. "Qanun Nimrat 25 li-Sanat 1920," 36.

76. Sections 184–187 and 208, in Qadri, *Code of Mohammedan Personal Law*, 47–48, 52–53.

77. For unsuitable homes, see J3, 539 (11 November 1898); J93, 445 (17 March 1906); J93, 731 (18 April 1906); J97, 1181 (26 June 1906); J97, 1185 (26 June 1906); J97, 1439 (21 August 1906); and J99, 1989 (15 December 1906). For lack of independent homes, see J4, 767 (1 June 1898); and J99, 1765 (4 November 1906). For far homes, see J3, 591 (7 May 1898); and J185, 1615 (18 February 1914).

78. J3, 539 (11 November 1898).

79. J5, 797 (8 June 1898); J8, 1740 (20 December 1898); J97, 1475 (29 August 1906); and J100, 4582 (9 December 1906).

80. J5, 859 (26 May 1898); J97, 1411 (14 August 1906); J99, 1761 (4 November 1906); J184, 1114 (15 January 1914); and J195, 30 (8 November 1914).

81. See J1, 201 (19 February 1898); J4, 714 (25 May 1898); J194, 4208 (21 October 1914); and J264, 97 (11 November 1922), where the wife offered no reason for her departure.

82. J1, 5 (1 January 1898); J91, 263 (18 February 1906); J92, 164 (28 January 1906); J184, 1396 (3 February 1914); and J261, 2618 (2 September 1922). See also sections 207 and 213–214, in Qadri, *Code of Mohammedan Personal Law*, 52, 54; Esposito, *Women in Muslim Family Law*, 25; and Shaham, *Family and the Courts*, 72.

83. J1, 5 (1 January 1898); J91, 263 (18 February 1906); and J261, 2618 (2 September 1922).

84. J92, 164 (28 January 1906); and J184, 1396 (3 February 1914).

85. J1, 29 (5 January 1898); J2, 350 (21 March 1898); and J4, 621 (12 May 1898).

86. Shaham, *Family and the Courts*, 96.

87. Esposito, *Women in Muslim Family Law*, 25; and Shaham, *Family and the Courts*, 73.

88. Sections 209 and 211, in Qadri, *Code of Mohammedan Personal Law*, 53. A husband's excessive verbal and/or physical abuse was grounds for a wife's refusal to return home in the national courts, which were beyond the jurisdiction of the Islamic courts. See Shaham, *Family and the Courts*, 81, 92–93.

89. Gordon, *Heroes*, 258. An exception is J5, 833 (26 June 1898).

90. J97, 1181 (26 June 1906); and J93, 731 (18 April 1906), and its follow-up, J100, 1660 (17 October 1906), respectively.

91. J4, 767 (1 June 1898).

92. J4, 767 (1 June 1898).

93. Section 93, in *La'ihat Tartib al-Mahakim al-Shar'iyya wa-l-Ijra'at al-Muta'alliqa bi-ha*, 19.

94. I1, 60 (13 January 1915); I19, 234 (3 January 1923), appealing J261, 2634 (5 October 1922); I19, 244 (8 January 1923); I22, 1206 (8 October 1923); I47, 464 (8 January 1930); I47, 468 (8 January 1930); I50, 1538 (18 June 1930); I50, 1952 (4 September 1930); I51, 51 (12 November 1930); I51, 58 (13 November 1930); I51, 95 (19 November 1930); and I51, 136 (24 November 1930).

95. Badran, *Feminists, Islam, and Nation*, 126, 131–132.

96. As quoted and translated by Badran, *Feminists, Islam, and Nation*, 131–132. See also Hasan, "al-Niza' al-'A'ili," *al-Mar'a al-Misriyya* 2, no. 10 (December 1921), 376–377.

97. Ahmad al-Sawi Muhammad, "Ma Qilla wa-Dalla," *al-Ahram* 58, no. 17189 (14 October 1932), 1.

98. As quoted and translated by Badran, *Feminists, Islam, and Nation*, 132.

99. Although abolished in 1967, police enforcement lasted until the 1980s. See Fluehr-Lobban and Bardsley-Sirois, "Obedience," 41. Also see Sonbol, "Law and Gender Violence," 282; and Badran, *Feminists, Islam, and Nation*, 132.

100. J1, 29 (5 January 1898); J91, 263 (18 February 1906); J93, 581 (3 April 1906); J93, 683 (14 April 1906); J97, 1185 (26 June 1906); J99, 1761 (4 November 1906); and J194, 4208 (21 October 1914).

101. J3, 591 (7 May 1898); J5, 797 (8 June 1898); J8, 1740 (20 December 1898); J93, 693 (15 April 1906); J184, 1124 (17 January 1914); J184, 1396 (3 February 1914); J195, 178 (23 November 1914); and J261, 2618 (2 September 1922).

102. J99, 1889 (15 December 1906); J185, 1591 (16 February 1914); and I51, 95 (19 November 1930).

103. J99, 1889 (15 December 1906).

104. For the average salary in 1913, see Muhammad al-Bardisi, "I'rad al-Shubban 'an al-Zawaj," *al-Ahram* 38, no. 10881 (15 December 1913), 1; and 'Abd al-'Aziz Isma'il, "I'rad al-Shubban 'an al-Zawaj," *al-Ahram* 38, no. 10893 (27 December 1913), 2.

105. For support, see J1, 29 (5 January 1898); J2, 350 (21 March 1898); J4, 621 (12 May 1898); J99, 1889 (15 December 1906); and J194, 4240 (24 October 1914). For homes, see J3, 539 (11 November 1898); J3, 591 (7 May 1898); J5, 797 (8 June 1898); J8, 1740 (20 December 1898); J93, 581 (3 April 1906); J93, 683 (14 April 1906); J97, 1185 (26 June 1906); J97, 1475 (29 August 1906); and J264, 97 (11 November 1922). For advanced dowers, see J1, 5 (1 January 1898); and J91, 263 (18 February 1906).

106. Section 171, in Qadri, *Code of Mohammedan Personal Law*, 44–45. For examples, see J93, 731 (18 April 1906); J99, 1935 (9 December 1906); J184, 956 (5 January 1914); J184, 996 (10 January 1914); J184, 1110 (15 January 1914); J184, 1138 (17 January 1914); and J195, 178 (23 November 1914).

107. I1, 60 (13 January 1915); I1, 98 (7 February 1915); I1, 99 (13 February 1915); I19, 234 (3 January 1923), appealing J261, 2634 (5 October 1922); I19, 244 (8 January 1923); I22, 1206 (8 October 1923); I47, 464 (8 January 1930); I47, 468 (8 January 1930); I47, 652 (30 January 1930); I50, 1913 (27 August 1930); I50, 1952 (4 September 1930); I51, 51 (12 November 1930); I51, 58 (13 November 1930); I51, 95 (19 November 1930); and I51, 136 (24 November 1930).

108. J93, 445 (17 March 1906); J93, 759 (22 April 1906); J184, 1124 (17 January 1914); and J185, 1591 (16 February 1914).

109. J186, 1474 (10 February 1914); J261, 2548 (22 August 1922); J264, 127 (14 November 1922); and J264, 499 (12 December 1922).

110. J184, 1348 (31 January 1914), appealing J182, 774 (24 December 1913); J261, 2536 (21 August 1922); I22, 1306 (31 October 1923); and I47, 681 (5 February 1930).

111. J261, 2542 (22 August 1922).

112. See J264, 499 (12 December 1922); and Shaham, *Family and the Courts*, 83.

113. Tucker, *House of the Law*, 66.

Chapter 4

1. Muhammad 'Izz al-Din Hafiz, "Mushkilatuna al-Ijtima'iyya wa-Kayfa Yumkin Halluha," *al-Nahda al-Nisa'iyya* 13, no. 12 (December 1935), 404.

2. Kholoussy, "Nationalization of Marriage," 324–332. I would like to thank the American University in Cairo Press for permission to use the main argument and a short segment of the aforementioned article in this chapter.

3. Musallam, *Sex and Society*, 11.

4. Section 217, in Qadri, *Code of Mohammedan Personal Law*, 56.

5. Section 324, in Qadri, *Code of Mohammedan Personal Law*, 82.

6. Esposito, *Women in Muslim Family Law*, 29–31.

7. Cooper, *Women of Egypt*, 214, 219. Also see Baron, "Making and Breaking of Marital Bonds," 286n54.

8. Cromer, *Modern Egypt*, 157, 159.

9. Tucker, *Women in Nineteenth-Century Egypt*, 53–55.

10. "Al-Ihsaʾ al-Hayawi li-Misr," *al-Siyasa al-Usbuʿiyya* 3, no. 127 (11 August 1928), 19; Junaydi, *Azmat al-Zawaj fi Misr*, 56; Ahmad al-Sawi Muhammad, "Ma Qilla wa-Dalla," *al-Ahram* 59, no. 17569 (4 November 1933), 1; and Husni al-Shintinawi, "al-Bayanat Tarifa ʿan al-Talaq wa-l-Zawaj," *al-Ahram* 58, no. 17172 (27 September 1932), 7.

11. Cuno, "Divorce," 211.

12. Baron, "Making and Breaking of Marital Bonds," 286n54; and Cuno, "Divorce," 200n16.

13. Fargues, "Terminating Marriage," 271.

14. The divorce rates in the census registers are especially problematic because they count the number of divorced individuals *at a given moment* every ten years. Because divorced Egyptians could and apparently did remarry quickly (see Fargues, "Terminating Marriage," 258), these figures were much lower than the number of recorded divorces per marriages. They are still worth noting because the fact that divorced individuals were remarrying quickly did not resolve the perception of a country full of divorced couples. See Ministry of Finance, *Census of Egypt Taken in 1917*, 18–19; Ministry of Finance, *Population Census of Egypt, 1927*, 66, 64; and Ministry of Finance, *Population Census of Egypt, 1937*, 116, 108.

15. "Fi al-Mahakim al-Sharʿiyya: Yatlaquha wa-Yarajʿuha," *al-Ahram* 57, no. 16603 (26 February 1931), 9.

16. Sh. ʿA. A., "Kayfa Urid an Atazawwaj: 4," *al-Ahram* 57, no. 16699 (6 June 1931), 1–2; Junaydi, *Azmat al-Zawaj fi Misr*, 56; Zaynab al-Maraghi, "Azmat al-Zawaj," *al-Usbuʿ* 2, no. 59 (17 April 1935), 4; Ahmad al-Sawi Muhammad, "Ma Qilla wa-Dalla," *al-Ahram* 56, no. 16441 (14 September 1930), 1; and Zawja Muhattama, "Azmat al-Zawaj," *al-Usbuʿ*, 2, no. 57 (31 March 1935), 4.

17. Junaydi, *Azmat al-Zawaj fi Misr*, 56–57.

18. ʿAbdu al-Barquqi, "al-Talaq," *al-Marʾa al-Misriyya* 1, no. 6 (June 1920), 193.

19. Al-Sawi Muhammad, "Ma Qilla wa-Dalla," *al-Ahram* 59, 1. See also Mahdi al-Din Sa'id, "Kayfa Urid an Atazawwaj: 66," *al-Ahram* 57, no. 16721 (28 June 1931), 2.

20. Nelson, *Doria Shafik*, 62–65.

21. Badran, *Feminists, Islam, and Nation*, 130; and Fargues, "Terminating Marriage," 256.

22. Cromer, *Modern Egypt*, 157, 159.

23. Nelson, *Doria Shafik*, 62, 64.

24. Al-Sawi Muhammad, "Ma Qilla wa-Dalla," *al-Ahram* 56, 1.

25. Labiba Ahmad, "al-Talaq," *al-Nahda al-Nisa'iyya* 5, no. 54 (June 1927), 193–194; Muhammad Hijazi, "al-Zawaj," *al-Mar'a al-Jadida* 1, no. 12 (4 December 1924), 111; al-Maghribi, "al-Talaq fi al-Islam," *al-Mu'ayyad al-Usbu'i* 1, no. 27 (25 October 1907), 4; Munira, "al-Zawaj al-Qahri," *al-Mar'a al-Misriyya* 1, no. 6 (June 1920), 211–213; and Sayyid Muhammad Nasir, "Kayfa Urid an Atazawwaj: 3," *al-Ahram* 57, no. 16699 (6 June 1931), 1.

26. Sa'id, "Kayfa Urid an Atazawwaj," 2.

27. A Muslim man's license to have up to four wives comes from the Qur'an 4:3 and 4:129.

28. As cited by Fargues, "Terminating Marriage," 256. See also Blackman, *Fellahin*, 38; and Butcher, *Things Seen in Egypt*, 37–38.

29. See Kholoussy, "Nationalization of Marriage," 333–334. Although not necessarily an accurate assessment because polygamy need not be mentioned in court unless it was the point of contention, my survey of thousands of court records between 1898 and 1936 turned up a meager three cases that referenced polygamy: J3, 538 (30 March 1898); J93, 445 (17 March 1906); and J195, 161 (22 November 1914).

30. See Kholoussy, "Nationalization of Marriage," 332–338.

31. A. F., "al-Firaq," *al-Mar'a al-Misriyya* 2, no. 5 (May 1921), 180–184; Junaydi, *Azmat al-Zawaj fi Misr*, 56; and "Talaq al-Ghadban," *al-Ahram* 57, no. 16812 (17 March 1933), 9.

32. Al-Hilal, "al-Talaq wa-l-Zawaj," *al-Nahda al-Nisa'iyya* 9, no. 70 (January 1931), 250. See also A. F., "al-Firaq," 183–184; and "al-Mahakim al-Shar'iyya: al-Talaq wa-Ta'addud Alfaz," *al-Ahram* 57, no. 16812 (26 September 1931), 9.

33. Sa'id, "Kayfa Urid an Atazawwaj," 2. See also Ahmad, "al-Talaq," 193–194; al-Barquqi, "al-Talaq," 193; Hijazi, "al-Zawaj," 111; al-Maghribi, "al-Talaq fi al-Islam," 4; Munira, "al-Zawaj al-Qahri," 211–213; and Nasir, "Kayfa Urid an Atazawwaj," 1.

34. Badran, *Feminists, Islam, and Nation*, 127; Baron, "Making and Breaking of Marital Bonds," 285–287; Booth, *May Her Likes Be Multiplied*, 201; and Kholoussy, "Nationalization of Marriage," 330.

35. A. F., "al-Firaq," 183–184.

36. For a rare exception, see Ahmad al-'Askari, "al-Haya al-Zawjiyya wa-Kayfa Nuriduha," *al-Ahram* 57, no. 16726 (3 July 1931), 7.

37. Amin, *Liberation of Women*, 97; Muhammad 'Abd al-Hamid Khalil, "Kayfa Urid an Atazawwaj: 51," *al-Ahram* 57, no. 16713 (20 June 1931), 8; Mustafa al-Qabbani, "Kayfa Urid an Atazawwaj: 52," *al-Ahram* 57, no. 16713 (20 June 1931), 8; and "Taqyid al-Talaq," *al-Mu'ayyad al-Usbu'i* 1, no. 28 (1 November 1907), 1. See also Anderson, "Recent Developments in Shari'a Law V," 287–288; and Ziadeh, *Lawyers*, 126n52.

38. Badran, *Feminists, Islam, and Nation*, 129–130.

39. There are too many articles to cite here, but newspapers, such as *al-Ahram*, covered the EFU's campaign in the late 1920s and frequently interviewed Huda Sha'rawi and Sayza Nabarawi, who spearheaded the campaign.

40. Sh. 'A. A., "Kayfa Urid an Atazawwaj: 4," 1–2.

41. Rashad Mahmud Nigm, "Kayfa Urid an Atazawwaj: 15," *al-Ahram* 57, no. 16704 (11 June 1931), 8.

42. Kholoussy, "Nationalization of Marriage," 325.

43. "Marsum bi-Qanun Raqam 25 li-Sanat 1929," 208–211. Also see Kholoussy, "Nationalization of Marriage," 325.

44. Anderson, "Recent Developments in Shari'a Law V," 278–288; Baron, "Making and Breaking of Marital Bonds," 285; Esposito, *Women in Muslim Family Law*, 29, 51; and Shaham, *Family and the Courts*, 14.

45. Hatem, "Enduring Alliance," 27.

46. "Marsum bi-Qanun Raqam 25 li-Sanat 1929," 203.

47. Anderson, *Islamic Law*, 26; and Esposito, *Women in Muslim Family Law*, 50.

48. Kholoussy, "Nationalization of Marriage," 332.

49. J1, 2 (12 January 1898); J2, 308 (15 March 1898); J3, 485 (13 April 1898); J5, 847 (17 May 1898); J7, 1213 (13 September 1898); J8, 1714 (17 December 1898); J97, 1229 (4 July 1906); J97, 1391 (7 August 1906); J100, 1738 (31 October 1906); J100, 1740 (31 October 1906); J184, 1032 (12 January 1914); J184, 1152 (18 January 1914); J183, 1305 (26 January 1914); J186, 1520 (12 February 1914); J185, 1589 (16 February 1914); J186, 1676 (22 February 1914); J186, 1706 (24 February 1914); J186, 1798 (2 March 1914); J188, 2248 (1 April 1914); J195, 197 (24 November 1914), and its related detention case, H20, 958 (24 June 1915); H21, 1232 (1 October 1915); J257, 1266 (17 March 1922); J258, 2047 (11 June 1922), and its appeal, I21, 999 (16 July 1923); J259, 1846 (17 May 1922); J261, 2620 (2 September 1922); J262, 3083 (18 October 1922); J264, 249 (23 November 1922); J264, 261 (25 November 1922); I20, 707 (23 April 1923); H46, 893 (28 October 1923); and I22, 1293 (29 October 1923).

50. J3, 535 (14 April 1898); J5, 910 (31 March 1898); and J91, 311 (27 February 1906).

51. J195, 59 (11 November 1914).

52. J195, 59 (11 November 1914).

53. Esposito, *Women in Muslim Family Law*, 34. If the repudiated wife was pregnant, then her waiting period did not end until she gave birth. See Section 316, in Qadri, *Code of Mohammedan Personal Law*, 80. A divorced wife was required to remain in the marital abode during her waiting period if her ex-husband decreed. See J1, 10 (1 January 1898); J4, 690 (19 May 1898); J6, 959 (13 July 1898); J91, 361 (6 March 1906); J97, 1559 (25 September 1906); J258, 1625 (25 April 1922); J260, 2315 (13 July 1922); and J260, 2387 (22 July 1922).

54. Section 324, in Qadri, *Code of Mohammedan Personal Law*, 82.

55. I1, 82 (6 February 1915).

56. J97, 1459 (28 August 1906); J97, 1505 (11 September 1906); J184, 1274 (26 January 1914); J184, 1404 (3 February 1914); J184, 1424 (4 February 1914); J184, 1460 (9 February 1914); J185, 1505 (11 February 1914); J195, 176 (23 November 1914); J254, 845 (4 February 1922); and J258, 1711 (30 April 1922), and its related case, H44, 218 (25 January 1923).

57. J91, 227 (14 February 1906), appealing J92, 2 (2 January 1906); J185, 1427 (4 February 1914); J185, 1553 (14 February 1914); J185, 1833 (4 March 1914), appealing J185, 1691 (23 February 1914); I1, 59 (12 January 1915), appealing J195, 171 (23 November 1914); J264, 17 (5 November 1922); I50, 1551 (19 June 1930); and I50, 1754 (28 July 1930).

58. J258, 1667 (27 April 1922); J262, 3125 (21 October 1922); I21, 789 (21 May 1923); I21, 811 (23 May 1923); I21, 883 (13 June 1923); I22, 1252 (17 October 1923); I50, 1572 (23 June 1930); I51, 55 (13 November 1930); and I51, 57 (13 November 1930).

59. J97, 1197 (26 June 1906); J99, 1909 (4 December 1906); J184, 1046 (12 January 1914); J184, 1424 (4 February 1914); J261, 3148 (23 October 1922); and I51, 135 (24 November 1930).

60. J262, 3125 (21 October 1922).

61. I21, 883 (13 June 1923). Also see Article 3 of "Qanun Nimrat 25 li-Sanat 1920," 36.

62. As cited by Anderson, "Recent Developments in Shari'a Law IV," 196. For examples, see J264, 225 (22 November 1922); and I22, 1262 (17 October 1923). Also see J261, 2532 (21 August 1922), for a rare but unsuccessful ex-wife's attempt to obtain divorce alimony long after she remarried another.

63. J3, 509 (16 April 1898); J3, 581 (27 April 1898); J4, 691 (22 May 1898); J100, 1864 (25 November 1906); and J184, 992 (10 January 1914). Also see J184, 1056 (12 January 1914); and J186, 1648 (19 September 1914).

64. Al-Sawi Muhammad, "Ma Qilla wa-Dalla," *al-Ahram* 56, 1; and "Fi al-Mahakim al-Shar'iyya: Yatlaquha wa-Yaraj'uha," 9.

65. See J3, 451 (7 April 1898). For examples of a third party taking a divorced couple to court because they continued to live together without formally remarrying, see J3, 610 (10 May 1898); and J193, 4213 (21 October 1914).

66. For successful attempts, see J4, 760 (29 May 1898); J6, 1065 (28 July 1898); and I1, 69 (24 January 1915). For unsuccessful attempts, see I2, 18 (20 November 1915); and J257, 1226 (12 March 1922).

67. See, respectively, J4, 741 (23 May 1898); and J6, 923 (5 July 1898).

68. J4, 678 (18 May 1898).

69. Abu 'Abd Allah, "al-Sa'ada fi al-Zawaj," *al-Nahda al-Nisa'iyya* 12, no. 8 (September 1934), 264.

70. Mir-Hosseini, *Marriage on Trial*, 32.

71. J195, 161 (22 November 1914).

72. Abdal-Rehim, "Family and Gender Laws."

73. "Al-Zawja allati Tatluq Nafsaha," *al-Ahram* 58, no. 17253 (17 December 1932), 8. See also "Fi al-Mahakim al-Shar'iyya: Zawja Tatluq Nafsaha," *al-Ahram* 58, no. 16989 (24 March 1932), 10.

74. Sections 137 and 139, in Qadri, *Code of Mohammedan Personal Law*, 36–37.

75. I50, 1986 (10 September 1930).

76. Tucker, *Women in Nineteenth-Century Egypt*, 54.

77. Esposito, *Women in Muslim Family Law*, 32.

78. J4, 695 (23 May 1898); J5, 848 (19 June 1898); and J100, 1880 (18 November 1906). For nineteenth-century cases, see Tucker, *Women in Nineteenth-Century Egypt*, 54.

79. In J5, 862 (5 June 1898) and J97, 1473 (29 August 1906), the husband consented to accord his wife a divorce by mutual agreement (*khul'*), but in J2, 430 (3 April 1898), he did not and his wife was not granted one. Also see J3, 477 (11 April 1898).

80. Tucker, *Women in Nineteenth-Century Egypt*, 54.

81. Islamic law enabled an adult unmarried woman to demand support from her father or, in his absence, another paternal relative. See Shaham, *Family and the Courts*, 168–169. Also see J92, 168 (28 January 1906).

82. Law 1 of 2000 reinstated a version of divorce by mutual agreement (*khul'*) in which a wife did not need her husband's consent to obtain a divorce. The controversy that surrounded the law indicates that most Egyptians were not familiar with this Islamic form of divorce. See Tadros, "Third Option." My survey of court records confirms that *khul'* became exceedingly uncommon by the 1920s,

whereas divorce in exchange for money (*mubara'a* or *talaq 'ala mal*) continued
to be practiced in twentieth-century Egypt. This latter form of divorce closely
resembled *khul'* because it also occurred by mutual consent of the spouses, but
it differed because it was revocable and because husbands could also initiate the
divorce. For examples, see J1, 87 (12 December 1898); J97, 1473 (29 August 1906);
J100, 1872 (28 November 1906); J258, 1627 (25 April 1922); J262, 3041 (15 October
1922); J264, 251 (23 November 1922); H44, 162 (4 January 1923), contesting J257,
1402 (3 April 1922); I21, 836 (30 May 1923), appealing J264, 175; and I47, 454
(6 January 1930).

83. Kholoussy, "Nationalization of Marriage," 326.

84. "Qanun Nimrat 25 li-Sanat 1920," 37–38. See Kholoussy, "Nationalization of Marriage," 326–327, for an analysis of the third ground for female-initiated divorce.

85. "Tatluq li-Faqr Zawjiha," *al-Ahram* 58, no. 16864 (17 November 1931), 8.
Also see "Talaqatha al-Mahkama," *al-Ahram* 56, no. 16405 (9 August 1930), 5.

86. Galal Husayn, "Qanun al-Ahwal al-Shakhsiyya," *al-Ahram* 46, no.
13164 (29 June 1920), 2.

87. "Fi al-Mahakim al-Shar'iyya: Yatazawwajuha ba'd 'Ana'," *al-Ahram* 57,
no. 16873 (26 November 1931), 9.

88. Article 4 of "Qanun Nimrat 25 li-Sanat 1920," 37.

89. I51, 86 (17 November 1930); and I51, 94 (19 November 1930). The transcripts do not indicate why their requests were refused.

90. J259, 2010 (16 June 1922); and I21, 920 (25 June 1923), respectively.

91. J262, 2893 (3 October 1922).

92. J184, 1408 (4 February 1914).

93. See "Qanun Nimrat 25 li-Sanat 1920," 37; and "Marsum bi-Qanun
Raqam 25 li-Sanat 1929," 205, respectively.

94. Al-Barquqi, "al-Talaq," 193.

95. Kholoussy, "Nationalization of Marriage," 329.

96. As cited and translated by Kholoussy, "Nationalization of Marriage,"
329.

97. Kholoussy, "Nationalization of Marriage," 329–330.

98. "Qanun Nimrat 25 li-Sanat 1920," 37. It was not until Article 12 of
Law 25 of 1929 that desertion in and of itself was presented as a wife's ground
for divorce. See "Marsum bi-Qanun Raqam 25 li-Sanat 1929," 204. See also
Kholoussy, "Nationalization of Marriage," 328.

99. "Qanun Nimrat 25 li-Sanat 1920," 37. See also Kholoussy, "Nationalization of Marriage," 328.

100. J257, 1172 (5 March 1922). Also see J264, 257 (23 November 1922).

101. Kholoussy, "Nationalization of Marriage," 327–338. Also see Sonbol, "Adults and Minors," 238.

102. Tucker, *Women in Nineteenth-Century Egypt*, 54.

103. Kholoussy, "Nationalization of Marriage," 328. Also see Sonbol, "Reforming Personal Status Laws," 97.

104. "Marsum bi-Qanun Raqam 25 li-Sanat 1929," 204. Also see Kholoussy, "Nationalization of Marriage," 327.

105. Hatem, "Enduring Alliance," 27, 29.

106. I50, 1584 (26 June 1930).

107. "Fi al-Mahakim al-Shar'iyya: al-Tatliq li-l-Darar," *al-Ahram* 57, no. 16693 (31 May 1931), 9; "al-Talaq li-l-Darar," *al-Ahram* 57, no. 16816 (30 September 1931), 8–9; and "Fi al-Mahakim al-Shar'iyya: Tatlubu Tatliq li-l-Darar," *al-Ahram* 58, no. 16934 (28 January 1932), 9.

108. "Fi al-Mahakim al-Shar'iyya: al-Tatliq li-l-Darar," 9.

109. "Fi al-Mahakim al-Shar'iyya: Tatluba Tatliq li-l-Darar," 9.

110. "Fi al-Usra wa-l-'A'ila: al-Talaq li-l-Darar!" *al-Ahram* 59, no. 17481 (8 August 1933), 8; and "Fi al-Usra wa-l-'A'ila: al-Talaq li-l-Darar!" *al-Ahram* 59, no. 17520 (16 September 1933), 8, respectively.

Chapter 5

1. "Al-Tarbiya al-Manziliyya," *al-Siyasa al-Usbu'iyya* 1, no. 14 (12 June 1926), 4.

2. Badran, *Feminists, Islam, and Nation*, 63; Baron, "Mothers," 278; Baron, *Women's Awakening*, 159; and Booth, *May Her Likes Be Multiplied*, 109–170.

3. Baron, *Women's Awakening*, 158–159. Also see Giladi, *Children of Islam*; and Giladi, *Infants*.

4. Sections 365, 366, and 395, in Qadri, *Code of Mohammedan Personal Law*, 94, 101.

5. Sections 384 and 385, in Qadri, *Code of Mohammedan Personal Law*, 98. See J5, 804 (5 April 1898); J8, 1719 (18 December 1898); J92, 102 (20 January 1906); J184, 1470 (9 February 1914); J195, 191 (24 November 1914); and I50, 2218 (29 October 1930). Also see Khadduri and Liebesny, *Law in the Middle East*, 54, 156–158; and Tucker, *House of the Law*, 113, 117, 138.

6. Gavanas, *Fatherhood Politics*, 7; and Lupton and Barclay, *Constructing Fatherhood*, 37.

7. Mustafa Gad Abu al-'Ila, "Kayfa Nu'adu al-Fata li-l-Zawaj?" *al-Ma'rifa* 2, no. 16 (August 1932), 468–470, 480; Hasan Ahmad Abu Dhahab, "al-Zawaj fi Misr," *al-Hisan* 3, no. 1 (24 March 1928), 5–6; 'Abd al-Rahman 'Ajiz, "al-Zawaj," *al-Siyasa al-Usbu'iyya* 1, no. 53 (12 March 1927), 7; Amin, *Liberation of Women*,

11–34, 81–82; ʿAbd al-Hamid al-Disuqi, "Azmat al-Zawaj fi Misr," *al-Usbuʿ* 2, no. 53 (17 March 1935), 10; Mahmud Hifni, "Azmat al-Zawaj: 3," *al-Shubban al-Muslimin* 2, no. 3 (December 1930), 208–213; Muhammad Farid Junaydi, *Azmat al-Zawaj fi Misr*, 35–41, 87–98; Mustafa al-Maraghi, "Iʿrad al-Shubban ʿan al-Zawaj: 1," *al-Hidaya al-Islamiyya* 4, no. 6 (March 1932), 319–326; Mustafa al-Maraghi, "Iʿrad al-Shubban ʿan al-Zawaj: 2," *al-Hidaya al-Islamiyya* 4, no. 7–8 (April–May 1932), 319–324; "Mashakil Ijtimaʿiyya Khatira," *al-Afkar* 23, no. 7 (18 September 1926), 3; Muhammad Masʿud, "al-Idrab ʿan al-Zawaj," *al-Nahda al-Nisaʾiyya* 5, no. 53 (May 1927), 176–177; Mustafa Sadiq al-Rafiʿi, "al-Taʾisha," *al-Risala* 3, no. 99 (20 July 1935), 963–967; "al-Tarbiya al-Manziliyya," 4; and "Wazifat al-Marʾa," *al-Jins al-Latif* 1, no. 5 (November 1908), 151–153.

8.   Badran, *Feminists, Islam, and Nation*, 63, 135–137; Baron, "Mothers," 278; Baron, *Women's Awakening*, 125, 158–167; and Booth, *May Her Likes Be Multiplied*, 127–137.

9.   Abu Dhahab, "al-Zawaj fi Misr," 5–6; Abu al-ʿIla, "Kayfa," 468–470, 480; ʿAjiz, "al-Zawaj," 7; Amin, *Liberation of Women*, 11–34, 81–82; al-Disuqi, "Azmat al-Zawaj fi Misr," 10; Hifni, "Azmat al-Zawaj," 208–213; Junaydi, *Azmat al-Zawaj fi Misr*, 35–41, 87–98; al-Maraghi, "Iʿrad al-Shubban ʿan al-Zawaj: 1," 319–326; al-Maraghi, "Iʿrad al-Shubban ʿan al-Zawaj: 2," 319–324; "Mashakil," 3; Masʿud, "al-Idrab ʿan al-Zawaj," 176–177; al-Rafiʿi, "al-Taʾisha," 963–967; "al-Tarbiya al-Manziliyya," 4; and "Wazifat," 151–153.

10.   For examples of articles in secular periodicals, see Abu al-ʿIla, "Kayfa," 468–470, 480; "Mashakil," 3; and "al-Tarbiya al-Manziliyya," 4. For examples of articles in religious journals, see Hifni, "Azmat al-Zawaj," 208–213; and al-Maraghi, "Iʿrad al-Shubban ʿan al-Zawaj: 1," 319–326.

11.   Mitchell, *Colonising Egypt*, 113; and El Shakry, "Schooled Mothers."

12.   Booth, "*Woman in Islam*," 190–191. See also Badran, *Feminists, Islam, and Nation*, 141.

13.   Pollard, *Nurturing the Nation*, 197.

14.   Zaynab al-Hakim, "ʿAlaqat al-Abaʾ bi-l-Abnaʾ," *al-Maʿrifa* 3, nos. 3–4 (July–August 1933), 305–312; Najib al-Hawawini, "al-Zawaj wa-l-Abawiyya," *al-Jins al-Latif* 1, no. 4 (October 1908), 101–106; T. F., "Ila al-Ummihat wa-l-Abaʾ," *al-Ahram* 28, no. 775 (1 September 1903), 1; "Nawahin wa-Tahdhirat li-l-Abaʾ wa-l-Ummihat," *al-Marʾa al-Misriyya* 8, nos. 5–6 (May 1927), 298–299; "Wajibat al-Abaʾ Nahwa al-Abnaʾ," *Fatat al-Sharq* 11, no. 1 (October 1916), 143–148; and "Wajibat al-Abaʾ wa-l-Abnaʾ," *al-Hilal* 12, no. 1 (October 1903), 25.

15.   ʿAbd al-Muʿti Hajjaj, "Ila al-Abaʾ," *al-Ahram* 32, no. 8905 (3 July 1907), 1–2; Mahmud Effendi al-Sarki, "Ma Huwa Wajib al-Abaʾ Nahwa Awladihim," *al-Haya* 1, no. 9 (1 February 1900), 140–143; and Mahmud Effendi al-Sarki,

"Wazifat al-Ab," *al-Haya* 1, no. 6 (5 November 1899), 88–92. Also see Baron, *Egypt as a Woman*, 33; and Booth, "*Woman in Islam*," 10.

16. Russell, *Creating the New Egyptian Woman*, 3.

17. Rotundo, *American Manhood*; and Tosh, *Manliness*, 109–111, 129–143, 159–160.

18. Sections 395 and 365, in Qadri, *Code of Mohammedan Personal Law*, 101, 94. Also see 'Abd al-Rahman 'Abd al-Wahid, "Nafaqat al-Saghir wa 'ala Man Tajibu," *al-Muhama al-Shar'iyya* 6, nos. 6–8 (March–May 1935), 526; and Shaham, *Family and the Courts*, 175–177, 179.

19. On mothers' hiring nannies and nursemaids, see Balsam 'Abd al-Malik, "Amradna al-Ijtima'iyya," *al-Mar'a al-Misriyya* 3, no. 4 (April 1922), 129–134; Baron, *Women's Awakening*, 160–163; and El Shakry, "Schooled Mothers," 137, 141–142, 147. On mothers' indulgence, see Shabb, "Ma Qilla wa-Dalla," *al-Ahram* 61, no. 18000 (18 January 1935), 1. On mothers' lack of hygiene, see Baron, *Women's Awakening*, 159–160; and El Shakry, "Schooled Mothers," 135–148. On mothers' ignorance, see Labiba Ahmad, "Azmat al-Zawaj al-Hadira fi Misr," *al-Nahda al-Nisa'iyya*, 10, no. 11 (November 1932), 361–363; Jarmain Bumun, "Akhlaq al-Fata al-'Asriyya," *al-Nahda al-Nisa'iyya* 14, no. 5 (May 1936), 151–152; "Hall Mushkilat al-Zawaj," *al-Nahda al-Nisa'iyya* 13, no. 11 (November 1935), 370–371; and "al-Haya al-Zawjiyya: 2," *al-Manar* 8, no. 4 (21 April 1905), 141–147.

20. 'Aziza Al-Hakim, "Manahij al-Ta'lim La Takhluq Zawaj," *al-Isha'a* 4, no. 1 (20 January 1936), 13.

21. Booth, *May Her Likes Be Multiplied*, 127.

22. Badran, *Feminists, Islam, and Nation*, 64–65; Baron, *Women's Awakening*, 167; Booth, *May Her Likes Be Multiplied*, 178; and El Shakry, "Schooled Mothers," 127–128.

23. El Shakry, "Schooled Mothers," 126–170. See also Stoler, "Carnal Knowledge," 71–73.

24. Badran, *Feminists, Islam, and Nation*, 63; Baron, *Women's Awakening*, 158–163; and El Shakry, "Schooled Mothers," 127.

25. For various European pronatalist policies, see Davin, "Imperialism and Motherhood"; Moeller, *Protecting Motherhood*; and Riley, "Free Mothers." On population control in early twentieth-century Egypt, see Fikri Abaza, "Mushkilat al-Zawaj fi Misr," *al-Hilal* 41, no. 4 (February 1933), 457–465; and El Shakry, *Great Social Laboratory*, 145–194.

26. Chakrabarty, "Difference-Deferral," 51.

27. Shabb, "Ma Qilla wa-Dalla," 1.

28. Section 382, in Qadri, *Code of Mohammedan Personal Law*, 97.

29. J6, 1024 (3 August 1898).

30. J6, 1024 (3 August 1898).

31. Shaham, *Family and the Courts*, 93–94.

32. J97, 1561 (26 September 1906).

33. J97, 1389 (7 August 1906); J99, 1799 (10 November 1906); J254, 649 (10 January 1922); J261, 2566 (28 August 1922); and I22, 1259 (17 October 1923). Also see J183, 1263 (24 January 1914).

34. J188, 2440 (15 April 1914); I50, 1907 (27 August 1930); and I51, 108 (19 November 1930). Also see J195, 213 (25 November 1914).

35. Tucker, *Women in Nineteenth-Century Egypt*, 60.

36. "Al-Qahwajiyya wa-Hadanat Ibnaha al-Saghir," *al-Ahram* 58, no. 17043 (21 May 1932), 8.

37. I47, 454 (6 January 1930).

38. Elsadda, "Gendering the Nation," 3.

39. Russell, *Creating the New Egyptian Woman*, 84; and El Shakry, "Schooled Mothers," 127–128.

40. Egyptian press debates about mixed marriage between Egyptian men and European women during the British occupation also reveal that the issue of contention for Egyptian opponents to mixed marriage was the effects of a European wife's foreign national identity, not her non-Muslim religion, on the offspring of such interracial unions. See Kholoussy, "Stolen Husbands."

41. Sections 365 and 395, in Qadri, *Code of Mohammedan Personal Law*, 94, 101.

42. Khadduri and Liebesny, *Law in the Middle East*, 154.

43. J93, 627 (9 April 1906).

44. Baron, "Mothers," 271–288; and Baron, *Women's Awakening*, 168–187.

45. Kholoussy, "Stolen Husbands," 224.

46. As cited and translated by Kholoussy, "Stolen Husbands," 222.

47. Sulayman, *al-Ajanib fi Misr*, 22.

48. Khadduri and Liebesny, *Law in the Middle East*, 137.

49. For scholarly accounts of this scandal, see Ayalon, *Press in the Arab Middle East*, 57–59, 164, 170, 233–237; Baha' al-Din, *Ayyam la-ha Tarikh*, 49–65; Baron, *Egypt as a Woman*, 34–35; Baron, "Making and Breaking of Marital Bonds," 275–276; Kelidar, "Shaykh 'Ali Yusuf"; Marsot, "Revolutionary Gentlewoman," 263; and al-Namnam, *Rasa'il*.

50. Esposito, *Women in Muslim Family Law*, 21, 155; Sonbol, "Adults and Minors," 248; and Tucker, *Women in Nineteenth-Century Egypt*, 52.

51. Ayalon, *Press in the Arab Middle East*, 164, 170, 237; Baha' al-Din, *Ayyam la-ha Tarikh*, 49–65; Baron, *Egypt as a Woman*, 34–35; Baron, "Making and Breaking of Marital Bonds," 275–276; Kelidar, "Shaykh 'Ali Yusuf," 18–19; Mar-

sot, "Revolutionary Gentlewoman," 263; and al-Namnam, *Rasa'il*, 5–61. For a published transcript of this case, see "Hukm Mawdu' al-Kafa'a fi al-Zawaj," *al-Muhama Shar'iyya* 1, no. 1 (October 1930), 65–85. Most newspapers reported on the three-week trial on a daily basis. See, for example, *al-Sharq* and *al-Ahram* between 21 July 1904 and 11 August 1904, the duration of the trial.

52. See Ayalon, *Press in the Arab Middle East*, 164; Baron, *Egypt as a Woman*, 35; and Kelidar, "Shaykh 'Ali Yusuf," 18–19. For examples of al-Sadat's supporters, see "Qadiyat al-Sadat wa-Sahib al-Mu'ayyad," *al-Manar* 7, no. 11 (13 August 1904), 440; and "Qadiyat al-Zawjiyya," *al-Liwa'* 4 (October-December 1904), 149–150.

53. For examples attacking Yusuf, see "al-Qadiyatan," *al-Liwa'* 4 (October–December 1904), 26–28; and "Qadiyat al-Zawjiyya," 149–150. For examples supporting Yusuf, see issues of his own newspaper, *al-Mu'ayyad*, published between 11 August 1904 and 18 September 1904.

54. J91, 269 (19 February 1906); J92, 288 (25 February 1906); J92, 378 (10 March 1906); and J99, 1611 (9 October 1906).

55. J92, 378 (10 March 1906). Also see J188, 2338 (7 April 1914).

56. "Fi al-Mahakim al-Shar'iyya: 'Adm al-Kafa'a bayn al-Zawjayn," *al-Ahram* 56, no. 16396 (31 July 1930), 5.

57. Adwar 'Abdu Sa'd, "Hadhihi Jarimat al-Mujtama'," *al-Usbu'* 2, no. 61 (2 May 1935), 1; "Fi al-Mahakim al-Shar'iyya: 'Adm al-Kafa'a bayn al-Zawjayn," 5; "Fi al-Mahakim al-Shar'iyya: al-Kafa'a bayn al-Zawjayn," *al-Ahram* 57, no. 16855 (8 November 1931), 9; "Fi al-Mahakim al-Shar'iyya: Naziriyya Jadida fi Da'awat al-Kafa'at," *al-Ahram* 56, no. 16418 (22 August 1930), 5; "Fi al-Mahakim al-Shar'iyya: 'Sawaq' Yuhibb Hafidat al-Basha," *al-Ahram* 57, no. 16674 (12 May 1931), 9; and "Fi al-Mahakim al-Shar'iyya: al-Sayyida Tatazawwaj Khadimha," *al-Ahram* 57, no. 16941 (4 February 1932), 8.

58. Esposito, *Women in Muslim Family Law*, 155; and Section 62, in Qadri, *Code of Mohammedan Personal Law*, 15.

59. Baron, *Egypt as a Woman*, 35.

60. Sh. al-Dusuqi, "al-Zawaj wa-l-Hubb," *al-Jins al-Latif* 1, no. 10 (April 1909), 310.

61. Armanusa, "al-Zawaj wa-Dahayahu," *al-Mar'a al-Misriyya* 1, no. 5 (May 1920), 181–183; H. Kh. Fawzi, "al-Mutallaqa al-Ba'isa," *al-Nahda al-Nisa'iyya* 4, no. 42 (May 1926), 191–192; and Munira, "al-Zawaj al-Qahri," *al-Mar'a al-Misriyya* 1, no. 6 (June 1920), 211–213.

62. 'Abd al-'Aziz al-Bashari, "Huriyyat al-Fatiyat fi Ikhtiyar al-Zawaj," *al-Hilal* 45, no. 1 (November 1936), 15–19; Mansur Fahmi, "Hawla al-Zawaj al-Qahri," *al-Mar'a al-Misriyya* 8, no. 2 (February 1927), 95–96; and "Zawaj bidun Ikhtiyar," *al-Muqtataf* 66, no. 3 (March 1925), 346.

63. Al-Bashari, "Huriyyat al-Fatiyat fi Ikhtiyar al-Zawaj," 15–19; Fahmi, "Hawla al-Zawaj al-Qahri," 95–96; Munira, "al-Zawaj al-Qahri," 211–213; Mustafa al-Qabbani, "Kayfa Urid an Atazawwaj: 52," *al-Ahram* 57, no. 16713 (20 June 1931), 8; and "Zawaj bidun Ikhtiyar," 346. Exceptions include Mustafa Kamal 'Ali Faraj al-Mutawalli, "Kayfa Urid an Atazawwaj: 17," *al-Ahram* 57, no. 16704 (11 June 1931), 8; and Saniyya Zahir, "Da'waha Takhtar!" *al-Mar'a al-Misriyya* 17, nos. 1–2 (January–February 1936), 3–5.

64. Armanusa, "al-Zawaj wa-Dahayahu," 181–182.

65. 'A'isha 'Abd al-Rahman, "Mushkilat al-Zawaj: 5," *al-Nahda al-Nisa'iyya* 11, no. 4 (April 1933), 120.

66. J264, 505 (12 December 1922).

67. Also see I19, 368 (31 January 1923), in which Khalil unsuccessfully appealed the original ruling.

68. J1, 55 (11 January 1898); J3, 533 (20 April 1898); J4, 715 (27 May 1898); J4, 759 (31 May 1898); J8, 1720 (18 December 1898); J8, 1721 (19 December 1898); J8, 1748 (15 December 1898); J91, 381 (7 March 1906); J92, 272 (20 March 1906); J92, 290 (25 February 1906); J183, 989 (6 January 1914); J184, 1230 (21 January 1914); J184, 1314 (28 January 1914); J185, 1423 (4 February 1914); J186, 1572 (16 February 1914); J195, 65 (11 November 1914); J261, 2544 (22 August 1922); J261, 2606 (31 August 1922); J261, 2626 (3 September 1922); and J265, 148 (10 November 1922). Also see H19, 782 (5 May 1915); H19, 798 (9 May 1915); H19, 813 (15 May 1915); H20, 991 (8 July 1915); H20, 1006 (13 July 1915); H20, 1037 (26 July 1915); H20, 1074 (9 August 1915); H20, 1078 (16 August 1915); H21, 1225 (9 October 1915); H44, 144 (1 January 1923); H44, 264 (8 February 1923); H44, 337 (1 March 1923); and H46, 847 (10 October 1923).

69. J91, 73 (14 January 1906); J264, 179 (19 November 1922); and I50, 1941 (1 September 1930). For husbands' appeals to reduce alimony, also see J97, 1323 (24 July 1906); J185, 1593 (17 February 1914); J195, 52 (10 November 1914); J261, 2576 (28 August 1922); I19, 240 (3 January 1923); I20, 735 (2 May 1923); I22, 1219 (8 October 1923); I47, 465 (8 January 1930); I47, 466 (8 January 1930); I50, 1602 (30 June 1930); I50, 1893 (21 August 1930); I51, 46 (12 November 1930); I51, 62 (13 November 1930); and I51, 129 (20 November 1930).

70. J91, 125 (23 January 1906); J91, 151 (27 January 1906); J185, 2013 (17 March 1914); and I2, 38 (7 December 1915).

71. J92, 290 (25 February 1906); and J186, 1572 (16 February 1914), respectively.

72. J186, 1908 (9 March 1914).

73. J1, 84 (16 January 1898); J2, 378 (26 March 1898); J2, 390 (24 March 1898); J3, 474 (11 April 1898); J3, 534 (14 April 1898), and its appeal J4, 683 (10 May

1898); J5, 802 (8 June 1898); J5, 805 (9 June 1898); J5, 813 (5 June 1898); J7, 1159 (18 August 1898); J7, 1186 (8 September 1898); J91, 237 (14 February 1906); J92, 150 (27 January 1906); J92, 376 (7 March 1906); J97, 1311 (18 July 1906); J99, 1791 (10 November 1906); J184, 1034 (12 January 1914); J194, 4194 (19 October 1914); J195, 194 (24 November 1914); H19, 838 (23 May 1915), and its appeal H20, 1000 (12 July 1915); H21, 1249 (17 October 1915); J259, 1854 (18 May 1922); J259, 1856 (18 May 1922); J261, 3156 (24 October 1922); I19, 248 (7 January 1923); H44, 177 (11 January 1923); I21, 1066 (20 August 1923); I47, 421 (1 January 1930); I50, 1981 (8 September 1930); I50, 2007 (17 September 1930); I50, 2014 (18 September 1930); and I51, 59 (13 November 1930). For ex-husbands' appeals, see J99, 1747 (3 November 1906); I1, 70 (24 January 1915); I2, 26 (30 November 1915); I20, 484 (28 February 1923); I20, 626 (2 April 1923); I20, 627 (2 April 1923); I20, 696 (23 April 1923); I21, 810 (23 May 1923); I50, 1617 (2 July 1930); I51, 45 (17 July 1930); and I51, 72 (17 November 1930).

74. Sections 369 and 389, in Qadri, *Code of Mohammedan Personal Law,* 94, 99.

75. Section 393, in Qadri, *Code of Mohammedan Personal Law,* 101. See J3, 494 (14 April 1898); J93, 455 (18 March 1906); J99, 1743 (31 October 1906); J260, 2361 (18 July 1922); and I22, 1200 (3 October 1923).

76. Shaham, *Family and the Courts,* 179. For examples of the father's paternal relatives demanding custody, see J186, 1916 (9 March 1914); J186, 2032 (17 March 1914); J261, 2622 (3 September 1922); and J264, 85 (9 November 1922). For fathers demanding custody, see J1, 31 (6 January 1898); J2, 381 (27 March 1898); J3, 500 (23 March 1898); J3, 524 (19 April 1898); J3, 607 (10 May 1898); J8, 1723 (19 December 1898); J8, 1751 (27 December 1898); J92, 94 (17 January 1906); J97, 1561 (26 September 1906); J99, 1633 (14 October 1906); J99, 1821 (13 November 1906); J99, 1929 (5 December 1906); and J261, 2528 (21 August 1922).

77. J1, 31 (6 January 1898); J3, 524 (19 April 1898); J3, 607 (10 May 1898); J8, 1723 (19 December 1898); J8, 1751 (27 December 1898); J92, 94 (17 January 1906); J99, 1633 (14 October 1906); J99, 1929 (5 December 1906); and J261, 2528 (21 August 1922).

78. Badran, *Feminists, Islam, and Nation,* 128. See J2, 381 (27 March 1898), in which a mother manipulated her child's birth date.

79. J99, 1821 (13 November 1906); and I50, 1980 (8 September 1930), respectively.

80. See J3, 500 (23 March 1898), for an example of a mother refusing to hand over her child; and see I50, 1980 (8 September 1930); I51, 49 (12 November 1930); and I51, 128 (20 November 1930), for examples of appeals.

81. Sections 382 and 383, in Qadri, *Code of Mohammedan Personal Law*, 97; Shaham, *Family and the Courts*, 178; and Tucker, *House of the Law*, 128.

82. J2, 293 (13 March 1898); J3, 530 (20 November 1898); J8, 1722 (19 December 1898); J99, 1963 (11 December 1906); J183, 1075 (12 January 1914); J186, 1892 (8 March 1914); J260, 2393 (24 July 1922); and J262, 3185 (26 October 1922). Also see J97, 1405 (14 August 1906).

83. J2, 293 (13 March 1898); and J3, 530 (20 April 1898).

84. J8, 1722 (19 December 1898); and J99, 1963 (11 December 1906). Even a widow who remarried after her husband's death could lose custody of her children to his relatives. See J184, 1126 (17 January 1914); and J185, 1707 (24 February 1914).

85. J186, 1842 (4 March 1914).

86. I50, 2011 (17 September 1930).

87. "Urid an Akhudh Waladi," *al-Ahram*, 58, no. 17057 (4 June 1932), 8.

88. "Marsum bi-Qanun Raqam 25 li-Sanat 1929," 206. Also see Esposito, *Women in Muslim Family Law*, 54; and Shaham, *Family and the Courts*, 179.

89. I50, 1676 (14 July 1930); I50, 1900 (25 August 1930); and I51, 73 (17 November 1930).

90. I50, 1676 (14 July 1930).

91. I50, 1900 (25 August 1930).

92. "Marsum bi-Qanun Raqam 25 li-Sanat 1929," 217.

Chapter 6

1. There are too many articles to cite here, but a search of issues published in 2007 and 2008 by international media, such as the BBC and the *New York Times*, and Egyptian newspapers, such as *al-Ahram Weekly* and *Daily News Egypt*, reveals numerous articles. Mona Abaza, Ghada 'Abd al-'Aal, Barbara Ibrahim, and Diane Singerman are just a few of the experts who have granted interviews or written about the Egyptian marriage crisis of the early twenty-first century.

2. Hatem, "Enduring Alliance," 19.

3. Safran, "Abolition of the Shar'i Courts," 20–21.

4. Bier, "Mothers of the Nation," 146–198.

5. Cuno, "Divorce," 196.

6. Balsam 'Abd al-Malik, "al-Zawaj," *al-Mar'a al-Misriyya* 1, no. 4 (April 1920), 113–117; and Muhammad 'Izz al-Din Hafiz, "Mushkilatuna al-Ijtima'iyya wa-Kayfa Yumkin Halluha," *al-Nahda al-Nisa'iyya* 13, no. 12 (December 1935), 404–407.

Bibliography

Primary and secondary source legal texts, census registers, books, articles, and dissertations in Arabic and English are listed together under "Other Sources" to facilitate cross-referencing. Published Arabic-language primary source periodicals and unpublished Islamic court records are cited in full in the chapter notes.

Unpublished Primary Sources Located in the Egyptian National Archives

Mahkamat Misr al-Ibtida'iyya al-Shar'iyya: al-Ahkam al-Habsiyya [Cairo Islamic Court of First Instance: Detention Verdicts]. Reg. nos. 1–61 (19 April 1911–19 January 1928).

Mahkamat Misr al-Ibtida'iyya al-Shar'iyya: al-Ahkam al-Isti'nafiyya [Cairo Islamic Court of First Instance: Appellate Verdicts]. Reg. nos. 1–51 (7 November 1914–12 February 1930).

Mahkamat Misr al-Ibtida'iyya al-Shar'iyya: al-Ahkam al-Juz'iyya [Cairo Islamic Court of First Instance: Summary Verdicts]. Reg. nos. 1–324. (1 January 1898–19 January 1928).

Published Periodicals Located in the Egyptian National Library

Al-Afkar [Reflections], 1903–1937

Al-Ahali [The Indigenous Population], 1932–1947

Al-Ahram [The Pyramids], 1876–present

Al-'A'ila al-Qibtiyya [The Coptic Family], 1909

Anis al-Jalis [The Intimate Companion], 1898–1908

Al-Balagh al-Usbu'i [The Weekly Report], 1926–1930

Fatat al-Sharq [Young Woman of the East], 1906–1939

Fatat Misr [Young Woman of Egypt], 1930

Al-Fukaha [Humor], 1926–1934

Al-Haya [Life], 1899–1915

Al-Hidaya al-Islamiyya [The Society of Islamic Guidance], 1928–1939

Al-Hilal [The Crescent], 1892–1960

Al-Hisan [The Ladies], 1925–1954

Al-Isha'a [News], 1932–1936

Al-Jins al-Latif [The Fair Sex], 1908–1925

Al-Liwa' [The Standard], 1900–1907

Al-Manar [The Lighthouse], 1898–1940

Al-Mar'a al-Jadida [The New Woman], 1924–1925

Al-Mar'a al-Misriyya [The Egyptian Woman], 1920–1939

Al-Ma'rifa [Knowledge], 1931–1934

Misr al-Fata [Young Egypt], 1938–1940

Misr al-Haditha al-Musawwara [Modern Egypt Illustrated], 1927–1930

Al-Mu'ayyad [The Strengthened], 1889–1915

Al-Mu'ayyad al-Usbu'i [The Strengthened Weekly], 1907–1910

Al-Muhama al-Shar'iyya [The Islamic Legal Bar], 1929–1954

Al-Muqtataf [The Anthology], 1885–1952

Al-Nahda al-Nisa'iyya [The Women's Awakening], 1921–1939

Al-Risala [The Message], 1933–1953

Al-Sayyidat wa-l-Banat [Ladies and Girls], 1903–1906

Al-Sayyidat wa-l-Rijal [Ladies and Men], 1921–1930

Al-Shara'i' [Prescriptions of Islamic Law], 1913–1919, 1934–1939

Al-Sharq al-Jadid [The New East], 1924–1930

Al-Shubban al-Muslimin [The Young Muslim Men's Association], 1929–1939

Al-Siyasa al-Usbu'iyya [The Political Weekly], 1926–1949

Al-Sufur [The Unveiling], 1915–1925

Al-Thaghr [The Mouth], 1929

Al-'Urwa al-Wuthqa [The Firm Tie], 1905

Al-Usbu' [The Week], 1933–1947

Other Sources

Abdal-Rehim, Abdal-Rehim Abdal-Rahman. "The Family and Gender Laws in Egypt During the Ottoman Period." In *Women, the Family, and Divorce Laws in Islamic History*, ed. Amira El Azhary Sonbol, 96–111. Syracuse, NY: Syracuse University Press, 1996.

Abdel Kader, Soha. *Egyptian Women in a Changing Society, 1899–1986.* Boulder, CO: Lynne Rienner, 1987.

Abdel-Malek, Anouar. *Egypt: Military Society—The Army Regime, the Left, and Social Change Under Nasser,* trans. Charles Lam Markmann. New York: Vintage, 1968.

Abu-Lughod, Lila. "The Marriage of Feminism and Islamism in Egypt: Selective Repudiation as a Dynamic of Postcolonial Cultural Politics." In *Remaking Women: Feminism and Modernity in the Middle East,* ed. Lila Abu-Lughod, 255–269. Princeton, NJ: Princeton University Press, 1998.

Agmon, Iris. *Family and Court: Legal Culture and Modernity in Late Ottoman Palestine.* Syracuse, NY: Syracuse University Press, 2006.

Ahmed, Leila. *Women and Gender in Islam: Historical Roots of a Modern Debate.* New Haven, CT: Yale University Press, 1992.

Amin, Qasim. *The Liberation of Women and the New Woman,* trans. Samiha Sidhom Peterson. Cairo: American University in Cairo Press, 2000 [1899, 1900].

Anderson, James N. D. *Islamic Law in the Modern World.* New York: New York University Press, 1959.

———. "Law Reform in Egypt: 1850–1950." In *Political and Social Change in Modern Egypt,* ed. P. M. Holt, 209–230. London: Oxford University Press, 1968.

———. "Recent Developments in Islamic Law IV." *Muslim World* 41, no. 3 (1951): 186–198.

———. "Recent Developments in Islamic Law V." *Muslim World* 41, no. 4 (1951): 271–288.

'Arabi, Ahmad 'Abd al-Aziz. *Yusr al-Mahr wa-Athara fi al-Iqdam 'ala al-Zawaj fi al-Islam* [The facility of the dower and its writings on the enterprise of marriage]. Cairo: al-Amana, 1997.

Arabi, Oussama. *Studies in Modern Islamic Law and Jurisprudence.* The Hague, Netherlands: Kluwer Law International, 2001.

Arnold, David, and David Hardiman, eds. *Subaltern Studies VIII.* Delhi: Oxford University Press, 1994.

Asad, Talal. *Formations of the Secular: Christianity, Islam, Modernity.* Stanford, CA: Stanford University Press, 2003.

Ayalon, Ami. *The Press in the Arab Middle East: A History*. New York: Oxford University Press, 1995.

Badran, Margot. *Feminists, Islam, and Nation: Gender and the Making of Modern Egypt*. Princeton, NJ: Princeton University Press, 1995.

Baer, Gabriel. *Studies in the Social History of Modern Egypt*. Chicago: University of Chicago Press, 1969.

Baha' al-Din, Ahmad. *Ayyam la-ha Tarikh* [Days of history]. Cairo: Dar al-Shuruq, 1991.

Balibar, Etienne. "The Nation Form: History and Ideology." In *Race, Nation, Class: Ambiguous Identities*, ed. Etienne Balibar and Immanuel Wallerstein, trans. Chris Turner, 86–106. London: Verso, 1991.

Baraka, Magda. *The Egyptian Upper Class Between Revolutions, 1919–1952*. Reading, U.K.: Ithaca Press, 1998.

Baron, Beth. *Egypt as a Woman: Nationalism, Gender, and Politics*. Berkeley: University of California Press, 2005.

———. "The Making and Breaking of Marital Bonds in Modern Egypt." In *Women in Middle Eastern History: Shifting Boundaries in Sex and Gender*, ed. Nikki R. Keddie and Beth Baron, 275–291. New Haven, CT: Yale University Press, 1991.

———. "Mothers, Morality, and Nationalism." In *The Origins of Arab Nationalism*, ed. Rashid Khalidi, Lisa Anderson, Muhammad Muslih, and Reeva S. Simon, 271–288. New York: Columbia University Press, 1991.

———. *The Women's Awakening in Egypt: Culture, Society, and the Press*. New Haven, CT: Yale University Press, 1994.

Beinin, Joel, and Zachary Lockman. *Workers on the Nile: Nationalism, Communism, Islam, and the Egyptian Working Class, 1882–1954*. Princeton, NJ: Princeton University Press, 1987.

Berque, Jacques. *Egypt: Imperialism and Revolution*, trans. Jean Stewart. London: Faber and Faber, 1972.

Bier, Laura. "From Mothers of the Nation to Daughters of the State: Gender and the Politics of Inclusion in Egypt, 1922–1967." Ph.D. dissertation, New York University, 2006.

———. "Prostitution and the Marriage Crisis: Bachelors and Competing Masculinities in 1930s Egypt." Paper presented at the annual meeting for the Middle East Studies Association, San Francisco, CA, 20 November 2001.

Blackman, Winifred S. *The Fellahin of Upper Egypt: Their Religious, Social, and Industrial Life with Special Reference to Survivals from Ancient Times*. London: Frank Cass, 1968 [1927].

Blewett, Mary H. "Manhood and the Market: The Politics of Gender and Class

Among the Textile Workers of Fall River, Massachusetts." In *Works Engendered: Toward a New History of American Labor*, ed. Ava Baron, 168–176. Ithaca, NY: Cornell University Press, 1991.

Booth, Marilyn. *May Her Likes Be Multiplied: Biography and Gender Politics in Egypt*. Berkeley: University of California Press, 2001.

———. "*Woman in Islam*: Men and the 'Women's Press' in Turn-of-the-20th-Century Egypt." *International Journal of Middle East Studies* 33, no. 2 (May 2001): 171–201.

Botman, Selma. *Egypt from Independence to Revolution, 1919–1952*. Syracuse, NY: Syracuse University Press, 1991.

Brown, Nathan. *The Rule of Law in the Arab World: Courts in Egypt and the Gulf*. Cambridge, U.K.: Cambridge University Press, 1997.

———. "Shari'a and State in the Modern Middle East." *International Journal of Middle East Studies* 29, no. 3 (August 1997): 359–376.

Butcher, E. L. *Things Seen in Egypt*. London: Seeley, Service, 1931.

Cannon, Byron. *Politics of Law and the Courts in Nineteenth-Century Egypt*. Salt Lake City: University of Utah Press, 1988.

Chakrabarty, Dipesh. "The Difference-Deferral of a Colonial Modernity." In *Subaltern Studies VIII*, ed. David Arnold and David Hardiman, 50–88. Delhi: Oxford University Press, 1994.

Chatterjee, Partha. *Nationalist Thought and the Colonial World: A Derivative Discourse?* London: Zed Books, 1986.

———. *The Nation and Its Fragments: Colonial and Postcolonial Histories*. Princeton, NJ: Princeton University Press, 1993.

Clark, Anna. *Women's Silence, Men's Violence: Sexual Assault in England, 1770–1845*. London: Pandora, 1987.

Cole, Juan Ricardo. "Feminism, Class, and Islam in Turn-of-the-Century Egypt." *International Journal of Middle East Studies* 13, no. 4 (November 1981): 387–407.

Cooper, Elizabeth. *The Women of Egypt*. New York: F. A. Stokes, 1914.

Cott, Nancy F. *Public Vows: A History of Marriage and the Nation*. Cambridge, MA: Harvard University Press, 2000.

Coury, Ralph M. "Who 'Invented' Egyptian Arab Nationalism? Part 1." *International Journal of Middle East Studies* 14, no. 3 (August 1982): 249–281.

———. "Who 'Invented' Egyptian Arab Nationalism? Part 2." *International Journal of Middle East Studies* 14, no. 4 (November 1982): 459–479.

Cromer, Evelyn Baring. *Modern Egypt*, v. 2. London: Macmillan, 1908.

Cuno, Kenneth M. "Divorce and the Fate of the Family in Modern Egypt." In *Family in the Middle East: Ideational Change in Egypt, Iran, and Tunisia*, ed. Kathryn M. Yount and Hoda Rashad, 196–216. New York: Routledge, 2008.

———. "Joint Family Households and Rural Notables in 19th-Century Egypt." *International Journal of Middle East Studies* 27, no. 4 (November 1995): 485–502.

———. *The Pasha's Peasants: Land, Society, and Economy in Lower Egypt, 1740–1858.* New York: Cambridge University Press, 1992.

Cuno, Kenneth M., and Michael J. Reimer. "The Census of Nineteenth-Century Egypt: A New Source for Social Historians." *British Journal of Middle Eastern Studies* 24, no. 2 (November 1997): 193–216.

Davidoff, Leonore, and Catherine Hall. *Family Fortunes: Men and Women of the English Middle Class, 1780–1850.* Chicago: University of Chicago Press, 1987.

Davin, Anna. "Imperialism and Motherhood." *History Workshop Journal* 5, no. 1 (1978): 9–65.

Deeb, Marius. "Bank Misr and the Emergence of a Local Bourgeoisie in Egypt." *Middle Eastern Studies* 12, no. 3 (October 1976): 69–86.

Dhillon, Navtej Singh. "The Wedding Shortage." *Newsweek International*, 5 March 2007. http://www.newsweek.com/id/36381. Last accessed 15 August 2009.

Doumani, Beshara, ed. *Family History in the Middle East: Household, Property, and Gender.* Albany: State University of New York Press, 2003.

———. "Writing Family: *Waqf*, Property, and Gender in Tripoli and Nablus, 1800–1860." *Comparative Studies in Society and History* 40, no. 1 (1998): 3–41.

Duben, Alan, and Cem Behar. *Istanbul Households: Marriage, Family, and Fertility, 1880–1940.* Cambridge, U.K.: Cambridge University Press, 1991.

Dunne, Bruce W. "Sexuality and the 'Civilizing Process' in Egypt." Ph.D. dissertation, Georgetown University, 1996.

Eley, Geoff, and Ronald Grigor Suny. "Introduction: From the Moment of Social History to the Work of Cultural Representation." In *Becoming National: A Reader*, ed. Geoff Eley and Ronald Grigor Suny, 3–38. New York: Oxford University Press, 1996.

Elias, Norbert. *Court Society*, trans. Edmund Jephcott. New York: Pantheon Books, 1983.

Elsadda, Hoda. "Gendering the Nation: Conflicting Masculinities in Selected Short Stories by Mustafa Sadiq al-Rafiʻi." Paper presented at the American University in Cairo, Egypt, 13 December 2003.

———. "Imaging the 'New Man': Gender and Nation in Arab Literary Narratives in the Early Twentieth Century." *Journal of Middle East Women's Studies* 3, no. 2 (spring 2007): 32–55.

Esposito, John L. *Women in Muslim Family Law*, 2nd ed. Syracuse, NY: Syracuse University Press, 2001.

Fahmy, Khaled. *All the Pasha's Men: Mehmed Ali, His Army, and the Making of Modern Egypt*. Cambridge, U.K.: Cambridge University Press, 1997.

Fahmy, Khaled, and Rudolph Peters. "The Legal History of Ottoman Egypt." *Islamic Law and Society* 6, no. 2 (1999): 129–135.

Fargues, Philippe. "Family and Household in Mid-Nineteenth-Century Cairo." In *Family History in the Middle East: Household, Property, and Gender*, ed. Beshara Doumani, 23–50. Albany: State University of New York Press, 2003.

———. "Terminating Marriage." In *The New Arab Family*, ed. Nicholas S. Hopkins, 247–273. Cairo: American University in Cairo Press, 2003.

Fleischmann, Ellen. *The Nation and Its "New" Women: The Palestinian Women's Movement, 1920–1948*. Berkeley: University of California Press, 2003.

Fluehr-Lobban, Carolyn, and Lois Bardsley-Sirois. "Obedience (TA'A) in Muslim Marriage: Religious Interpretation and Applied Law in Egypt." *Journal of Comparative Family Studies* 21, no. 1 (1990): 39–53.

Foucault, Michel. *The History of Sexuality*, v. 1, trans. Robert Hurley. New York: Vintage Books, 1990 [1978].

Gavanas, Anna. *Fatherhood Politics in the United States: Masculinity, Sexuality, Race, and Marriage*. Urbana: University of Illinois Press, 2004.

Gellner, Ernest. *Nations and Nationalisms*. Ithaca, NY: Cornell University Press, 1983.

Gershoni, Israel. *The Emergence of Pan-Arabism in Egypt*. Tel Aviv, Israel: Tel Aviv University, 1981.

Gershoni, Israel, and James P. Jankowski. *Egypt, Islam, and the Arabs: The Search for Egyptian Nationhood, 1900–1930*. New York: Oxford University Press, 1986.

———. *Redefining the Egyptian Nation, 1930–1945*. New York: Cambridge University Press, 1995.

———, eds. *Rethinking Nationalism in the Arab Middle East*. New York: Columbia University Press, 1997.

Ghassoub, Mai, and Emma Sinclair-Webb, eds. *Imagined Masculinities: Male Identity and Culture in the Modern Middle East*. London: Saqi, 2000.

Ghurbal, Muhammad Shafiq. *Tarikh al-Mufawadat al-Misriyya al-Britaniyya, 1882–1939* [A history of the Egyptian-British negotiations, 1882–1939]. Cairo: Dar al-Qalam, 1952.

Giladi, Avner. *Children of Islam: Concepts of Childhood in Medieval Muslim Society*. New York: St. Martin's Press, 1992.

————. *Infants, Parents, and Wet Nurses: Medieval Islamic Views on Breastfeeding and Their Social Implications*. Leiden, Netherlands: Brill, 1999.

Goldberg, Ellis. "Peasants in Revolt: Egypt 1919." *International Journal of Middle East Studies* 24, no. 2 (May 1992): 261–280.

Goldschmidt, Arthur, Jr. *Modern Egypt: The Formation of a Nation-State*. Boulder, CO: Westview, 1988.

Gordon, Linda. *Heroes of Their Own Lives: The Politics and History of Family Violence—Boston, 1880–1960*. New York: Viking, 1988.

Goswami, Manu. *Producing India: From Colonial Economy to National Space*. Chicago: University of Chicago Press, 2004.

Haddad, Yvonne Y. "Islam, Women, and Revolution in Twentieth-Century Arab Thought." *Muslim World* 74, nos. 3–4 (July–October 1984): 137–160.

————. "Sayyid Qutb: Ideologue of Islamic Revival." In *Voices of Resurgent Islam*, ed. John L. Esposito, 67–98. New York: Oxford University Press, 1983.

Hartog, Hendrik. *Man and Wife in America: A History*. Cambridge, MA: Harvard University Press, 2000.

Hatem, Mervat. "The Enduring Alliance of Nationalism and Patriarchy in Muslim Personal Status Laws: The Serial Case of Modern Egypt." *Feminist Issues* 6, no. 1 (1986): 19–43.

Heineman, Elizabeth D. *What Difference Does a Husband Make? Women and Marital Status in Nazi and Postwar Germany*. Berkeley: University of California Press, 1999.

Hobsbawm, Eric. *Nations and Nationalisms Since 1780: Programme, Myth, Reality*. Cambridge, U.K.: Cambridge University Press, 1990.

Hobsbawm, Eric, and Terence Ranger, eds. *The Invention of Tradition*. Cambridge, U.K.: Cambridge University Press, 1983.

'Imara, Muhammad. *Al-Islam wa-l-Mar'a fi Ra'y al-Imam Muhammad 'Abdu* [Islam and women in the opinion of Imam Muhammad 'Abdu]. Cairo: Dar al-Hilal, 1979.

Jacob, Wilson Chacko. "Working Out Egypt: Masculinity and Subject Formation Between Nationalism and Colonial Modernity, 1870–1930." Ph.D. dissertation, New York University, 2005.

Jankowski, James. *Egypt's Young Rebels: "Young Egypt," 1933–1952*. Stanford, CA: Stanford University Press, 1975.

Junaydi, Muhammad Farid. *Azmat al-Zawaj fi Misr* [The marriage crisis in Egypt]. Cairo: Hijazi, 1933.

Kelidar, Abbas. "Shaykh ʿAli Yusuf: Egyptian Journalist and Islamic National-ist." In *Intellectual Life in the Arab East, 1890–1939*, ed. Marwan R. Buheiry, 10–20. Beirut: American University of Beirut Press, 1981.

Kessler-Harris, Alice. *A Woman's Wage: Historical Meanings and Social Conse-quences.* Lexington: University Press of Kentucky, 1990.

Khadduri, Majid, and Herbert J. Liebesny. *Law in the Middle East.* Washing-ton, DC: Middle East Institute, 1955.

Kholoussy, Hanan. "The Nationalization of Marriage in Monarchical Egypt." In *Re-Envisioning Egypt, 1919–1952*, ed. Arthur Goldschmidt Jr., Amy J. Johnson, and Barak Salmoni, 317–350. Cairo: American University in Cairo Press, 2005.

———. "Stolen Husbands, Foreign Wives: Mixed Marriage, Identity Forma-tion, and Gender in Colonial Egypt, 1909–1923." *Hawwa: Journal of Women in the Middle East and the Islamic World* 1, no. 2 (2003): 206–240.

———. "Talking About a Revolution: Gender and the Politics of Marriage in Early Twentieth-Century Egypt." *Graduate Researcher: Journal for the Arts, Sciences, and Technology* 1, no. 2 (2003): 25–34.

Kozma, Liat. "Women on the Margins and Legal Reform in Late Nineteenth-Century Egypt, 1850–1882." Ph.D. dissertation, New York University, 2006.

La'ihat al-Mahakim al-Sharʿiyya bi-l-Aqtar al-Misriyya [Procedures of the Is-lamic courts in the Egyptian districts]. Cairo: al-Matbaʿa al-Miriyya, 1880.

La'ihat Tartib al-Mahakim al-Sharʿiyya wa-l-Ijra'at al-Mutaʿalliqa bi-ha [Orga-nization and procedures of the Islamic courts]. Cairo: al-Matbaʿa al-Miriyya, 1897.

La'ihat al-Wukala' Amama al-Mahakim al-Sharʿiyya [Procedures of lawyers be-fore the Islamic courts]. Cairo: al-Matbaʿa al-Mawsuʿat, 1900.

Lane, Edward William. *An Account of the Manners and Customs of the Modern Egyptians.* London: East-West, 1978 [1836].

Lockman, Zachary. "Imagining the Working Class: Culture, Nationalism, and Class Formation in Egypt, 1899–1914." *Poetics Today* 15, no. 2 (summer 1994): 157–190.

Lupton, Deborah, and Lesley Barclay. *Constructing Fatherhood: Discourses and Experiences.* London: Sage, 1997.

Marsot, Afaf Lutfi al-Sayyid. *Egypt's Liberal Experiment: 1922–1936.* Berkeley: University of California Press, 1977.

———. "The Revolutionary Gentlewoman in Egypt." In *Women in the Muslim World*, ed. Lois Beck and Nikki R. Keddie, 261–276. Cambridge, MA: Har-vard University Press, 1978.

———. *A Short History of Modern Egypt*. Cambridge, U.K.: Cambridge University Press, 1985.

"Marsum bi-Qanun Raqam 25 li-Sanat 1929" ["Statute 25 of 1929"]. In *Majmu'at al-Qawanin wa-l-Marasim wa-l-Awamir al-Malakiyya li-l-Thalathat al-Ashur al-Awla min Sanat 1929* [Collection of the laws, regulations, and royal decrees for the first three months of 1929], 203–219. Cairo: al-Matba'a al-Amiriyya, 1930.

Messick, Brinkley. *The Calligraphic State: Textual Domination and History in a Muslim Society*. Berkeley: University of California Press, 1993.

el-Messiri, Sawsan. *Ibn al-Balad: A Concept of Egyptian Identity*. Leiden, Netherlands: Brill, 1978.

Milad, Salwa 'Ali. *Watha'iq al-Khul'* [Documents of divorce by mutual consent]. Alexandria, Egypt: Matba'at al-Iskandariyya, 1996.

Ministry of Finance. *The Census of Egypt Taken in 1907*. Cairo: National Printing Department, 1909.

———. *The Census of Egypt Taken in 1917*, v. 1. Cairo: Government Press, 1920.

———. *Population Census of Egypt, 1927*, v. 1. Cairo: Government Press, 1931.

———. *Population Census of Egypt, 1937*. Cairo: Government Press, 1942.

Mir-Hosseini, Ziba. *Marriage on Trial: A Study of Islamic Family Law*. London: I. B. Tauris, 1991.

Mitchell, Timothy. *Colonising Egypt*. Berkeley: University of California Press, 1991.

Moeller, Robert G. *Protecting Motherhood: Women and the Family in the Politics of Postwar West Germany*. Berkeley: University of California Press, 1993.

Mosse, George L. *Nationalism and Sexuality: Respectability and Abnormal Sexuality in Modern Europe*. New York: Howard Fertig, 1985.

Musallam, Basim. *Sex and Society in Islam: Birth Control Before the Nineteenth Century*. Cambridge, U.K.: Cambridge University Press, 1983.

Najmabadi, Afsaneh. *Women with Mustaches and Men without Beards: Gender and Sexual Anxieties of Iranian Modernity*. Berkeley: University of California Press, 2005.

al-Namnam, Hilmi. *Rasa'il al-Shaykh 'Ali Yusuf wa-Safiyya al-Sadat* [The letters of Shaykh 'Ali Yusuf and Safiyya al-Sadat]. Cairo: Mirette, 2002.

Nasif, Malak Hifni. *Al-Nisa'iyyat* [Women's issues]. Cairo: Multaqa al-Mar'a wa-l-Dhakira, 1998 [1910].

Nelson, Cynthia. *Doria Shafik, Egyptian Feminist: A Woman Apart*. Gainesville: University Press of Florida, 1996.

Nolan, Mary. "Housework Made Easy: The Taylorized Housewife in Weimar

Germany's Rationalized Economy." *Feminist Studies* 16, no. 3 (fall 1990): 549–577.

———. *Visions of Modernity: American Business and the Modernization of Germany.* Oxford, U.K.: Oxford University Press, 1994.

Ouzgane, Lahoucine, ed. *Islamic Masculinities.* London: Zed, 2006.

Owen, Roger. "The Population Census of 1917 and Its Relationship to Egypt's Three Nineteenth-Century Statistical Regimes." *Journal of Historical Sociology* 9, no. 4 (1996): 457–472.

Pedersen, Susan. *Family, Dependence, and the Origins of the Welfare State: Britain and France, 1914–1945.* Cambridge, U.K.: Cambridge University Press, 1993.

———. "National Bodies, Unspeakable Acts: The Sexual Politics of Colonial Policy Making." *Journal of Modern History* 63, no. 4 (December 1991): 647–680.

Peirce, Leslie. *Morality Tales: Law and Gender in the Ottoman Court of Aintab.* Berkeley: University of California Press, 2003.

Piterberg, Gabriel. "The Tropes of Stagnation and Awakening in Nationalist Historical Consciousness: The Egyptian Serial Case." In *Rethinking Nationalism in the Arab Middle East,* ed. James Jankowski and Israel Gershoni, 42–61. New York: Columbia University Press, 1997.

Pollard, Lisa. *Nurturing the Nation: The Family Politics of Modernizing, Colonizing, and Liberating Egypt, 1805–1923.* Berkeley: University of California Press, 2005.

Qadri, Muhammad Pasha. *Code of Mohammedan Personal Law According to the Hanafite School,* trans. Wasey Sterry and N. Abcarius. London: Spottiswoode, 1914 [1875].

———. *Kitab al-Ahkam al-Shar'iyya fi al-Ahwal al-Shakhsiyya 'ala Madhhab al-Imam Abi Hanifa al-Nu'man* [The book of the Islamic Code of Personal Status based on the school of Imam Abi Hanifa al-Nu'man]. Cairo: Ministry of Justice, 1875.

"Qanun Nimrat 25 li-Sanat 1920" ["Law 25 of 1920"]. In *Majmu'at al-Qawanin wa-l-Marasim al-Muta'alliqa bi-l-Shu'un al-'Amma li-l-Thalathat al-Ashur al-Awla min Sanat 1920* [Collection of the laws and regulations pertaining to public affairs for the first three months of 1920], 36–38. Cairo: al-Matba'a al-Amiriyya, 1921.

Rabinow, Paul. *French Modern.* Cambridge, MA: MIT Press, 1989.

al-Rafi'i, 'Abd al-Rahman. *Fi A'qab al-Thawra al-Misriyya* [In the throes of the Egyptian revolution], 3 vols. Cairo: Dar al-Ma'arif, 1947–1951.

———. *Thawrat 1919* [The 1919 revolution], 3 vols. Cairo: Dar al-Ma'arif, 1949–1967.

Ramadan, 'Abd al-'Azim Muhammad Ibrahim. *Tatawwur al-Haraka al-Wataniyya al-Misriyya* [The development of the Egyptian nationalist movement], 4 vols. Cairo: Dar al-Kitab al-'Arabi, 1987.

Riley, Denise. "The Free Mothers: Pronatalism and Working Women in Industry at the End of the Last War in Britain." *History of Workshop Journal* 11, no. 1 (spring 1981): 59–118.

Rizk, Yunan Labib. "A Diwan of Contemporary Life (461): Wedding Woes." Al-Ahram Weekly On-Line, 26 September–2 October 2002. http://weekly. ahram.org.eg/2002/605/chrncls.htm. Last accessed 15 August 2009.

———. "A Diwan of Contemporary Life (490): Money and Marriage." Al-Ahram Weekly On-Line. 17–23 April 2003. http://weekly.ahram.org.eg/2003 /634/chrncls.htm. Last accessed 15 August 2009.

———. "A Diwan of Contemporary Life (609): Ministry of Education Centennial." *Al-Ahram Weekly On-Line*, 11–17 August 2005. http://weekly.ahram. org.eg/2005/755/chrncls.htm. Last accessed 15 August 2009.

Ross, Ellen. *Love and Toil: Motherhood in Outcast London, 1870–1914*. New York: Oxford University Press, 1993.

Rotundo, E. Anthony. *American Manhood: Transformations in Masculinity from the Revolution to the Modern Era*. New York: Basic, 1993.

Russell, Mona L. *Creating the New Egyptian Woman: Consumerism, Education, and National Identity, 1863–1922*. New York: Palgrave Macmillan, 2004.

Ryzova, Lucie. "Egyptianizing Modernity Through the 'New *Effendiya*': Social and Cultural Constructions of the Middle Class in Egypt Under the Monarchy." In *Re-Envisioning Egypt, 1919–1952*, ed. Arthur Goldschmidt Jr., Amy J. Johnson, and Barak Salmoni, 124–163. Cairo: American University in Cairo Press, 2005.

Sabean, David Warren. *Property, Production, and Family in Neckarhausen, 1700–1870*. Cambridge, U.K.: Cambridge University Press, 1990.

Safran, Nadav. "The Abolition of the Shar'i Courts in Egypt." *Muslim World* 48, no. 1 (January 1958): 20–28.

———. *Egypt in Search of a Political Community*. Cambridge, MA: Harvard University Press, 1961.

Salim, Latifa Muhammad. *Al-Mar'a al-Misriyya wa-l-Taghyir al-Ijtima'i, 1919–1945* [Egyptian women and societal change, 1919–1945]. Cairo: al-Hay'a al-Misriyya al-'Amma li-l-Kitab, 1984.

Scott, Joan Wallach. *Gender and the Politics of History*. New York: Columbia University Press, 1988.

Shaham, Ron. *Family and the Courts in Modern Egypt: A Study Based on Decisions by the Islamic Courts, 1900–1955*. Leiden, Netherlands: Brill, 1997.

Shakir, Ahmad Muhammad. *Nizam al-Talaq fi al-Islam* [The system of divorce in Islam]. Cairo: Dar al-Matba'a al-Qawmiyya, 1936.

El Shakry, Omnia. *The Great Social Laboratory: Subjects of Knowledge in Colonial and Postcolonial Egypt.* Stanford, CA: Stanford University Press, 2007.

————. "Schooled Mothers and Structured Play: Child Rearing in Turn-of-the-Century Egypt." In *Remaking Women: Feminism and Modernity in the Middle East*, ed. Lila Abu-Lughod, 126–170. Princeton, NJ: Princeton University Press, 1998.

Sinha, Mrinalini. *Colonial Masculinity: The "Manly Englishman" and the "Effeminate Bengali" in the Late Nineteenth Century.* Manchester, U.K.: Manchester University Press, 1995.

————. "The Lineage of the 'Indian' Modern: Rhetoric, Agency, and the Sarda Act in Late Colonial India." In *Gender, Sexuality, and Colonial Modernities*, ed. Antoinette Burton, 207–221. London: Routledge, 1999.

Sonbol, Amira El Azhary. "Adults and Minors in Ottoman *Shari'a* Courts and Modern Law." In *Women, the Family, and Divorce Laws in Islamic History*, ed. Amira El Azhary Sonbol, 236–256. Syracuse, NY: Syracuse University Press, 1996.

————. "Law and Gender Violence in Ottoman and Modern Egypt." In *Women, the Family, and Divorce Laws in Islamic History*, ed. Amira El Azhary Sonbol, 277–289. Syracuse, NY: Syracuse University Press, 1996.

————. "Reforming Personal Status Laws in Egypt." *Middle East Insight* 15, no. 6 (November–December 2000): 96–97, 116.

————, ed. *Women, the Family, and Divorce Laws in Islamic History.* Syracuse, NY: Syracuse University Press, 1996.

Stern, Steve J. *The Secret History of Gender: Women, Men, and Power in Late Colonial Mexico.* Chapel Hill: University of North Carolina Press, 1995.

Stoler, Ann Laura. "Carnal Knowledge and Imperial Power: Gender, Race, and Morality in Colonial Asia." In *Gender at the Crossroads of Knowledge: Feminist Anthropology in the Postmodern Era*, ed. Micaela di Leonardo, 51–101. Berkeley: University of California Press, 1991.

————. *Carnal Knowledge and Imperial Power: Race and the Intimate in Colonial Rule.* Berkeley: University of California Press, 2002.

————. *Race and the Education of Desire: Foucault's History of Sexuality and the Colonial Order of Things.* Durham, NC: Duke University Press, 1995.

al-Subqi, Amal Kamil. *Al-Haraka al-Nisa'iyya fi Misr, 1919–1952* [The women's movement in Egypt]. Cairo: al-Hay'a al-Misriyya al-'Amma li-l-Kitab, 1986.

Sulayman, Mahmud Muhammad. *Al-Ajanib fi Misr* [Foreigners in Egypt]. Cairo: Ein for Human and Social Studies, 1996.

Tadros, Mariz. "The Third Option." *Al-Ahram Weekly On-Line*. 31 October–6 November 2002. http://weekly.ahram.org.eg/2002/610/li2.htm. Last accessed 15 August 2009.

Ta'rifat al-Rusum al-Muqarrara bi-l-Mahakim al-Shar'iyya [Price list of scheduled fees of the Islamic courts]. Cairo: Matba'at Bulaq, 1886.

Thompson, Elizabeth. *Colonial Citizens: Republican Rights, Paternal Privilege, and Gender in French Syria and Lebanon*. New York: Columbia University Press, 2000.

Tignor, Robert L. *Modernization and the British Rule in Egypt, 1882–1914*. Princeton, NJ: Princeton University Press, 1966.

———. *State, Private Enterprise, and Economic Change in Egypt, 1918–1952*. Princeton, NJ: Princeton University Press, 1984.

Toledano, Ehud R. *State and Society in Mid-Nineteenth-Century Egypt*. New York: Cambridge University Press, 1990.

Tosh, John. *Manliness and Masculinities in Nineteenth-Century Britain: Essays on Gender, Family, and Empire*. Harlow, U.K.: Pearson Education, 2005.

Tucker, Judith E. *In the House of the Law: Gender and Islamic Law in Ottoman Syria and Palestine*. Berkeley: University of California Press, 1998.

———. "Marriage and Family in Nablus, 1720–1856: Toward a History of Arab Marriage." *Journal of Family History* 13, no. 2 (1988): 165–179.

———. "Revisiting Reform: Women and the Ottoman Law of Family Rights, 1917." *Arab Studies Journal* 4, no. 2 (1996): 4–17.

———. "Ties That Bound: Women and Family in Eighteenth- and Nineteenth-Century Nablus." In *Women in Middle Eastern History: Shifting Boundaries in Sex and Gender*, ed. Nikki R. Keddie and Beth Baron, 233–252. New Haven, CT: Yale University Press, 1991.

———. *Women in Nineteenth-Century Egypt*. Cambridge, U.K.: Cambridge University Press, 1985.

Ullman, Sharon R. *Sex Seen: The Emergence of Modern Sexuality in America*. Berkeley: University of California Press, 1997.

Vatikiotis, P. J. *The History of Modern Egypt from Muhammad Ali to Mubarak*, 4th ed. Baltimore: Johns Hopkins University Press, 1991.

Vitalis, Robert. *When Capitalists Collide: Business Conflict and the End of Empire in Egypt*. Berkeley: University of California Press, 1995.

Walkowitz, Judith R. *The City of Dreadful Delight: Narratives of Sexual Danger in Late-Victorian London*. Chicago: University of Chicago Press, 1992.

White, Luise. "Matrimony and Rebellion: Masculinity in Mau Mau." In *Men and Masculinities in Modern Africa*, ed. Lisa A. Lindsay and Stephan F. Miescher, 177–191. Portsmouth, NH: Heinemann, 2003.

Wildenthal, Lora. "Race, Gender, and Citizenship in the German Colonial Empire." In *Tensions of Empire: Colonial Cultures in a Bourgeois World*, ed. Frederick Cooper and Ann Laura Stoler, 263–283. Berkeley: University of California Press, 1997.

Wood, Elizabeth A. *The Baba and the Comrade: Gender and Politics in Revolutionary Russia*. Bloomington: Indiana University Press, 1997.

Zayid, Mahmud. *Egypt's Struggle for Independence*. Beirut: Khayats, 1965.

Ze'evi, Dror. "The Use of Ottoman Shari'a Court Records as a Source for Middle Eastern Social History: A Reappraisal." *Islamic Law and Society* 5, no. 1 (February 1998): 35–56.

Ziadeh, Farhat J. *Lawyers, the Rule of Law, and Liberalism in Modern Egypt*. Stanford, CA: Hoover Institution, 1968.

Index

Note: Page numbers in italic type indicate illustrations.

dowers, 69; on household provision, 37–39, 44–45, 68–69; marriage crisis as understood through, 3; on minor brides, 53–55; reorganization of, 126; research on, 17–18, 126; on spousal abuse, 69–71, 147*n*88; types of, 17–18; and wifehood, 50, 67–74; witnesses in, 90; women's status in, 46–47. *See also* Alimony; Court system

Courts of First Instance, 17, 45
Courts of Summary Justice, 17
Court system: abolishment of Islamic, 17, 125–26; access to, 18; Britain and, 5, 16; personnel in, 13, 16, 37, 69, 72, 73, 126; reorganization of, 4, 17; research using, 13, 15–18; state regulation of, 16–17. *See also* Court cases; Islamic law
Coverture, 30
Cromer, Lord, 79, 82
Custody of children, 3, 12, 18, 20, 100, 107–11, 117–21, 122, 125, 126, 161*n*76, 162*n*84

al-Dahshuri, Nabawiyya, 89
al-Dalal, Hasan 'Amr, 113–14
Darar (maltreatment), 97
Daughter of the Nile Union, 34
Dependency (*hadana*), of children, 101, 107–10, 117–21
Detention cases, 17, 46–47, 131, 141*n*129
Dhillon, Navtej Singh, 123
al-Din, Asiya Salih Nur, 54, 55
Disease, 93
Disobedience. *See* Obedience of wives
al-Disuqi, 'Abd al-Hamid, 62
Divorce, 20, 77–98; causes of, 83, 85; and child support/custody, 118–20; class and, 81–83; court cases on, 87–97; in exchange for money, 154*n*82; female contractual right to, 91–92; female-initiated, 90–93; imprisonment as reason behind, 94–95; Islamic law on, 78, 86, 90–92, 95, 97–98; judicial, 53–54,

91–93, 95–97; legislation on, 10, 78, 85–90, 93–94; male-initiated, 85–90; maltreatment as reason behind, 97; minor brides and, 53–55; by mutual agreement, 91–93, 153*n*82; oath of, 78–79, 85–87, 89–90; poverty as reason behind, 94; press coverage of, 80–81, 85, 90, 92, 95, 97; process of, 78–79; rates of, 79–80, 83, 87, 149*n*14; revocable/irrevocable, 79, 80, 87, 89, 96; significance of, 77–78; waiting period ('*idda*) for, 78–79, 87–89, 93, 96, 152*n*53; wives' options for, 91–95
Domestic confinement. *See* Female seclusion
Domestic management. *See* Household management, by women
Dower (*mahr*), 19, 24, 28–36, 39, 43, 69, 86, 112; advanced portion (*muqaddam*) of, 28–29, 33–35, 69, 72, 148*n*105; amount of, 28–29, 31–33; court cases on, 69; deferred portion (*mu'akhkhar*) of, 28, 35, 78, 87, 88, 91, 92, 93; demands for, 29–33, 36, 47; disputes over, 34, 73; Islamic law on, 30, 33–34, 67, 79, 87, 89, 113; limits on, 33–35; press coverage of, 2, 25, 32–35, 44, 111; purposes of, 29; uses of, 30–31
Dunne, Bruce, 9

Economy: marriage crisis and, 19, 23–36, 43–47; nationalism and, 26–28; World War I and, 25
Education: of bachelors, 35–36, 49, 99; for childrearing responsibilities, 100–102, 106; class and, 36, 60; and employment prospects, 26–27; government promotion of, 26, 60–61; in household management, 64, 67; religious, 63; types of, 60–61; Western-style, 49, 60; of women, 49, 59–65, 67, 100, 106
Effendi, 7
EFU. *See* Egyptian Feminist Union

column). *See under* 'Abd al-Rahman, 'A'isha
Marsot, Afaf Lutfi al-Sayyid, 5
Masculinity. *See* Men and masculinity
Mas'ud, Muhammad, 58, 65Materialism, 7–8, 19, 24, 30–33, 36
Men and masculinity: and divorce, 78–79, 81–83, 85, 86, 92; and education, 36; and household provision, 36–39, 37, 68–74; marriage and, 23–24; marriage crisis and, 47; middle-class, 24; and sexuality, 57; threats to, 65; wives' behavior and, 72. *See also* Alimony (*nafaqa*); Bachelors; Fathers and fatherhood
Mexico, 46
Middle class: and alimony, 107–8, 117–18; anxieties of, 8–9; and child custody, 120–21; and childrearing, 105–6; development of Egyptian, 7; and divorce, 54–55, 91; and dowers, 34–35; economic hardships of, 24–26, 29; and education, 36, 49, 60–61; and the family, 122; and female seclusion, 51, 58, 64–65; and the fez, 133n21; and household provision, 37; and marriage, 10, 43, 113–14; marriage crisis and, 2, 4, 6–8, 24, 40, 49, 77, 79, 81–82; and masculinity, 24, 34, 36, 47; materialism of, 30–33; and nationalism, 12, 122; and obedience of wives, 68, 70, 72, 74; periodical readership among, 14; and the press, 2, 14–16, 65, 81, 90, 109–10, 112, 115; and wifehood, 50; and women's employment, 64, 108–9
Middle East Youth Initiative, 123
Minor brides, 6, 19, 50, 53–56, 92, 112
Mixed marriage, 110–11, 158n40
Mobility, class, 36
Modernity, 6, 7, 10, 20, 59, 62, 74, 78, 83, 86, 106, 110, 113
Modern marriage, 6, 20, 34–35, 43, 71, 78, 86, 116–17, 126

Morality: bachelor behavior and, 39–43; marriage and the promotion of, 19, 24, 45–47, 61; of women, 49, 51, 56–59, 61–63. *See also* Childrearing
Mothers and motherhood: childrearing role of, 20, 60, 99–102, 105–11, 118–20; criticisms of, 105–6; exaltation of, 101–2; family role of, 105; Islamic law on, 100, 107; nationalism and, 100–103, 105–7, 110–11, 121–22; press on, 102; Western ideals of, 102; working mothers, 107–10
al-Mu'ayyad (*The Strengthened*) [newspaper], 112
Mubara'a (divorce in exchange for money), 154n82
Mubarak, Sayyid, 119
Muhammad, Na'ima, 94
Mursi, Badr al-Zayn, 96
Mursi, Hanim, 94
Musa, Nabawiyya, 29
Muslim Brotherhood, 62
Mustafa, Fa'iqa Darwish, 120–21
Mustafa, Sayyid, 42–43
M. Z. K. (government employee), 52

Nabarawi, Sayza, 71, 151n39
Nafaqa (alimony). *See* Alimony (*nafaqa*)
al-Nahda al-Nisa'iyya (*The Women's Awakening*) [journal], 14, 31, 56, 63, 65, 77, 116
Nasser, Gamal Abdel, 5, 17, 124, 125
National courts, 17, 86, 125, 147n88
National identity and nationalism: characteristics of, 12; and childrearing, 99–103, 105–7, 111, 121–22; class and, 12; and divorce, 93–94; and the economy, 26–28; effendi and, 7; family and, 9–10, 103, 116–18; gender and, 11; Islam and, 59; law and, 12; marriage and, 3–4, 10–13, 23–24; and motherhood, 100–103, 105–7, 110–11, 121–22
Nightclubs, 40, 58